INTERNET DIRECT MAIL

THE COMPLETE GUIDE TO SUCCESSFUL E-MAIL MARKETING CAMPAIGNS

STEVAN ROBERTS
MICHELLE FEIT
ROBERT W. BLY

NTC Business Books

NTC/Contemporary Publishing Group

Library of Congress Cataloging-in-Publication Data

Bly, Robert W.
    Internet direct mail : the complete guide to successful e-mail marketing
campaigns / Robert W. Bly, Michelle Feit, and Stevan Roberts.
        p.   cm.
    ISBN 0-658-00136-1
        1. Internet marketing.   2. Electronic mail systems.
I. Feit, Michelle.   III. Roberts, Stevan, 1955–   III. Title.
HF5415.1265.B59   2000
658.8′4—dc21   00-55024

Interior design by Rattray Design

Published by NTC Business Books
A division of NTC/Contemporary Publishing Group, Inc.
4255 West Touhy Avenue, Lincolnwood (Chicago), Illinois 60712-1975 U.S.A.
Printed in the United States of America
International Standard Book Number: 0-658-00136-1
    02   03   04   05   06   LB   17   16   15   14   13   12   11   10   9   8   7   6   5   4   3

This book is dedicated to Evelyn Roberts, who gave me the gift of love, inspired me with her courage, and taught me that if we work hard enough, we can be anything we set our minds to achieve. Also to my loving wife Michelle, who provides a world of joy. Without your daily sacrifice I would never have reached so far. And to my sons William and Jonathan, who motivate me each day to embrace the future. You have enriched my life with your own.

—Steve Roberts

I would like to dedicate this book to the two most influential women in my life. To Marilyn Kaufman: Mom, thank you for your support and confidence, without which I could never have persevered. To my first boss, Edith Roman: Thank you for paving the way for my career. Both women were trailblazers in their own careers, and I feel honored to build on the momentum they established.

—Michelle Feit

To the memory of Robert McCarron.

—Bob Bly

There is a time coming . . . when many things will change.

—Sweet Medicine, Cheyenne folk hero

For I dipped into the future, far as human eye could see,
Saw the Vision of the world, and all the wonder that would be.

Saw the heavens filled with commerce, argosies of magic sails,
Pilots of the purple twilight, dropping down with costly bales.

—Alfred, Lord Tennyson

CONTENTS

ACKNOWLEDGMENTS

WE'D LIKE TO thank our editor, Danielle Egan-Miller, for having faith in us and this idea; and Fern Dickey, for her review of the book while in manuscript.

Thanks also to the people who contributed ideas and information, as well as those who allowed us to reprint articles or agreed to be interviewed for this book: Mina Chen, Royal Farros, Barry Green, Stefanie Healy, John Wright, Al Bredenburg, Trevor Levine, Ivan Levison, Michael Darviche, Paul Forringer, Rosalind Resnick, and Lenny Barshack. Apologies to anyone whose name we inadvertently omitted.

We are grateful to the authors of the following articles for their permission to reprint their work in this book:

Aaron, Michael, "E-Mail Marketing Has Many Faces," *DM News*, April 26, 1999, p. 20.

Andrews, Kelly J., "Opt-in E-Mail," *Target*, February 1999, p. 105. This article originally appeared in *Target Market* magazine. Copyright 1999 North American Publishing Company. Reprinted with permission.

Barshack, Lenny, "E-Mail: The Net's Killer App," *Target Marketing*, February 1999, p. 102. Copyright 1996 Bigfoot Partners, L.P.

Bredenberg, Al, "Direct Response Techniques Enhance Internet Efforts," *The Advantage from Microsoft Corporation*, August 1999, p. 5.

D'Arcangelo, Jim, "Path to E-Commerce Is Measurement," *DM News*, September 20, 1999, p. 28.

Darviche, Michael, "E-Mail Test Strategies," *DM News*, April 23, 1999, p. 22.

Dodson, Jody, "Increase Your Online Survey Response," *DM News*, September 13, 1999, p. 25.

Forringer, Paul, "Web Marketing Equals Constant Change," *DM News*, April 23, 1999, p. 24.

Frankel, Rob, "9 Easy Steps: How to Screw Up a Banner Campaign," www.searchz.com, July 30, 1999. Source: www.robfrankel.com.

Lewis, Maura, "Making Sense of Internet Metrics," *DM News*, April 23, 1999, p. 25.

Payne, John, "Leveraging Data to Gain Competitive Advantage," *DM News*, September 20, 1999, p. 24.

DIRECT MAIL IN THE INTERNET AGE

E-mail-len-ni-um (ē-māl-en-ē-um) *n*: The era, at the beginning of the twenty-first century, when direct marketing evolved from paper mail to electronic delivery over the Internet.

DIRECT MAIL, a mainstay of marketing for many small and large corporations alike, is rapidly becoming more expensive, at least in its traditional paper form, thanks to declining response rates and rising paper, printing, postage, and list rental costs.

Now a new type of direct mail, delivered over the Internet, is making direct marketing more cost-effective and profitable than ever before. There are dozens of books on traditional direct mail and many more on the Internet, websites, and e-business. But there has been no authoritative how-to guide to Internet direct mail for serious, legitimate marketers (as opposed to business opportunity, sex, online casino, and get-rich-quick promoters and spammers). Until now.

Internet Direct Mail fills this gap. It presents clear, practical, step-by-step instructions on how to create, send, and track the results of Internet direct mail: selecting products and offers, getting lists, writing the mailing, distributing it on the Internet, fulfilling orders and inquiries, and collecting and measuring response. With this book in hand, any businessperson will be able to quickly and easily compose an Internet mailing, e-mail it to thousands or millions of target prospects, and generate inquiries and orders—without getting spammed or flamed.

Internet direct mail has many advantages over traditional paper direct mail:

- It's faster. According to a recent survey from the Rylander Company, 75 percent of nationally distributed third-class bulk rate mail reaches its destination in two weeks. Internet direct mail can reach its target literally in seconds. You can get out a campaign, get results, and make money in days, even within hours, after sending your e-mail. This compares very favorably with traditional direct mail campaigns, which can take eight to twelve or more weeks to complete (from concept, copy, and design, through printing and mailing).

- Response is immediate. You start getting responses the day you send your message, and you will receive 90 percent of your responses in about four days. You know your results sooner, so you can plan the next campaign or rollout with confidence. Tests can be immediately tabulated and analyzed to give you answers on themes, sales appeals, products, offers, pricing, lists, and other test variables. In traditional direct mail, you get the majority of your responses to a third-class bulk mailing within four to five weeks after mailing. In Internet direct mail, you get almost all your responses within a week of transmission.

- Unlike conventional direct mail, which is limited by geographical boundaries (currencies, time zones, varying postal regulations, and postal systems of varying quality and reliability), e-mail is a global medium. "The single most revolutionary aspect of the Internet is the way it eliminates the time and place restrictions on business," writes Porter Stansberry in *Oxford Club Communiqué* (May 1, 1999, p. 4). "On the Internet, literally everyone in the world can buy a product or service at the same time."

Successful campaigns can easily be rolled out worldwide. Internet users can receive e-mail in 160 countries. Survey results published in *CIO WebBusiness* magazine (section 2, August 1, 1999, p.

12) indicate that half of Internet users speak a language other than English.

The nations with the greatest percentage of residents connected to the Internet are Iceland (32 percent), Finland (30 percent), Norway (30 percent), Sweden (29 percent), and the United States (28 percent). But language is not necessarily a barrier: according to a study from the Strategis Group, 51 percent of French Internet users spend most of their time on English-language websites.

- It's less complicated to produce. The typical Internet direct mailing is a typed e-mail message you create right on your computer screen. It doesn't require a professional graphic designer, Web developer, HTML programmer, or printer, unless you want to incorporate sophisticated graphics (an option we'll explore later in this book).

- It costs less to send. The cost to send a paper direct mailer—including printing, postage, mailing list rental, and production—is typically sixty to eighty cents each. At that rate, mailing 100,000 pieces would cost $60,000 to $80,000. By comparison, you can send your Internet mailing to the same number of prospects for a fraction of that cost—and in some cases, for only pennies per prospect. There is no postage, printing, or expensive graphic design. Organizations are finding that, for most tasks, switching processes to the Internet reduces costs over traditional means. For example, the Arizona Motor Vehicles Department has found the cost to process Web-based registration renewals is 76 percent less than regular counter transactions.

- It works as well as or better than regular direct mail, in many instances. E-mail increases response rates by making the purchase easy, fast, and at a time and place of the buyer's choice. Personalization, which increases response, is easy and inexpensive. You can create powerful presentations combining graphics, text, voice, video, audio, animation, color, and interactivity. According to an article in *Business 2.0* (November 1999), Jupiter Communications reports that targeted e-mail results in a sale 5 to 15 percent of the time, compared to 0.5 to 2 percent for banner ads.

The profit implications for marketers are staggering. At a cost of $600 per thousand—a typical industry figure—a mailing that generates the standard 2 percent response rate for an offer of a $30 product *will not even make a profit*. On the other hand, an Internet direct mail offer for the same product will turn a profit if the *entire mailing* produces only 1 percent response, or even less. And the response rates to Internet direct mail are actually higher, not lower, than conventional direct mail.

"When the dust from the transition to the new e-conomy settles, the corporate landscape will be strewn with the carcasses of organizations that were unable to adapt," warns Abbie Lundberg, editor of *CIO* magazine. "Don't let yours be among them."

"If you own a small company and you're not online or planning to be online within the next six months, you're heading toward obsolescence and you'll ultimately go out of business," says small business columnist Jane Applegate.

Internet entrepreneur and marketing expert Dr. Jeffrey Lant adds, "To succeed in the new millennium, you must succeed on the Internet." Internet direct mail is a marketing revolution . . . the wave of the future, where smart people will send out as many of their marketing communications as possible via e-mail . . . just as many companies are doing right this minute.

Many marketers already know what Internet direct mail is and receive it every day, but have no idea how to do their own. *Internet Direct Mail* shows you how to do it yourself—quickly, effectively, and affordably.

We do have one favor to ask. When you start your next e-campaign, add our e-mail addresses (listed in our bios at the back of the book) to your list. We'll be thrilled to receive your e-mail and learn what you're up to.

Continual updates to this book may be found at the Edith Roman Associates website, www.edithroman.com. They include updates and additions to our vendor list, new tips and strategies, and downloadable and viewable samples of new rich media and other Internet direct mail formats. This way, your edition of *Internet Direct Mail* will never be out of date. For additional updates on what's working in direct mail (online and conventional), and to view successful mailings, visit www.bly.com.

INTRODUCTION TO
INTERNET DIRECT MAIL

WELCOME TO THE twenty-first century! We call this new age of marketing the *e-maillennium*, which we define as "the era, at the turn of the century, when direct marketing evolved from paper mail to electronic delivery over the Internet."

You can't pick up a newspaper or magazine, or turn on the TV or radio, without hearing a story about the Internet. And in business, not a day goes by when executives don't think about the impact Internet technology will have on their business.

Everybody in business is aware of and forming strategies for dealing with the rising popularity of the Internet. Most marketers have an idea of the tremendous potential of the Internet. But while big ideas abound, actual how-to advice on what to do next and the steps you must take to implement these ideas is in short supply. That's the gap this book is written to fill.

This book is for marketers who want to start or jump-start their Internet direct mail efforts. If you do not know how to do Internet direct mail, we will show you step by step exactly what you must do to write your message, select your e-mail lists, send the message, and generate quality responses without getting flamed. If you already do direct mail on the Internet, we'll show you how to improve results while avoiding mistakes that can cost you sales, customer goodwill, or even your account with your ISP (Internet service provider).

There are many brilliant futurists writing brilliant, bestselling books on e-business and other aspects of business in the new digital economy. We are not part of their group. Two of us (Steve and Bob) are traditional direct marketers, with decades of experience, who have moved enthusiastically and excitedly into this new age of Internet direct mail. One of us (Michelle) is younger and a "child" of this electronic age, although she also has fifteen years' experience in direct marketing.

As direct marketers, however, our combined commitment is to get results and maximize response rates—not push you on this or that technology or concept. The direct mail we create, whether Internet or traditional, has to sell—or else! Everything in this book is aimed at helping you generate maximum response at minimal cost. To take any other approach in a direct marketing book, even one focusing on digital technology, would be cheating the reader. And that's something we refuse to do. It goes against every fiber of our being instilled by our combined fifty-plus years in the direct marketing industry.

Internet Direct Mail Works—and Here's the Proof

To begin with, some marketers question not merely whether Internet direct mail can work for them, but whether it can work at all. "Won't prospects complain we're spamming them?" is a common concern. Another is, "Isn't the Internet mainly filled with kids trying to entertain other kids? My customers don't go to the Internet when they have to buy our type of product!" A third question we hear frequently: "How can I make money on the Internet? Don't Internet prospects just want *free* stuff?" This issue is of special concern to direct marketers selling periodicals, books, and other "information products."

These are legitimate concerns, and they will be addressed throughout this book. But the question of whether Internet direct mail can actually work can only be answered in tests. And enough test campaigns have already been conducted to prove, beyond doubt, that

Internet direct mail works—and sometimes, to the chagrin of traditional direct marketers, even better than traditional direct marketing.

For instance, after delivering a speech at an Information Training Association (ITA) conference in April, Kendra Lee decided in October to send a mailing to the association's membership to generate leads. Lee's company, Denver-based KLA Group, creates sales training programs for high-tech Web organizations. Convinced that e-selling—the electronic selling conducted by individual salespeople—is a key growth area, Lee chose to conduct some testing while she promoted her firm.

Lee divided the list of the 446 ITA members she had decided to target into two groups—151 received personalized e-mail messages and 295 received direct mail pieces. Lee split the list alphabetically, selecting the first third who had e-mail addresses to receive an e-mail message; the remaining two-thirds received the direct mail piece. Lee divided the prospects this way because she didn't expect the e-mail to be a success; she thought the direct mail would do better, and she wanted to maximize her response.

Of the 151 e-mail recipients, Lee received twenty-six leads, three of which were waiting in her inbox when she arrived at work the next day. (The messages were sent after the close of business the previous day.)

Not one person responded to the paper mailing. And Lee and her sales rep had difficulty reaching those prospects by phone when making follow-up calls. However, two weeks after the initial direct mailing, Lee sent e-mail to 248 of the ITA members who initially had received paper letters. Twenty-nine recipients responded. Using e-mail, Lee generated a 29 percent combined response rate, and only nine of the total 399 who received the e-mail asked to be removed from her list. Lee credits the response rate to e-mail's simplicity.

There was one catch: Lee wasn't prepared to send more information via e-mail; she and her sales rep were ready to respond by mail and phone. So Lee had to quickly decide what information to send electronically. She comments, "You really need to be prepared. If prospects respond to you in minutes or hours, they expect you to respond in minutes or hours."

Lee believes that a digital version of a company's direct mail information is not always appropriate. "You don't want to send out your price before you know why a person is interested," she cites as an example. Even so, Lee and her rep have delivered more than twenty proposals via e-mail, without any phone conversations, and have closed three sales so far.

The test worked so well that this past February, Lee sent 200 electronic Valentine's Day cards to customers and prospects. She received thirty-five responses and five leads.

In many ways, the Internet is a direct marketing paradise, offering interactivity, instant access to product information, and the ability to purchase conveniently from home. E-mail is fast, inexpensive, manageable, easy to use, and uniquely personal. It is already established as an important communications tool, often surpassing the telephone for many forms of business and personal interaction.

Forrester Research estimates that in 1998, 500 million e-mail messages were sent per day—and that by 2002, that number will be 1.5 billion. This growth has significant implications for direct marketers looking to get their offerings in front of the right prospects.

A growing number of people now prefer e-mail to face-to-face meetings and letter writing. "The art of letter writing has changed with the times," observes Dear Abby in her syndicated column. "E-mail, faxes, and quick phone calls are time-savers for busy people." According to survey results published in *ComputerWorld* (May 10, 1999, p. 106), 20 percent of the respondents acknowledged using e-mail to avoid speaking with people.

In an interview with *Network Magazine* (December 1998, p. 66), Rich Guth, vice president of marketing for Sendmail (Santa Barbara, California), comments, "E-mail historically has been a convenience. But now it's the primary means of communication in corporate America." A report from Frost and Sullivan says e-mail has surpassed the telephone as the most commonly used tool for business communication, with more than 112 million e-mail boxes installed worldwide.

According to *American Demographics* magazine (November 1999, p. 72), 15 million people subscribe to free e-mail services, and 86 percent of Internet users have e-mail. A U.S. West survey of 500 people found that 53 percent of those surveyed said they send personal e-mail from work.

Warning: Unlike mail, which can be kept private and even shredded after it is read, e-mail is not quite as confidential. In a recent survey from the American Management Association, 27 percent of the companies said they store and review employee e-mail messages.

E-mail is increasingly being used as a means to receive business and personal news, entertainment, products, and even advertisements. People want to receive marketing materials when they've asked for them. Frequent travelers, for example, often ask that airlines e-mail them up-to-date information on discounted fares.

According to an article in *Sales & Marketing Management* (December, 1999), 46 percent of companies surveyed said they conduct e-mail marketing campaigns. "There is no more cost-effective way to reach individual customers, not to mention boost sales," the article observes.

When you buy a product, whether it's a new stereo or a piece of software, you are often given the option of receiving e-mail updates of new offers from the vendor. Software vendors, for example, will often send bug fixes or usage tips. When these e-mail updates appear in your inbox, you can read a short paragraph and then click on a link to quickly view a Web page with more information. Or you can delete the e-mail.

The vendors sending these e-mails can track your response and tailor future mailings to your preferences. For example, if a clothing manufacturer sends a single woman an e-mail containing four click-through website links—two for children's clothes, one each for women's and men's—they would quickly find out that she is only interested in, say, women's casual wear, or whatever her preferences are. Future mailings would be more targeted to her preferences, a benefit to both parties.

There is, of course, the issue of too much of a good thing, and if a vendor were to abuse its privilege, it would quickly lose customers. It is all too easy for an end user to reply to the vendor asking not to receive any further e-mails.

And although there are no statistics yet, surely there are some people who don't like and won't respond to e-mail—just as there are some who won't respond to traditional direct mail or telemarketing. "All of this compulsive checking and replying [to e-mail] necessarily carves up days into smaller and smaller bits," complains Tony Schwartz in *New York* magazine. "What gets sacrificed is the depth and richness that grows out of sustained, absorbed attention to a single task."

Lewis McCreary, editorial director of *CIO Enterprise* magazine, is even grouchier about e-mail. "At some point, you're forced to consider whether when the mode of expression is so empty and easy, it can count for much," writes McCreary in one of his magazine's editorials. "Because it is so darned cheap and easy to deploy recklessly, e-mail has now coagulated into an appalling slop of nearly indistinguishable content. Sane businesspeople wade into it with dread, since finding amid the drivel something you actually need or want can be a futile if not demeaning task."

Effective Web banner ads (see Chapter 9, page 165) garner click-throughs in the 0.5 percent to 2 percent range, and sometimes lower—response rates that are quite consistent with mail-based direct marketing. Some banners, especially those with multimedia, can generate 3 percent to 4 percent click-through. E-mail campaigns to existing customers, by comparison, can generate response rates of 5 to 20 percent or more! And that doesn't even begin to address the personalization and visual options that e-mail can bring to the table.

E-mail is not only a way to deliver a message to an interested audience, but also a way to tailor that message over time to make it as relevant as possible. Response rates to opt-in e-mail campaigns (see Chapter 7, page 127) are the kinds that marketers dream about—and the cost is incredibly low.

An Evolution, Not a Revolution

Many people talk of e-business as a revolution that is transforming the way business is done. Maybe. But many experienced direct marketers see it as more of an extension of what we've already been doing. The technology makes it more efficient and cheaper, but in terms of marketing, the Internet techies haven't invented anything that we hadn't already been doing in nonelectronic media for years.

One trait of the Internet culture that poses a challenge to many traditional marketers is the tendency of Internet users to give and get stuff for free, since direct marketers want to *sell* stuff. In Internet services, for instance, your ISP charges for e-mail capability. So does AOL. But NetZero and Onebox.com give away e-mail service for free! In exchange, they get a large database of active users they can turn around and sell to Internet marketers.

Or take any of the many health and nutrition sites on the Web, such as www.vitaminshoppe.com. Posted on such sites, free for the taking, are tons of information on health, nutrition, and fitness. Our traditional direct marketing clients—book and newsletter publishers—sell this information at handsome prices. But the websites give it away free. Why? To attract people to the site so they will order the nutritional supplements (described in the articles). Where do they order them? Directly from the site, which makes its money selling products, not information.

A new model for doing business? Not at all. Television has worked this way for years! Every night of the week, you can turn on your TV and watch elaborate productions—some that cost a million dollars or more an episode—without paying a dime. The networks give away this costly programming free. In exchange, they get millions of viewers they can turn around and sell to advertisers as expensive air time.

Or take controlled circulation magazines. They spend thousands of dollars to write, design, and print issues, then give them away without charge. Why? They deliver a guaranteed, quality audience to advertisers, who pay handsomely to reach them with ads.

Likewise, direct marketing on the Internet follows the model of direct marketing on paper almost exactly. A text e-mail is the equivalent of a typed sales letter, only online. The more elaborate graphic HTML and animated e-mails we are seeing these days are the electronic equivalent of color, dimensional, and pop-up direct mail.

E-mail marketers count *click-throughs*—the number of people receiving the e-mail who click on the link to the website—the same way direct marketers have always counted reply cards. A growing number of services, such as Match Logic and eTracks.com, measures not only click-throughs but also actual sales resulting from the e-mail. With this data, e-marketers perform break-even analysis—the critical calculation direct marketers live or die by.

The methods and mechanics are the same. The audience is virtually the same—people like you and us. The Internet simply makes it faster and easier. That's a plus, and there are very few drawbacks. For direct marketers, the Internet is an opportunity and not the threat some see it as.

The only real threat, in a sense, is the threat of being left behind because you're not participating. Like it or not, the Web is not only here to stay, but it's growing in usage and importance almost daily. If you don't start using e-marketing to your advantage, your competitors will. And on the Internet, the first in is the marketer who usually wins.

"The winner takes all in Internet space," writes Howard Baldwin in *CIO* magazine (November 1, 1999, p. 88). "Market leaders typically have insurmountable advantages over industry followers."

Want proof? Barnes & Noble has been in business for well over a century (it was started in 1873 as a student book exchange in Greenwich Village); Amazon.com for only a few years. But Amazon.com was the first bookseller on the Web; barnesandnoble.com was second. Today, Amazon.com has a market capitalization of almost $22 billion—around forty times greater than the barnesandnoble.com market capitalization of $520 million. Steve Leuthold, chairman of the Leuthold Group, a financial research organization in Minneapolis, predicts 20 percent or more of all retail volume will be done on the Web in the near future.

The Internet moves faster than offline media. Willy Gissen, an account supervisor at Levin Public Relations in White Plains, New York, observes that it took radio forty years to reach fifty million users. TV took thirteen years to reach fifty million users. The Internet did it in four years. According to an article in *Sales & Marketing Executive Report* (December 6, 1999), the number of small businesses with websites has doubled in each of the past three years.

Where We Stand Now

We are now at the dawn of the e-maillennium, an era in which direct marketing is rapidly evolving from paper mail to electronic delivery over the Internet. But where exactly do we stand? And what are the opportunities over the next several years?

Traditional paper direct mail is beginning to see increased competition from Internet direct mail, which features the advantages of lower cost, less production, faster delivery, and easier response. Print runs for paper catalogs and brochures are being reduced, and in some cases eliminated, as these marketing documents are posted on websites or burned into interactive CD-ROMS.

Although Internet marketing is exciting, has generated impressive early results, and has won many converts, it is still in the relatively early stages of acceptance. Despite the numerous books, seminars, products, software, and services focused on e-commerce, most companies aren't even close to conducting actual business on their websites, most of which are still just graphics and words posted on a server.

Proactive, aggressive Internet marketing right now is being primarily used by early adapters and innovators. While many businesspeople think it would be "nice" to be able to broadcast an e-mail to their customers and prospects, most haven't even put in place the mechanisms (such as e-mail addresses appended to customer and prospect records, and interactive order-accepting websites) to do so.

Every quarter, Edith Roman Associates, a mailing list company, conducts a survey via e-mail to determine the growth rate of Internet direct mail usage. As you can see from the most recent survey results available as this book went to press (see Figure 1.1), e-mail marketing is growing, but the overall usage is relatively small.

Several factors are changing that. To begin with, the Internet in general and business usage of the Internet in particular is growing at a rapid rate (see Figure 1.2). The more your customers are on the Internet and using it actively, the more successfully you can market to them using e-mail and the Web.

Second, the tools and technologies are becoming more powerful and sophisticated. Lots of these are explored throughout this book. Every day, we're discovering new ways to make Web marketing look better, reach the right audience, and generate more response, revenue, and returns.

Third, we're becoming more knowledgeable. We're at the early stages of conducting tests, measuring results, and learning what works

How to Read This Chart: Take a look at consumer catalogs. According to the chart, 44 percent of consumer catalogs are using more e-mail than in last quarter, 44 percent do not use e-mail, and 11 percent are using it less.

E-Mail Trend Results	Up % total	Up % industry	Same % total	Same % industry	Down % total	Down % industry	Do Not Use % total	Do Not Use % industry	Total % total
Associations, club or membership organizations	3	43	0	0	0	0	4	57	7
Catalog (consumer) or retail outlet	4	44	0	0	1	11	4	44	10
Catalog (business to business)	4	67	1	17	0	0	1	17	6
Computer hardware and software	4	29	4	29	0	0	6	43	15
Seminar provider	1	17	3	50	0	0	2	33	6
Financial direct marketer	1	11	2	22	0	0	6	67	10
Fund-raiser	1	100	0	0	0	0	0	0	1
Office equipment, electronic marketer	0	0	0	0	0	0	0	0	0
Other manufacturing/ industrial marketer	0	0	4	80	0	0	1	20	5
Publisher or subscription marketer	4	27	1	7	1	7	10	60	16
Other	6	27	3	14	0	0	14	59	23
Total	30	30	19	19	2	2	49	49	100

Figure 1.1. E-mail trend results

and what doesn't in e-marketing. Guiding principles, methods, and tactics are rapidly emerging. You can do better today because the pioneers of twelve months ago made mistakes we can learn from and avoid. The development and learning curve is that fast!

Fourth, the availability of good e-mail mailing lists—the initial stumbling block to doing Internet direct mail on a vast scale—is

Online purchasing

- One out of five Internet users buys products or shops online
- Average consumer spends $754 a year online
- $43 billion business-to-business Internet sales in 1998
- $7.8 billion consumer Internet sales in 1998
- 62 million online shoppers by 2002
- E-commerce growing 200% annually
- By 2003, business-to-business Internet sales were projected to reach $1.3 trillion—9.4% of total business-to-business annual sales

Source: Forrester Research, 1/5/99; *Research Alert*

Internet advertising and e-commerce

- $1.92 billion in U.S. advertising expenditures in 1998—consumer related 27%, computing 24%, financial 16%, telecom 11%, new media 7%
- Projected to reach $2.6 billion in 1999, $4.2 billion in 2000, $6.7 billion in 2001, $7.1 billion in 2002
- 10,000 domain names are registered daily at $70 each
- More than 2 million small businesses will be engaged in e-commerce by 2002
- E-mail marketing to reach $31 billion by 2002

Sources: e-Marketer, 3/30/99; PricewaterhouseCoopers, IAB 2/9/99; Forrester Research; *CIO WebBusiness*; *DM News; Internet World*

Internet users

- 97 million people in the United States have access to the Internet
- 1 billion people may be connected to the Internet by 2005
- 135 million people in the U.S. will be using e-mail by 2001
- 350 million Internet users by 2003
- 47% of U.S. adults use the World Wide Web
- U.S. population spends a combined 65 million hours per day on the Internet
- Average annual income of Internet users who access the Internet both at work and home is $67,500, versus $48,833 for home users only
- 3.4 billion e-mail messages sent in the U.S. in 1998
- 7 billion e-mail messages will be sent annually in the U.S. in 2000
- 250 billion e-mail marketing messages by 2002
- 63% of Internet users say they use e-mail often
- Average Internet user is online 6 hours a week
- 30 million overseas Internet users in 1997, projected at 184 million in 2002

Sources: Nielsen Media Research, 3/22/99; IDC, Direct Marketing Association; *Research Alert; Daily News; CIO WebBusiness* (6/1/99 and 9/1/99); *Sales and Marketing Management; DM News.*

Figure 1.2. Internet usage and growth

becoming less of a barrier as the number of lists on the market increases at a rapid rate. When we first started working in Internet direct mail, there were only a few dozen lists; today there are hundreds.

By the time this book is published, Internet mailing lists may also number in the thousands. In the United States, a total of more than one hundred million names are available on the thirty thousand conventional mailing lists. So far, the total number of names on e-lists is between two and ten million, depending on how you define a qualified, quality name. (See Chapter 4, page 73.)

Fifth, the cost of Internet direct mail, already low compared with traditional paper marketing, is decreasing. More efficient technology is driving transmission costs down. In conventional direct marketing, by comparison, the cost of almost everything—ad space, printing, postage—is continually increasing and shows no sign of slowing down.

Sixth, there has never been a better time than right now to exploit Internet direct mail as a weapon in your marketing arsenal. That's because the Internet is still new and exciting, and Internet direct mail, although on the rise, is a relatively underused medium. Early adapters of e-mail as a marketing tool can profit during the window of opportunity created by the hesitance of their competitors.

"The Web race belongs to the fastest and smartest players," writes Gregory Slayton in *DM News* (September 27, 1999, p. 28). "Hundreds of companies are experimenting with e-mail marketing today, and most are finding astonishing success."

Will e-marketing's effectiveness decline as its popularity grows? It's possible. Already, early evidence shows that response to banner ads may be waning. Paul Bringe, the late old-time direct mail writer, once said, "When the feed is scarce, the chickens will scratch at anything." Right now, doing aggressive e-campaigns sets you apart from your competition, giving you an edge. That edge may not be around forever. Why not get in now? Let's get started.

Six Steps to Internet Direct Mail Success

Internet marketing consultant Al Bredenberg recommends the following six-step process for putting together and executing successful Internet direct mail campaigns:

1. Planning

2. Determining your offer

3. List selection

4. Creative

5. Testing

6. Rollout

Let's go into each of these steps in brief now, as they will be covered in detail in the remainder of this book.

1. Planning As with any other promotional effort, planning for the direct e-mail campaign should arise from your business's overall marketing plan. Here are some questions you should answer in the beginning.

- What is the positioning of this product? (What does it do and who is it for?)
- Who is your target market?
- What is your competitive position?
- What are your sales objectives? (Be specific: number of sales, dollar amount of sales, profit margin.)
- What do you want to achieve with this e-mail campaign?
- Does this potential audience have access to the Internet?
- Does this potential market like to communicate via the Internet, or are they reluctant and infrequent users?

Besides answering questions like these, you will also need to plan for fulfillment, delivery, customer service, and other activities that will be affected by the campaign.

2. Determining Your Offer Basically, the *offer* means: What are you going to give them and what are they going to give you in return? Sometimes the offer is a straight sale: You're going to give them the product with its associated benefits, and they are going to give you money. It's also possible to structure more compelling offers, or offers that sound like an exceptional value. Perhaps you could offer a discount price for those who order over the Internet during this special campaign. Or maybe you could offer a free premium. Omaha Steaks has had success in e-campaigns with buy one, get one free offers. Whatever your offer, you should emphasize that in your ad copy.

3. *List Selection* Which list or lists you mail to will be determined mostly by the target market you've identified in your plan. Some list providers offer many e-mail lists with varying demographics or interest areas. Some providers own only one list, but they should be able to tell you what the characteristics or interests of their recipients are. For a more in-depth discussion on list selection, see Chapter 4, page 73.

4. *Creative* Creative refers to the concept, copy, design, and format of an advertising piece. Offer and list selection are probably the most critical choices you're going to make, but if you botch your creative, your campaign will fall on its face.

Here are some of the creative issues you'll need to deal with:

Concept and format

- What will be the overall objective of the piece you're writing? What overall theme, slant, or approach will you take?
- How will your message be structured? Will you use long or short copy? Some marketers have had success with a two-step approach: using a brief message to generate interest, then providing a longer presentation via a Web page or autoresponder.
- What response mechanism will you use? How do you want buyers or prospects to reply? Through a Web page? By e-mail? By telephone? Do you need a form? If so, how should it be designed?

Design

- Most e-mail is straight ASCII text—letters, numbers, and punctuation marks.

- Graphical e-mail is emerging, but is not yet prevalent. Even with straight text, however, there are some graphical elements you can employ: capital letters, bullets, lines, and white space.
- Keep in mind that some users will have their e-mail readers configured to display fixed fonts, whereas others will have proportional fonts. This means that your message will look different to different recipients. View your message both ways to make sure that it looks all right—and that you avoid trying to create cute pictures in ASCII.
- Rich media, with its multimedia and interactive attributes, has been proven to increase response to banner ads. Now *visual mail*—e-mail using rich media—is showing itself to be effective.*

Copy

- Copywriting is probably the single most important creative element in an e-mail campaign.
- Focus on your offer and on benefits. A benefit, of course, is what your product or service *does* for the customer or what recipients *get* out of it: Our product makes you money, saves you money, saves you time, or it helps you get ahead in your profession, or it makes you feel good about yourself.
- Use headlines to get attention. Grab their attention right away. Include a major selling point or benefit right in your main heading and opening copy. Use subheads to break up copy and to get across key selling points and benefits. Many people will read only your heads and will skim the rest of your message.
- Include a "call to action" in your message. Don't be ambiguous. Let the recipients know what you want them to do, and ask them to do it. Include a clear response vehicle and easy instructions for how to respond.

---

*Visual mail is a copywritten trademark of e-PostDirect.com. All rights reserved.

5. Testing Once you've selected your lists, created your message, and arranged all back-end processes, it's time to test. You may have found several lists that match your target market. Each list may have tens of thousands or hundreds of thousands of addresses. Test your mailing on smaller samples, perhaps only a few thousand per list. Then examine the response to see which lists "pull" the best. Code your tests to determine where response is coming from. You can also test various offers and creative approaches to find out what generates the highest response rate.

6. Rollout Once you have identified responsive lists and workable offers and creative approaches, it's time to roll out your campaign to a larger audience. Be sure to track the campaign and measure your response. Always run the numbers.

To Sum It All Up

- The Internet has permanently changed the way business is done in America and worldwide.
- Although tons of e-commerce solutions are being made available, methods of marketing on the Internet are in their infancy and only a limited number are available.
- A website is a necessity for Internet marketing, but a website alone is not effective at getting new customers through the Internet.
- Internet direct mail—sending unsolicited promotional e-mails to rented lists of Internet users—is generating huge responses at relatively low marketing cost and (as this book goes to press) is still an untapped gold mine for direct marketers.

What Sells Best on the Internet?

CAN YOUR EXISTING products be sold using Internet direct mail? Or are there only certain products, like software or airline tickets, that have been proven to sell on the Web? This chapter outlines how you can use Internet direct mail, where it seems to work best, and what your target prospects will respond to.

How Internet Direct Mail Can Help You Improve Your Marketing Results

Internet direct mail can be used to:

- acquire new customers
- sell more products to existing customers
- get orders for products or services
- generate requests for follow-up from a salesperson
- direct prospects to a website or page
- generate inquiries for more information
- create affinity programs
- announce new products, services, pricing, and policies

- promote special offers
- conduct market surveys
- renew policies, service contracts, and subscriptions
- promote upgrade offers
- remind customers to use accumulated frequent buyer bonus points
- invite people to participate in a seminar or online discussion
- precede or follow up a paper direct mailing or telemarketing effort—or both
- publish and distribute an online newsletter (e-zine)
- give last-minute reminders
- build brand awareness
- promote your online presence
- provide added value for customers
- convert Web surfers to online buyers
- build customer relationships
- keep your name in front of your customers and prospects
- increase frequency of communication at minimal cost

In an article in *Priorities* magazine (volume 4, issue 1), best-selling author Denis Waitley lists seven ways to make money on the Internet.

1. Sell your own product or services directly to end users—businesses and consumers—over the Internet.

2. Sell products and services, using the Internet to reach distribution channels.

3. Establish a new level of twenty-four hours a day, seven days a week customer service.

4. Create and sell content.

5. Control or provide content and sell advertising around it.

6. Become an Internet consultant or adviser yourself, helping others capitalize on this new global retail outlet as a revenue-producing business.

7. Build a network marketing or direct selling business using the Internet.

What Types of Products Can Be Sold via the Internet?

You can love the Internet. You can hate the Internet. But you ignore it at your peril.

We all know that the Internet has permanently changed the way business is done, overcoming geographic boundaries to doing business and providing customers with twenty-four-hour access to information, pricing, customer service, and order entry.

The Internet is a worldwide store that never closes. "It used to be that if you were lucky you could have one original idea in a lifetime," says David Wetherall, CEO of the dot-com company CMGI. "Now you can have one every day—you really can if you put your mind to it—and that's made possible by the nature of the Internet."

Any product you sell now offline can probably be sold more efficiently and cost-effectively on the Internet. IBM CEO Lou Gerstner says, "E-business has arrived for everyone. Every important business and institution is turning into a dot-com." Whether you sell products or services to businesses or consumers, there is opportunity for you to increase distribution and revenues on the Internet.

It is easy enough to find out what types of products sell best via the Internet. Start a notebook in which you list the different products you find offered online. Check websites, e-mails, and banner ads. You will soon have a large list of items that are being sold successfully via the Internet. If others are selling these types of products online, you can too.

Be careful of being an innovator. You might have stumbled upon a product that seems ideal for the Internet and said to yourself, "Nobody else is doing this, so I will capture the market." Maybe. But if the big players aren't doing it, there must be a reason. Most likely, they are convinced it won't work. Or, they tried it and failed. So be careful of being first. Be innovative in products or channels of distribution but not product categories.

According to the late Eugene Schwartz, one of the most successful direct marketing copywriters of all time, the following products sell extremely well through direct marketing: books, clothing, jewelry, insurance, collectibles, newsletters, magazines, children's items, CDs and audiocassettes, automobile accessories, real estate, household accessories, electronics, status symbols, magic and superstition products, time-savers, and leisure-time products. To this list we add hobby products, start-your-own-business plans, technical plans (for building your own house, helicopter, microbrewery), food, and gift items of all kinds. And, since all Internet selling is in effect "mail order," you will find that these mail-order products work very well online. Table 2.1 summarizes what people are buying online today.

As the table indicates, most online purchasing is for low-ticket consumer items. For high-ticket items, Internet users do product research on the Internet but then purchase through retail or other means.

Surveys indicate 83 percent of Internet users regularly research high-ticket items online. These products include computers (51 percent), appliances (24 percent), and furniture (8 percent).

Pure Internet selling—a transaction conducted 100 percent through the Web without the intervention of a live sales agent—seems to work best for simpler items with fixed per-unit prices.

For products that are more complex, are customizable, or require a price estimate or proposal, some companies are linking their websites to help desks, customer service centers, and other areas where live agents can intervene.

For instance, according to a survey from Jupiter Communications, almost half of online shoppers buying airline tickets over the Internet want to interact at some point during the transaction with a live customer service agent. By comparison, Amazon.com works so well because book buyers don't require this human intervention; fewer than one in ten online book buyers say they would like help from a live customer rep.

Some systems, such as those from AT&T WorldNet, enable a customer service agent to interact directly with the online shopper as he or she surfs the company's website. One such system lets the agent and customer speak on the phone while both view the same

Table 2.1 What People Buy Online

Computer hardware	42%
Nongame software	37%
Books	36%
Airline tickets	33%
Game software	32%
Catalog items	25%
Gifts	25%
Clothing/apparel	23%
Toys	15%
Sporting goods	11%
Cell phones, beepers	7%
Shoes	6%
Cosmetics	3%
Groceries	2%

Source: *Research Alert* (8/20/99)

on-screen Web pages, the viewing of which is controlled by the agent during the conversation, then relinquished to the customer after the live conversation.

The one problem with such a system is that many Internet users have just one phone line. So if they are online, they can't make a voice call at the same time. In these cases, software is available that enables customer service reps to chat with prospects while online. (One such program, LivePerson, is listed in Appendix A, page 230.)

Not everyone who responds to your e-mail and clicks through to your website will buy. According to *DM News* (December 21, 1998, p. 20), only half of Web users who research, browse, or comparison shop for products made an online purchase in 1998.

Many Internet operations grew out of one person's interest in, and love for, a particular type of product. For instance, if you like engraved prints, maybe you can sell them to other art collectors via the Internet. The advantage you have is you go into the venture with knowledge of and enthusiasm for the product. This usually comes across in your communications with customers.

One individual who was a handyman loved writing do-it-your-self articles for the newspaper but found it didn't pay much. Now he has his own website and has made a small fortune selling how-to home project information online.

If you don't have a product you're in love with and want to sell, think of a problem you have that you want to solve. Is there a product that can solve it and that you can create or buy somewhere and then sell it via the Internet?

For example, Frank Reick, a scientist and entrepreneur with a private pilot's license, once had a problem during a flight because he accidentally hit a certain control switch. An inventor, Reick devised a protector for the switch so he would not inadvertently hit it again. He then used mail order to sell many of these switches to other pilots. He now has a website he uses to market an engine additive of his own invention.

What Type of Customer Is the Typical Internet Buyer?

According to a new study by the Interactive Solutions Group, more than sixty million Americans surf the Web, representing 30 percent of the U.S. population age sixteen or older. The study results indicate that the buying habits, behaviors, and attitudes of Internet users increasingly reflect those of the general population.

It's impossible to stereotype Internet buyers, and you shouldn't try. However, many do have certain characteristics in common.

Internet users, by definition, are technology enthusiasts—or at least it's safe to say they aren't afraid of technology. If they were, they'd be shopping offline. "Web users are convenience junkies," says Ilise Benun, a self-promotion expert, "so everything they do online must be simple and save them time."

Internet users are rabidly enthusiastic about this new medium. Dr. Kimberly Young, a psychologist and author of *Caught in the Net* (1998, John Wiley & Sons), found in a survey of 496 Internet users that 80 percent could be classified as "addicted" to the Internet!

Web surfers are information seekers. Contrary to fears that electronics will make print obsolete, surveys show that Internet users tend to rely more on the printed word for information and read newspapers more than non-Internet people. According to a report from the U.S. Department of Commerce, *The Emerging Digital*

Economy, nearly 90 percent of Web users go online to get news and information.

Many Internet marketers serve as *infomediaries*. An infomediary is anyone or anything in the distribution channel that adds value to the buyer through information.

An example is The Diamond Co. Their website, www.thedia mondco.com, is packed with useful information on diamonds. "Our main concern is to educate the customer about diamonds, so they know what they are looking for when they come to us to shop," says manager David Levy.

Different pages on the Diamond Co. website offer explanations of the four Cs—cut, color, clarity, and carat weight—and give tips on purchasing. The site also displays available diamonds that can be purchased by e-mailing inquiries about a particular diamond, then arranging a phone call to consummate the purchase.

Internet buyers are often bargain hunters, so they're looking for savings. That's why discounts and sales work very well with this audience. According to a survey of 1,944 Web users who had not yet made an online purchase (*CIO WebBusiness*, section 2, October 1, 1999, p. 24), 65 percent said they would buy online only if offered a price discount. Look at E*TRADE (www.etrade .com) as an example. They get people to try their online trading service by offering the first trade free; in one promotion, E*TRADE actually offered to put $75 in the customer's account when he or she opened one!

Although people of all ages buy via the Internet, many of the Internet buyers are young and technically oriented. They do not have technophobia. They will buy online and conduct many other activities online, from job searches to dating. Results of a survey published in *CIO WebBusiness* (section 2, August 1, 1999, p. 16) show that 38.5 million youngsters ages five to eighteen will be online by 2002.

According to Ernst & Young, 64 percent of Internet shoppers are between forty and sixty-four years old. Two-thirds are male, 91 percent have attended college, and three-quarters have an annual income of $50,000 or higher. Their favorite online activities are summarized in Table 2.2.

Table 2.2 Favorite Online Activities

Downloading software	81%
E-mail	69%
Computer games	60%
News	43%
Home banking	35%
Online reservations	29%
Product research	29%
Portfolio management	28%
Educational materials	27%
Forums	20%
Chats	17%
Purchases	4%

Source: Ernst & Young

Internet buyers often look for items that are a bit interesting, different, or unusual. If there's a story to tell about your product, the Internet buyer wants to hear it. They like to be "romanced," talked to, and sold.

They have curious, active minds, and they want more information about products than the average buyer before making a purchase decision. Despite all the talk about illiteracy in North America, the Internet buyers tend to be information seekers—more so than the general public. Keep your e-mails concise, but have more back-up information available on your website.

The Internet buyers often are people who either dislike retail or don't live close to stores. As online sales are growing, offline retail business is declining. According to research from Jupiter Communications, 94 percent of online revenues generated in 1999 were generated by people buying products online that they would have otherwise bought offline. Only 6 percent of Internet sales were for purchases that would otherwise not have been made.

The Internet buyers look for convenience. They want to click on a banner, reply to an e-mail, go to a website, fill up an online shopping basket, give their order and credit card information, and be done with their shopping. They like looking through interesting Web pages, but they may not get the same enjoyment in stores. Stores are too crowded; they don't like dealing with store clerks; and driving to and parking at the mall is a pain in the neck.

Characteristics of the Successful Internet Product

Here's what to look for when evaluating products and their Internet potential. You don't need all of these factors to be successful, but you do need at least some of them.

The Product Is Not Available in Stores

The easier it is to get the product in stores, the more difficult it will be to sell it via the Internet. The ideal Internet product is available only via the Internet and not in stores. "Not available in stores" is a magnetic lure to many Internet buyers.

However, many products are sold both retail and via the Internet. For these products, the convenience of buying via the Internet is what attracts buyers. Take Amazon.com as an example. Internet users can get books in bookstores but prefer buying them on Amazon.com because it's easier.

Actually, as any author knows, all books are not as available in bookstores as nonauthors might think. The fact is, even the largest book superstore—with an inventory of 150,000 to 200,000 titles—has only a fraction of the 65,000-plus new books published each year and the nearly 1.5 million or so books in print. Amazon offers buyers a convenient source for titles they can't easily get in their local bookstores, especially for specialized and out-of-print books.

The Product Is Story-Rich

This means there is a lot you can say about the product. The story can include how it originated, how it was made, and, of course, the many benefits it offers users.

A good example is the increasing use of the Web to sell vitamins, herbs, and other nutritional supplements. These sites combine product descriptions with pages containing articles, medical papers, abstracts, and other extensive background information on zinc, ginkgo biloba, bilberry, and other natural ingredients.

Many customers using search engines to research a particular herb or mineral find themselves sent to a commercial website with an appropriate article. After they read the article and are convinced they want to try the supplement, they naturally order it from the website, since they are already on it.

Buyers cannot consistently and reliably get this depth of information from the average clerk working at a health food store. Some health food stores' employees are knowledgeable others are not. And, with many customers to service, the time they can spend answering your questions is limited.

The Internet, on the other hand, is always there. The health websites are open twenty-four hours a day, seven days a week, to answer questions and take orders. And there's almost no limit to the number of customers they can handle simultaneously.

The Product Can Be Priced for Internet Selling

A $6 product is difficult to sell via the Internet. The price is too low to profitably sell it directly from a space ad or direct mail package. You can only sell the $6 product if it's one of many items in a catalog.

Internet products ideally sell for at least $10. If you are going to promote the product via direct e-mail, it should sell for at least $25 or more. *E-tailers* (Internet retailers) who sell low-priced items encourage shoppers to buy multiple items at a time so that the total order is at least $25. They often do this by offering a discount, free shipping and handling, or a bonus gift for larger orders. For instance, gazelle.com, an online retailer of hosiery, has offered free shipping and handling for orders of $25 or more, as well as a free sports bag for orders of $40 or more.

The Product Has an Element of Fun, Mystery, or the Unusual

Internet buyers tend to respond to gimmicks, gadgets, and unusual, hard-to-find products. For example, one of us (Bob) recently bought his son a Venus's flytrap after reading about it on a nursery website that features carnivorous plants.

The Product Can Be Shipped

Ice cream is not widely sold via the Internet because it cannot be shipped to the consumer without melting. Delicate, fragile, and oversized items are also difficult to ship. The ideal Internet product is compact enough to be shipped economically and rugged enough that it won't break or spoil in transit.

Distribution and fulfillment often separate the successful websites from the failures. Sure, you can reach prospects and take orders electronically. But unless the product is electronic—software, data, or information—you have to deliver the goods physically to the customer. Some websites now allow shoppers to find items and sales online, then direct them to a retail outlet for purchasing and merchandise pick-up.

What about selling services over the Internet? Internet direct mail can be used to generate inquiries, which can be followed up to close the sale or generate an appointment with a sales rep. Any service that does not require a face-to-face meeting between service provider and customer can be completely transacted over the Internet. For instance, you can fill in a form on an astrologer's website, then he or she can calculate your horoscope and e-mail it back to you.

The Product Is Refillable or Requires Updating or Supplies

We will discuss in the next section the importance of having additional products, known as *back-end products*, to sell your Internet customers. A refillable product, or one that requires updating, has its own back end built into it.

A good example is Day-Timers. When you buy a Day-Timer, the company gains a customer who will in all likelihood come back each year to buy refill pages for the new year. Another good refillable Internet product is vitamins. When you use up the vitamins, you have to order more to keep up with the regimen.

Another example is iPrint.com, a company that sells printing of business cards, letterhead, and other business materials over the Internet. They make free or low-priced offers to get customers to buy from them once; their profit is on the repeat orders as people run out of stationery and need to replenish their supply.

The Product Is Different from Competing Products

Try to identify or create in your product one unique selling point that differentiates it from all other products in its class. Your copy will come across as much stronger if it focuses on a unique aspect of your product the consumer can't get when buying competing products.

Hamilton Knife, for example, sells a machine tool oil that makes tools last up to five times longer because of the superior lubrication. The lubrication is superior because the oil is literally magnetic, so it clings to the cutting edge better. In magnetic materials, the atoms are polarized, or aligned in one direction. Hamilton's ad headline, "Unique 'polarized oil' makes machine tools last 5 times longer," capitalizes on the unique difference of polarized oil versus regular oil. This is their unique selling proposition, which is explained at great length in their inquiry fulfillment materials.

The Product Is Part of a Bigger Line of Related Products

To succeed in the Internet, you cannot offer just one product, unless it needs replenishment, like vitamins or groceries. The reason is that the majority of the Internet businesses make the bulk of their profits on the back end—selling related products to people who have purchased the *front-end*, or primary, product.

The greatest expense on the Internet is acquiring a new customer. Direct marketing expert Murray Raphel explains that it costs five times as much to acquire a new customer as it does to sell additional products (the back-end product line) to existing customers. Therefore, if you do not have a back end—additional products to sell to people who have bought your main product from you—you are leaving a lot of profits on the table.

Order some Internet products. Write down the name of the product and the price on a sheet of paper in a notebook. Then keep track of other offers you get from the company. Write down these products and their prices on the sheet under the primary product. You will quickly learn how companies put together their front- and back-end product lines.

What makes for a good back-end product? A good back-end product complements the front-end product. For instance, Dan Poynter of Para Publishing (800-PARAPUB) sells as his front end *The Self-Publishing Manual*, a book on how to self-publish your own book. Many forms are involved in publishing a book (such as copyright forms and ISBN registration), so a natural back-end product for Dan, which he sells from his catalog, is a collection of all the necessary forms.

Jon Kremer of Ad-Lib Publications in Fairfield, Iowa, also sells information on how to self-publish and promote your own book. Recognizing that a major step in self-publishing is getting the book printed, he sells, as a back-end product, a directory of all the book printers in North America.

The Atkins Center, in New York City, publishes a newsletter, *Dr. Atkins' Health Revelations.* Their back-end products are vitamins and nutritional supplements recommended in the newsletter.

Back-end products should relate to the front-end product; that is, they ideally address the same consumer need, fear, concern, or problem. If you sell vitamins, for example, a book on blood pressure is a good back-end product; a book on investing in mutual funds, unrelated to health, is less appropriate.

Back-end products are usually smaller than the main product, less expensive to produce, and priced lower. But this is not always the case. A percentage of customers who buy your product will buy a related product at a much higher price, and upselling your list on more expensive offers can often be profitable.

How big a back end do you need to be profitable? The bigger, the better. However, you don't have to have a complete back-end product line when you begin. Start with a small number of back-end products, then add new ones as you create or find them.

If you sell a product in the $10 to $50 range as your front end, try to line up at least $100 to $200 worth of back-end products to start with. You can always expand later on.

How and When Do You Offer Back-End Products?

There are many ways to offer back-end products to Internet customers. If you send an e-mail designed to get the prospect to order a product, sell only your front-end product in the initial promotion. Do not confuse the reader by discussing other items in the first e-mail. The idea is to sell the person the front-end item first, making him or her a customer of your firm, and then sell related products. If you try to sell more than one product in the first promotion, you will probably depress your response.

The greatest profit opportunity for selling back-end products is through your website. Ideally, your website should serve as an online catalog of your entire back-end product line.

You can promote your back end in other ways, of course. For instance, you can periodically send an e-zine (electronic customer newsletter; see Chapter 9, page 185) promoting five or six of your offers. Or you can feature one of your back-end products in an e-mail to your list of existing Internet customers. Another option is to mail customers a print or CD-ROM catalog several times a year.

You can experiment with different back-end products by posting literature about them on your website. The low cost of Internet marketing allows you to add many products to your back end, not just those you make. Additional profits from selling other people's products on your site can be substantial.

When you find an item you want to offer, arrange with the manufacturer to order a small quantity on consignment or to have them drop ship to your customers. That way, you can test a product without making any significant investment in inventory or product development.

If orders are good and the product is profitable, arrange with the manufacturer to buy larger quantities at a deep discount, or you can continue to drop ship. Or, develop and produce your own product similar to the one you tested.

If a product is not profitable (meaning people don't order it), simply return your consignment inventory and delete the item's page from your site.

Sometimes a back-end item sells well for a time, then slows down or is replaced with a newer, more appropriate item. You can always get rid of the remaining inventory by offering the item on sale at 10 to 20 percent discount or more.

Another strategy is to order the old item as a premium or free gift. You tell customers that if they offer X dollars' worth of merchandise from your site, they get the item free. This works extremely well.

Since the back end can be modified and expanded gradually, creating and building a back-end product line is one of the few things in the Internet you can do at a reasonably slow pace. Once you have an ongoing, successful product line, it's fun to discover new products you can sell profitably as part of your back end.

Keep in mind that back-end products usually fill a gap in the customer's requirements that the front-end product does not address. Often this need or requirement is, in fact, created by the front-end product.

For instance, if you sell sales training materials on "how to sell more product by telephone," and your front-end product recommends use of a telephone headset, many of your customers will write you asking where they can get such a headset and which one you personally recommend. Why not arrange with the manufacturer of your preferred brand of headset for you to become a distributor, then sell your customers the headset directly—and make the profit yourself—when they call looking for it?

Sales Tax

According to the *San Jose Mercury News*, forty-six states and seven thousand local jurisdictions in the United States charge sales taxes, often on different items and at varying rates. Rates typically range from 5 to $8\frac{1}{4}$ percent.

On the Internet, sales tax is not often collected. You may want to consult your tax accountant on whether you should be charging sales tax to your Internet customers.

In a sense, all e-commerce is an electronic version of traditional mail-order marketing, in which the buying and selling is conducted remotely rather than in person. In e-commerce, the transaction takes place electronically over the Internet. In conventional mail order, the order is placed over the phone or mailed in. As an article in *Time* magazine (December 17, 1999, p. 129) explains, "Because e-tailers have no physical presence—such as a store or warehouse—in most states, they are not required to collect sales tax from customers."

Traditionally, mail-order operators in the United States collect sales tax only on orders placed by customers whose mailing addresses are in your state. Says mail-order attorney Kalvin Kahn in his book *Mail Order Laws*, "You need not collect and pay the sales tax of the state of your purchaser unless you have a 'physical presence'—an office, warehouse, or salespersons—in that state."

- **Tip:** If you sell software, your promotions—online and printed—should encourage prospects to visit your site and download a demo or evaluation copy. One software marketer found that prospects who downloaded an evaluation copy from the website—in response to a traditional (not e-mail) direct mail—were up to ten times more likely to purchase than those who mailed back a reply card requesting a CD-ROM.

- **Did you know?** Financial products are an increasingly popular offer on the Internet. Forrester Research estimates that by 2002, nearly 10 million Europeans will be seeking financial advice online, and 14.4 million Americans will be trading online. Online trading from day traders alone accounts for 15 percent of the NASDAQ volume.

According to the Direct Marketing Association, the 1992 Supreme Court decision in Quill Corporation vs. North Dakota Department of Revenue ruled in favor of direct marketers. It affirmed that, without congressional authorization, state governments can't force out-of-state mail-order companies to collect the sales taxes imposed by the state on in-state merchants.

Prior to Quill vs. North Dakota, there had been many proposals at both the federal and state levels to force mail-order firms to collect sales tax from all customers. The recent Supreme Court ruling, which upholds the 1967 ruling of National Bellas Hess, makes it illegal for states to ask you or try to force you to collect sales tax if you don't have a physical location in that state.

This law has been challenged several times over recent years. While it is still in place, one of the greatest threats to small mail-order operators is that the courts may someday require them to collect sales tax in every state. This would make order forms unbelievably complex and would be an administrative and accounting nightmare. Order forms would have to be redesigned, and computer software modified to account for the different sales tax rates in the various states. Software and tax rate tables would have to be updated annually since sales tax rates do change periodically.

If in the future e-marketers are required to collect sales tax, the sales tax can automatically be charged to the buyer's credit card. The credit card companies could then remit it to the state.

Canadian mail-order operators collect Goods and Services Tax (G.S.T.) on all orders from customers within Canada. The G.S.T. is currently 7 percent. Canadian mail-order operators do not charge sales tax on orders placed from customers in the United States. U.S. mail-order operators do not charge G.S.T. or any other sales tax on orders placed from customers in Canada.

Accept Credit Cards on Your Website

You can seriously increase your Internet orders by accepting credit cards as payment. It's easy and convenient for customers, and that makes it more likely they will order. An article in *The Interactive Multimedia Sourcebook 1997* says that nearly 90 percent of online shoppers pay by credit card. Yet according to *Business Week* (April 17, 2000, p. 10), only 28 percent of large businesses surveyed say they can process a credit card transaction online!

Mediamark Research reports that the average age of credit card holders in the U.S. is 45.6 years. Of 220 million Americans, 144 million have Visa, 93 million have MasterCard, 41 million have Discover, and 25 million have American Express, reports an article in *Upfront* newsletter. According to the article, having a merchant account can increase your sales volume 30 to 200 percent.

The only problem is that it's hard for some businesses, particularly small Internet businesses, to gain the ability to accept credit cards. Banks are very reluctant to authorize credit card acceptance, mainly because they have been burned too many times by fraudulent businesses.

So, many businesses go on, accepting only checks or money orders for payment, and miss out on the added sales they would get through credit cards. There is a way, though, for businesses that can't get bank authorization to accept credit cards.

Being able to accept credit cards is immensely helpful for conventional businesses but absolutely essential for businesses that want to market merchandise to consumers over the Internet. The Internet prospect prefers doing transactions and communicating online rather than offline. If you can complete the transaction completely online, you satisfy your customer and get his or her business. If you force the person to go offline during the transaction, you may lose the sale.

If you have a long-term good relationship with your bank, that gives you some powerful leverage. Be willing to use that leverage to get what you want. After all, banks are in business for the same reason as the rest of us—to serve their customers and to make a profit.

The major credit cards in the United States are Visa, MasterCard, Discover, and American Express. If your business caters to certain market segments, you may want to consider other types of credit cards. For example, if many of your customers are Japanese, you probably want to accept orders from JCB (Japan Credit Bureau) cardholders. For European customers, consider Diner's Club. You might also want to think about Carte Blanche cards.

To get established as a Visa and MasterCard merchant, start with your own bank. If you have a good relationship with them, they are your best bet. Another option you may want to add is American Express. They are easy to deal with and seem to have no bias against the Internet businesses.

The typical American Express cardholder has an affluent lifestyle, high household income, and is an impulse buyer. Many businesses give their employees American Express credit cards for travel and other business expenses. So if you are selling products or services to businesspeople, by all means call American Express for a merchant account application.

A suggestion when you fill out your merchant account applications, whether it be for your bank, American Express, or whomever: be truthful, but give them as high an average per-order dollar figure as you can. They like to see average orders of $20 or more.

Higher-average orders and higher sales volumes can reduce the percentage of each sale you will pay to the credit card issuer. This fee can vary anywhere from 1.5 percent to 5 percent, depending on your average order size, sales volume, and other factors. But even if you have to pay 5 percent, it's well worth it.

The easiest way to get a merchant account is to work with an independent sales organization (ISO), which acts as a mediary between small businesses and banks. They will charge an additional fee for each transaction, so you will be paying a bit more than the standard percentage charged for credit card transactions. There will also be an application fee. Here are the typical charges to expect, as of this writing.

- **Application fees:** Usually, these range from $95 to $400, and may or may not be refundable.
- **Point of sale terminal purchase or lease:** The terminal you use to process the charge and check for fraudulent numbers is usually available from a bank for around $300. You will only be able to get this price, though, if a bank authorizes you. If working through an ISO, prices will range from $400 to even as high as $1,500. You can usually lease the terminal, though, at an average of $45 per month. The best thing to do is to find an ISO that will provide computer software that can be used in place of a terminal. This will usually cost only around $150.
- **Service fees:** Banks charge between 2 and 5 percent for processing a credit card purchase. ISOs charge more, usually 3 to 7 percent. They also usually charge a per-transaction fee of 20 to 25 cents, and a monthly statement fee of $5 to $10.

Why all these fees? ISOs want to work only with legitimate businesses and ones that will stay with them for a long period of time—and if a business can afford these fees, they are considered less of a risk. Thus, the important thing to do is to shop around for an ISO. Get as much information as you can about each ISO you are considering, and read it thoroughly. Look for hidden charges and unreasonable requirements.

All of these services will require you to fill out an application. Be totally truthful with everything on the application and don't let the representative talk you into putting anything else down.

The reason is, if the banks affiliated with the ISO you use were to find out that any information on your application is false, you would probably be immediately cancelled and your business name and address would go on a blacklist. This would prevent you from being able to accept credit cards for an indefinite period of time. Don't let this happen to you.

Most of the ISOs out there are legitimate, but there are a few that may put down spurious information, rather than lose the fees they'd receive. Be sure to look everything over twice. If you do, you'll probably find an ISO that will work with you to expand your business through the acceptance of credit cards.

Another payment option is to work through a service bureau that can process the online payments for you. One such company (listed in Appendix A, page 239) is CyberCash, which promotes itself as "the leading provider of electronic commerce payment services." Their CyberCash CashRegister product, for instance, lets you accept secure credit card transactions over the Internet, including real-time authorization, voids, returns, and settlement. See Appendix A for information on how to contact credit card providers, ISOs, and CyberCash.

Another service bureau, 1ClickCharge (also listed in Appendix A, page 246), specializes in allowing online purchases for small dollar amounts—typically less than $20. They store the customer's credit card information, so the buyer doesn't have to reenter the card number and expiration date whenever he or she visits your site.

To Sum It All Up

- Internet marketing is direct response marketing that takes place over the World Wide Web instead of on paper.
- Internet buyers are looking for education and information about your products. You can increase your sales by supplying it to them—in your e-marketing campaigns and especially on your website.
- Allow the entire transaction to take place on the Web. Don't force prospects to call on the telephone or use snail mail, although you may want to give them the *option* of doing so.
- Accept credit cards on your website for true e-commerce.

CREATING THE MAILING

ARE THE RULES of copywriting changing in the e-maillennium, or does what worked in printed direct mail translate directly into Internet direct mail? As this book goes to press, the answers to those questions are being worked out in tests right now.

So far, results indicate that a lot of the copywriting techniques that boost response in paper direct mail—strong offers, powerful headlines, provocative lead-ins, enticing benefits, and appeals to the reader's self-interest—are just as necessary in Internet direct mail.

A concern among direct marketers who use long copy to sell products directly from their direct mail packages, rather than generate leads, is whether long copy is also effective in Internet direct mail. Can the Internet be used to sell newsletters, magazines, software, seminars, and other products traditionally sold through copy-heavy print packages?

Early results show that shorter Internet direct mail generally works better than lengthy e-mail; force people to scroll through pages of an e-mail message, and you risk losing them. If the whole selling message can't fit on the e-mail, a two-step approach can work: You arouse the reader's interest and get him or her to click on a response form designed specifically for the e-mail campaign and on the Web. Once you get the prospect there, additional copy on the Web page can complete the selling job and get the order.

Plain or Fancy?

Most people think of e-mail as plain text messages, and the majority of the 3.4 trillion e-mail messages in 1998 were sent in this format.

Straight text is the simplest, most popular, easiest, and least costly e-mail marketing format. In fact, the programming and design costs are zero. Just type your message, and you're done.

But text e-mail doesn't take advantage of the graphic and interactive capabilities of the Internet. That's why you might want to consider two other formats: *enhanced graphics* (HTML) and *visual mail*.

With enhanced graphics e-mail, HTML is used to add color, fonts, different type sizes, drawings, photos, and other visuals to the e-mail message. You can send an e-mail that looks more like a designed Web or catalog page than a memo or letter. This is ideal for catalog marketers and others selling tangible goods.

Not every PC user can read HTML files. Therefore, make sure your transmission bureau uses dual-mode "sniffer" technology. This technology automatically determines whether recipients can read HTML files. If they can, they get the HTML version. If not, they are sent a straight text version instead.

Usage of e-mail enhanced with HTML graphics is on the rise. In some, the HTML is used simply to display fonts and put headlines and subheads in color. In others, it adds images to the text. HTML e-messages take longer to send and require more bandwidth to transmit, but they don't take any longer for the recipient to view. Depending on the list, there can be no extra cost for sending HTML, or it can run an additional $10 to $50 per thousand names.

HTML e-mail can outpull plain text messages by as much as 20 percent, both in click-through and conversion rates. Perhaps those who receive HTML and click are more Internet savvy and more willing to purchase online. According to an article in *American*

Demographics (June 2000, p. 44), an eMarketer survey found that 80 percent of e-mail users owned computers capable of managing HTML e-mail.

Visual mail goes a step further, adding motion and interaction to the e-mail. Graphics, animation, video, music, sound effects, multimedia, and audio are incorporated into a self-contained file that is sent as an attachment to an e-mail or a link to a Web page. In the industry, this is known as *rich media*.

With rich media, you can create dynamic presentations that have much greater impact than traditional static e-mail. For instance, if you are marketing a consulting service, your visual mail, when opened by the recipient, could show a short scene of two executives discussing the problem your service can help solve.

Graphics can make a difference. Mina Chen of Doubleday Interactive told us that increasing headline type size by one point, displaying it in red instead of black, and indenting the first paragraph increased response on one e-marketing message an incredible 184 percent!

The preferred format for visual e-mail is to embed the rich media into the e-mail message, much like an HTML graphic would be. The rich-media file is automatically opened and displayed when the e-mail is opened.

Certain rich-media visual presentations require the user to have a plug-in. Many recipients will quickly delete an e-mail rather than bother to download the plug-in as instructed.

As an alternative, the rich-media presentation can be e-mailed as an attached file in a self-running format. Data compression techniques are used to compress this file to an acceptable size. Be careful about sending a rich-media or other e-mail requiring the recipient to open an attachment. On the plus side, some recipients have commented to us that the attachments make the e-mail seem more personal and important. But most e-mail systems give a warning about opening attachments from an unknown source. The warning mentions the possibility of downloading an attachment with a virus, so it scares people. If the recipients don't know you, they might instantly delete the whole message as soon as this warning appears.

Prospects don't like to waste time downloading large files. Proprietary compression programs enable visual mail presentations to be "shrunk" to a manageable file size—typically 200K or less.

Structuring the Message

Contrary to the popular misconception that people don't read anymore, real prospects with a genuine interest in your offer *want* product information and *will* read long copy—even on the Internet!

Yet people are busier than ever, so your e-mail should use the following structure (as shown in Figure 3.1).

At the beginning of the e-mail, put a "From" line and a "Subject" line. The e-mail "From" line identifies you as the sender if you are e-mailing to your house file. If you're e-mailing to a rented list, the "From" line might identify the list owner as the sender. This shows the recipient that the e-mail is not spam, but rather a communication from someone with whom they already have an established relationship.

The "Subject" line should be constructed like a short attention-grabbing, curiosity-arousing outer envelope teaser, compelling recipients to read further—without being so blatantly promotional it turns them off. If you can tease the reader and force him or her to read the e-mail to satisfy curiosity, your subject line will increase readership and response. Example: "Advice from Bill Gates" is better than "Bill Gates on innovation." The latter sounds like just another lecture or article, but the former arouses curiosity. What exactly would Bill Gates want to tell you?

Subject lines should be as short as possible to get the point across quickly. Standard e-mail readers can accommodate a subject line of up to sixty characters, but many don't display them all. So long subject lines can get cut off.

In the first paragraph, state the offer and provide an immediate response mechanism, such as clicking on a link connected to a Web page. This appeals to Internet prospects with short attention spans.

After the first paragraph, present expanded copy that covers the features, benefits, proof, and other information the buyer needs to make a decision. This appeals to the prospect who needs more details than a short paragraph can provide.

To: Sam August@zelco.com

Return address handles
bounces/opt-outs

From: Zelco Publishing

Subject: Renew now!

Dear <Sam>:   *Personalized*
opening salutation

Please take a few moments now to renew your FREE subscription to
Zelco by clicking on the easy-to-use hyperlink below.

We are happy to continue your FREE subscription to Zelco, but we need
to hear from you now in order to guarantee delivery of future issues.

Customized URL to
facilitate tracking

To renew your FREE subscription, just click on
http://www.zelco.com/cgi-bin/ch?c=3456&sam@zelco.com/orderform

(or copy and paste it into your browser) and complete the renewal
information online.

Don't delay. Renew Today!

This messsage is brought to you on behalf of Zelco Publications in
an effort to simplify the renewal process for you and to keep your
FREE subscription coming to you. Any feedback you have on this
type of notice is welcome.

Opt-out
instruction

If you wish to stop receiving such messages, please click on this link:
http://www.zelco.com/cgi-bin/ch?c=zp&e=sam@zelco.com
Or, reply to this email with the word "remove" in the subject line. For
better service, please be sure to include the following information in
your reply:

Customized copy using
house file data fields

Your name: Sam August
Your Subscription Account#: 3456

Thank you!

Figure 3.1 Personalized message

Choose a style that fits your audience and your content. In some e-mails, this body of information is presented as a series of short paragraphs separated by lines or asterisks. Others present it as a continuous letter.

Another successful format is the e-zine (Internet magazine), in which the e-mail resembles a short newsletter containing multiple items. Each short section covers one product or service. Each section has a link to a page on your website providing more information on that product.

More on Subject Lines

"It's gotten so bad that I am now surfing my e-mail, deleting as many messages as possible, and barely skimming the rest. And my decisions are based on the subject line," reports Ilise Benun, a self-promotion specialist.

According to Benun, your subject line must answer one or more of the following questions.

Who is the e-mail from? Make sure your name or company name comes up in the "From" field, so your message is easily recognizable.

What is it about? These tell us enough to decide whether we care.

- "Yoga classes at Healing Arts"
- "Support the NEA"
- "Your Website Planner"

What does the recipient have to do and when?

- "C'mon back to Idea Site"
- "Self-Promotion Workshop in NYC 10/19"

Also, no one has any patience for vague or deceptively intriguing subject lines, so don't use anything like:

- "Hello"
- "We need your help"
- "Make 10K a month"
- "My computer is fixed"

The subject line must say who you are or what you do—or both. Remember that your subject line is the marketing equivalent of a teaser on a direct mail package's outer envelope or the headline on a print ad. It has to get the reader's immediate attention. If the readers perceive the subject line as promotional, irrelevant, or boring, they'll delete your e-mail on the spot.

Use an energetic, to-the-point subject line. That's what people see first. If you're using the word "Free," make it the first word. (You don't want it to get cut off in the reader's "Subject" window by mistake!) Example: "FREE templates for JetSoft customers!" instead of "Get your fabulous templates FREE!"

Like a memo, an e-mail message needs a subject or reference line to help your reader quickly identify what you're communicating. Make your subject line as specific as you can without creating a complete sentence. To avoid boring your reader, don't use the very same wording as the first line of your message.

The "From" Line

Some e-marketers think the "From" line is trivial and unimportant; others have told us they think it's critical. Internet copywriter Ivan Levison says, "I often use the word 'Team' in the FROM line, which makes it sound as if there's a group of bright, energetic, enthusiastic people standing behind the product." For instance, if you are sending an e-mail to a rented list of computer people to promote a new software product, your "Subject" and "From" lines might read as follows (in this example, the sender is Adobe Software; the recipients are Adobe customers who own an earlier version of PageMill):

TO: Name
FROM: The Adobe PageMill Team
SUBJECT: Adobe PageMill 3.0 limited-time offer!

If the e-mail is from a well-known company, put the company name in the "From" line. For instance, since most computer users are Microsoft users, they will read an e-mail that says it's from Microsoft.

Warning: Despite the fact that *free* is a proven, powerful response-booster in traditional direct marketing, and that the Internet culture has a bias in favor of free offers rather than paid offers, some e-marketers avoid *free* in the subject line. The reason is the spam filter software some Internet users have installed to screen their e-mail. These filters eliminate incoming e-mail that they determine to be advertising, and many identify any message with FREE in the subject line as promotional.

If your company name is not well known, do not use it in the "From" line—recipients will think the message is spam and delete it. A better strategy would be to use your own name in the "From" line. They might think it's a personal message and at least look at it a bit rather than instantly delete it.

The Lead

Deliver a miniversion of your complete message right in the first paragraph. Within the first paragraph, include your response mechanism—a link to a Web page or form that serves as the response mechanism for the offer.

The offer and response mechanism should be repeated in the close of the e-mail, but they should almost always also appear at the very beginning. That way, busy Internet users who don't have time to read, and give each e-mail only a second or two, get the whole story.

A short-form e-mail marketing message may consist of only a few lines or a few paragraphs. If you want more detail, you should still start with a powerful lead that sums up the offer and asks for action. Then you can follow with a series of bullets or short paragraphs that give more details. But the first paragraph must always tell the recipients why you are contacting them and what you are offering them, with a clickable link to more information or a response mechanism.

If you put multiple response links within your e-mail message, 95 percent of click-through responses will come from the first two. Therefore, you should probably limit the number of click-through links in your e-mail to three. An exception to this might be an e-newsletter or e-zine broken into five or six short items, where each item is on a different subject and therefore each has its own link.

Writing the Body Copy

Remember that when you're restricted to ASCII characters, you give up all your formatting tools. You're working without bold, italics, underlining, and graphics. This means you have to lay things out very simply. Here are some guidelines to follow when writing Internet direct mail messages.

• Don't use big blocks of text. Organize your message into modules using simple borders created out of asterisks, dollar signs, or dashes.

• Use wide margins. You don't want to have weird wraps or breaks. Limit yourself to about fifty-five to sixty characters per line. If you think a line is going to be too long, insert a character return. Set your margins at 20 and 80 to keep sentence length to sixty characters; this ensures that the whole line gets displayed on the screen without odd text breaks.

• Take it easy on the all-caps. You can use WORDS IN ALL CAPS, but do so carefully. They can be a little hard to read—and in the world of e-mail, all-caps give the impression that you're shouting.

• Get the important points across quickly. If you want to give a lot of product information, add it lower down in your e-mail message. People who need more information should scroll down for it. The key benefits and deal should be communicated in the first screen, or very soon afterward.

• Lead off the message copy with a killer headline. You need to get a terrific benefit right up front. Pretend you're writing envelope teaser copy or are writing a headline for a sales letter.

- Watch your tone. When you're writing e-mail it's easy to sound sarcastic or cutting without meaning to. Be sure you're not giving unintended offense. Watch the jokes. They're a lot less funny in ASCII!

- Don't use emoticons (see Glossary, page 317). If you want to use happy faces (or whatever) in your personal mail, that's fine, but keep them out of your business e-mail. They're terminally cute.

- Information is the gold in cyberspace. Trying to sell readers with a traditional hyped-up sales letter won't work. People online want information, and lots of it. You'll have to add solid material to your puffed-up sales letter to make it work online. Refrain from saying your service is "the best" or that you offer "quality." Those are empty, meaningless phrases. Be specific. How are you the best? What exactly do you mean by quality? And who says it besides you? And even though information is the gold, readers don't want to be bored. They seek, like all of us, excitement. Give it to them.

- In Internet direct mail, copy is king. Graphics can make a big difference, when you use them. But a tailored message, compellingly expressed, is what motivates people to click for more information. Avoid putting too much emphasis on design and functionality at the expense of a well-crafted marketing message, as some e-marketers do.

- Internet copy should have an appropriate balance between "tension" (hard-selling) and "relief" (information). You must quickly convince the readers to take the next step. But educating them in the process builds confidence in your product and in you as an authority in the problem or field your product deals with.

- In general, short is better. This is not the case in classic mail-order selling, where, as a general principle, "the more you tell, the more you sell." E-mail is a unique environment. Readers are quickly sorting through a bunch of messages and aren't disposed to stick with you for a long time. Unlike other kinds of sales writing, where long copy outsells short copy, the standard for e-mail is different.

The tradition in Internet direct mail of using short copy poses a problem for marketers whose paper direct mail typically depends on long copy to make the sale. Increasingly, we find that longer e-mail copy can work for these firms.

The key is to incorporate the benefit, offer, and response link into the first paragraph or two of your long-copy message. Those people who are more comfortable on the Internet, or are familiar with the product, might want to click on the link at the top without reading the rest of the message. Others who need to be sold before they click and purchase can delve further into the copy.

And don't forget to test! We all know that one of the exciting things about direct mail is that you can use it to answer vital marketing questions. You can find out which list works best, which price point makes the most money, which creative approach is the winner, and so on. The same thing holds true for your e-mail campaigns.

What can you test? How about pitting a warm, personal message from a specific person against a more formal, longer, anonymous presentation of the offer? Or how about testing an HTML-based or visual approach against a straight text e-mail?

Opt-Out Language

Another key component of your e-mail message, especially when mailing to your own house file, is the opt-out language.

The opt-out statement prevents flaming from recipients who feel they have been spammed, by stating that your intention is to respect their privacy and making it easy for them to prevent further promotional e-mails from being sent to them. All they have to do is use their e-mail software's reply function and type "unsubscribe" or "remove" in the subject line.

The following text is a model opt-out statement. You can use it as is or modify it to fit your own e-campaigns:

"We respect your online time and privacy and pledge not to abuse this medium. If you prefer not to receive further e-mails of this type from us, please reply to this e-mail and type 'Remove' in the subject line."

Think about the way you sort through e-mail, especially when you have a backlog of messages. A busy prospect will delete e-mails rapidly unless something immediately grabs his or her attention. From an informal survey of corporate executives (that is, asking our friends and colleagues), we estimate that the average executive gets fifty to eighty e-mails daily. The clutter forces them to read, scan, make decisions about reading, and delete e-mail much more quickly than they would if the inbox in their messaging systems were not so cluttered.

Proofread

Proofread all Internet copy—Web pages and e-mails—before it is posted or transmitted. Many potential buyers are sensitive to grammatical errors. They feel if you are not careful about your writing, you may not be careful about their business, either.

Poor grammar is perhaps a symptom of our technological age, where anybody with a keyboard can produce his or her own slick-looking printed materials. Many of these people seem not to realize they have—or don't bother to use—the spell checker their e-mail service provides for checking text messages.

In addition to running a spell check, proof each document manually. Spell checkers miss many errors. Once, the training manager at a Big Six accounting firm hired one of us (Bob) to teach business writing to his employees. He said, "Please stress proofreading in the seminar." He then showed us a major proposal one of his employees submitted to a major client. The cover described the firm as "Certified Pubic Accounts."

Typos online, just like offline, are an embarrassment and reflect poorly on your firm. In an October 11, 1999, e-mail broadcast to subscribers, AOL promised to "asure" better and faster service for members. If they can't spell it, you wonder whether they can do it.

"If you can't get someone to proof your cyber epistles, read them through yourself, at least once or twice, before clicking

'Send,'" advises Julie Meyer in an article in *Opportunity World* magazine (October 1999, p. 46). Spell check will catch "acomodation" but it won't alert you if you wrote about "at avalanche." Concludes Meyer, "There's a reason computers still need people to operate them."

More DM Tips

The following tips, based on years of tested paper direct mail experience, seem so far to hold true in the online world as well.

• Before you begin anything, write down the purpose of the mailing. This will help you focus your copy. You could be interested in building a list . . . or getting new subscribers to a magazine . . . or getting volunteers for your organization. But remember: more than one purpose may serve to confuse your reader—and destroy the effectiveness of your mailing.

• When writing the text, begin with very short sentences—and use very simple words. State the major benefits of what you are selling. Make it easy to get "into" the copy.

• Be sure to write from the buyer's point of view. Tell how your product is going to make his or her life easier, more enjoyable, more productive. Appeal to human values, even if you are selling computer microchips.

• Before you begin to write, make a list of all the benefits that your product could bring. Then make note of the three most important benefits on that list. When you write your copy, be sure to start with those three major benefits.

• Testimonials from satisfied customers are the strongest way to bring believability to your copy. Also, reviews from critics and the endorsement of someone the public trusts can lend a note of credibility.

• A free trial and a money-back guarantee will work wonders—if your buyer is uncertain about accepting your offer. And be sure to give at least a month to examine your product. The longer you give, the fewer returns you will get. Why is this? Simply this:

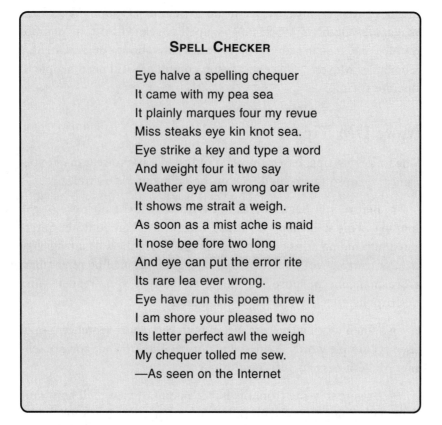

SPELL CHECKER

Eye halve a spelling chequer
It came with my pea sea
It plainly marques four my revue
Miss steaks eye kin knot sea.
Eye strike a key and type a word
And weight four it two say
Weather eye am wrong oar write
It shows me strait a weigh.
As soon as a mist ache is maid
It nose bee fore two long
And eye can put the error rite
Its rare lea ever wrong.
Eye have run this poem threw it
I am shore your pleased two no
Its letter perfect awl the weigh
My chequer tolled me sew.
—As seen on the Internet

people are lazy. They forget to return the product and become accustomed to seeing it around the house or office.

• Using dual media for the same basic message will improve your results dramatically. Publisher's Clearing House uses TV to say "watch your mailbox for our latest sweepstakes mailing"—and the mailing results soar. This is why online marketing complements, rather than competes with, offline marketing.

• When writing copy, emphasize the benefits of your product. Write from the buyer's point of view—and show how your product fills the human needs of the buyer: the need for love, the need for financial security, the need for social recognition, for status, and more.

• The use of a celebrity will add considerably to the credibility of your copy. (But it must be the right celebrity.) The result: a 25 percent lift in response with a good celebrity endorsement.

• When do you write long copy? When do you keep it short? Some time ago, the rule was this: Always write long copy—so long as you keep it interesting. The rule no longer applies. As a result of TV and the Internet, the average attention span is much shorter. Consequently, it's better to keep copy on the short side, with this exception: when your audience is composed of known readers, you can use long copy.

• Want to increase sales dramatically? Easy! Offer three easy, small payments—rather than one large payment. One large publisher says that you can get a 20 percent lift by using this simple device.

• What's the value of a good headline? According to Frank Vos, the headline accounts for 60 percent of the success of any ad. How do you write a winning headline? Here are five good rules: Keep it short. Use the word *you*. When possible, use the words *free*, *new*, *now*. Ask a challenging question. Put a benefit in the headline.

• After you have finished, show the copy to several people who do not know anything about what you are selling. See whether the copy does a good job of making the deal absolutely clear. Ask whether there are any points that are fuzzy. Make certain that everything is crystal clear.

• When selling a business product, don't forget that most middle managers have discretionary buying power up to $100. In other words, they can buy anything they want without asking the boss— if the price is less than $100. Thus, it's wise to position your price at $99 rather than $125.

Case Study: Free Shopping

Eli Katz, founder of The Fragrance Counter, says that one e-campaign that worked well was to send prospects and customers an e-mail advising them of a "free shopping" opportunity. The e-mail stated that on a certain day, shopping would be free for one hour; however, it did not disclose the hour. (This technique was also recently used in a radio campaign by Visa.)

The shoppers, of course, had no way of knowing whether they were shopping during the free hour. If they were fortunate enough to buy online during that hour, their accounts were not charged.

Katz says the e-marketing increased revenue for that day by 400 percent, and it remained high in the days that followed. He warned that if the tactic was used too often, people might wait for the next free shopping day to be offered, which could hurt business.

They held a total of four free shopping days; the e-mail announcing the first is reprinted below.

****

You are receiving this e-mail because of your relationship with The Fragrance Counter or The Cosmetics Counter. Please scroll to the bottom of this message to find out how to change your e-mail preferences. Thank you!

****

Dear AOL Shopper,

Want something for nothing? Join Shop4FREE! Your favorite fragrance and gift source, <A href="aol://4344:1188.home.4010324.569435945">The Fragrance Counter</A>, is giving away a FREE hour of shopping for AOL shoppers only! If you shop during the WINNING HOUR on Wednesday, October 27th, every item in your shopping cart will be FREE!!!

Just place your order on October 27th between 8 A.M. and midnight (EST), and you may win the whole order for FREE. Absolutely, totally, completely free! We'll select the hour at random; all you have to do is select your favorite gift sets, fragrances, cosmetics, men's cologne, or other holiday beauty treats! An e-mail will be sent out the following day to our winners and our other participants, so get ready to shop!

<A href="aol://4344:1188.home.4010324.569435945">The Fragrance Counter </A>ibeauty.com . . . coming soon!

Click here for <A href="aol://4344:1188.winners.4010212.604430318">
Shop4FREE information.</A>

****

This message was sent to your e-mail address: elikatz@aol.com. If you do not
wish e-mail communications from The Fragrance Counter in the future, simply
click here: <A href="mailto:unsubscribeibeauty3@click.ibeauty.com">unsub
scribe-ibeauty3@click.ibeauty.com</A>. You do not need to include a message.
Your e-mail address will be removed immediately!

****

Response Options and Measurement

Every direct e-mail message should contain multiple response
options for both Internet and non-Internet replies. Internet response
options can include clicking on a link embedded in the text that
sends the recipient to your website or clicking on an e-mail address
the recipient can use to send you an immediate reply. These can be
your general addresses, but even better is a unique Web or e-mail
address. This makes responses easier to track, and a unique URL
has the added benefit of bringing the prospect to a Web page
designed specifically for handling inquiries for the offer advertised
in the e-mail campaign.

The most common non-Internet reply mechanism is a toll-free
number to call. This can be your general toll-free number, but a special 800 number specifically for Internet response makes results easier to track. To maximize responses, include a special offer in your
Internet e-mail, such as a bonus gift, free shipping, or discount. Even
better, make it clear that the offer is available only to customers and
prospects receiving this special e-mail promotion.

With these reply mechanisms in place, you can get a good sense
of the response your e-mail campaign is generating. One common
measure is click-throughs (the number of people who clicked on a
URL embedded in the e-mail message).

Many click-throughs bring the prospect to a Web page presenting more information and encouraging further response, such as

completing a registration form, downloading a file, or placing an order. Measuring how many click-throughs go to this higher level of response gives an even clearer sense of whether the e-campaign is working.

With the low cost of e-campaigns compared to conventional direct mail, you can mail and test more, and more easily. Do so. The options for designing and writing e-campaigns are becoming clearly defined, but what works best is not yet well known. Test your offers, messages, formats, response mechanisms, lists, and list segments. Keep track of the results and you will gradually discover what your prospects and customers respond to in e-mail marketing, giving you an edge in future success.

You can only e-mail your customers if you have their addresses, so start collecting them now. Is there a place for prospects to write their e-mail addresses on the reply cards you use in traditional direct mail reply cards? Is it prominent? Don't make the e-mail address space an afterthought. Use every design trick you can think of to get the prospect to include his or her e-mail address.

If you make an offer that encourages the reader to visit your website, make sure you use a unique website address (URL) leading him or her to a page especially designed for capturing responses to that particular e-mail offer. On that custom-designed page you can thank customers for responding to your e-mail, take them by the hand, and lead them along toward the sale. You don't want to send them to your general-purpose home page and force them to search for your e-mail offer.

Tips for Maximizing Your Response Rates

To maximize response, give your recipient an incentive to click through and fill out your online form. Convincingly explain the benefits of submitting the completed form, registering with your website, and requesting the materials or information you are offering to send.

Consider using promotions and contests, new member sign-up programs, "buyer's club" discounts, and other devices to build repeat visits to the website (after the initial click-through) and a sense of community.

Freebies and discounts, effective in traditional direct mail, also work well in Internet direct mail. A savings of $5 to $20 off on the initial purchase can be effective in getting a first-time customer to order something from your site. ToyTime.com offered as its Christmas promotion in 1999 a $20 coupon good for the next purchase when the customer spent $75 or more at the site. The goal was to get the customer to buy at least twice—traditionally, a multibuyer (person who buys two or more times) is considered a more valuable customer in direct marketing than a one-time buyer.

Since you need permission to e-mail people—unlike in regular direct mail, where no permission is required—you can get more people to give you this permission by offering incentives. In effect, you are "paying" them for the right to communicate with them, for purposes of commerce, online. This is called *permission marketing*, a term coined by Seth Godin in his book *Permission Marketing*.

Tip: If you are offering a bonus program where site registrants build bonus points based on purchases, show them their point counter on the screen. And load it right at the start—before they have even bought anything—with some free points (100 to 500 is an attractive-sounding range), simply as a reward for registration. Once they have a bonus "account" already loaded with points, they will be more inclined to visit and use the site, to check their point total, and to not waste the points they have already earned. Post the rewards (discounts, merchandise, other incentives) you offer for different levels of bonus point accumulation. Changing these incentives monthly or more frequently also provides an added incentive to revisit your site and see what's new.

Sig File

A *sig file* is your electronic "signature" at the end of an e-mail. We don't mean a scanned digital facsimile of your handwritten signature. Rather, a sig file is like an electronic letterhead, only at the end of the message rather than the beginning. Like a letterhead, a good sig file gives your name, address, and other contact information, enabling the recipients to contact you any way they want—offline or online.

According to the conventions of the Internet, the sig file is the one place you can put an advertising message where it won't be considered spam—even if sent to people who have not agreed to receive e-mail from you. So, many e-marketers add a slogan, tag line, or other brief descriptor of what they do.

Your e-mail service almost certainly permits you to create a standard sig file. Its contents automatically appear at the end of any e-mail, individual or mass, you send. If you don't know how to create your sig file, call your e-mail service or ISP for instructions.

Internet Direct Mail Formats and Examples

Here are some different models of Internet direct mail. You can follow a particular model, mix and match them to suit your campaign, or create and test your own.

Short-Form Promotional E-Mail, Lead-Generation

This is a brief e-mail, usually taking a single screen, that is clearly promotional in nature. It resembles a traditional one-page direct mail sales letter written to generate sales leads.

KIDASA Software mailed the following message to an e-mail list representing the subscribers to the trade journal *Electronic Products*. Response to the offer was 10 percent.

FROM: "The Milestones Etc.Team" ep@mail5.enlist.com

TO: warren_deeb@edithroman.com

SUBJECT: Download Milestones, Etc. Now!

Dear Warren Deeb,

Are you a project manager? Do you find project management software to be more trouble than it's worth? Are you looking for a truly EASY way to schedule and track your projects? You need MILESTONES, ETC!

Click this Web link and a free trial copy is yours: http://www.kidasa.com/miles

Milestones, Etc. is designed for engineers, managers, and ANYONE who needs to schedule and track projects. It's by far the easiest project scheduling tool on the market today. Milestones, Etc. offers a simple "click and drag" solution that will let you put together brilliant, presentation-ready schedules and timelines and Gantt charts in minutes.

HOW WILL IT BENEFIT YOU?

- Drastically reduce your scheduling time
- Easily communicate and sell your project's objectives
- Effortlessly track and monitor your project's progress
- Win more customer and coworker recognition

IMPORTANT

The software is not a watered down version of Milestones, Etc. You'll try the actual, fully functioning version of software that's used by demanding managers, team leaders, planners, and administrators every single day. Here's a key code you can use to unlock the software through May, 1999: 004-000502-KA8701

A personal note: I know you get a lot of e-mail. I just want to personally assure you that Milestones, Etc. is worth the trouble. If you regularly schedule and manage projects, Milestones, Etc. can make your life easier. All I ask is for a chance to prove it. http://www.kidasa.com/miles

Sincerely,
Sue Butler, President
KIDASA Software, Inc.
(512) 328-0167 or (800) 765-0167
sbutler@kidasa.com

E-Mail Series

Communicating with your audience using a series of messages is often more effective than the one-shot approach. And with the speed and low cost of the Internet, an e-mail series can be sent much more quickly, closer together, and with more precise timing than a paper direct mail series.

Here are some e-mails from a series that *Electronic Products*, the magazine mentioned earlier, used to qualify and renew subscribers to their controlled circulation publication.

Electronic Products is a controlled circulation trade publication with 120 thousand subscribers who are electrical engineers, managers, and other professionals involved in electronic products. The goal of their e-mail program was to enhance the renewal process while reducing mailing costs. As a controlled circulation publication, they do not charge for subscriptions. But subscribers are required to complete a qualification form. If they meet the criteria of a qualified subscriber, they receive the magazine free.

Response to the e-mailings asking people to renew over the Internet was approximately 20 percent. This is roughly equivalent to the response rates *Electronic Products* was getting with direct mail, but with substantially lower cost per renewal.

Additional e-mailings, also shown here, asked new and existing subscribers to opt in and agree to receive promotional e-mails—enabling *Electronic Products* to rent their subscriber names as an opt-in e-list. In less than a year, this effort expanded the size of the publisher's opt-in list from six thousand to twenty-six thousand names.

Subscription Renewal This e-mail was used to renew subscribers online. It went to subscribers for whom *Electronic Products* already had an e-mail address. Since the list was not clean, bounce-back rate (e-mails returned because of incorrect Internet addresses) was unusually high—20 to 25 percent. This decreased in subsequent e-mailings as the list was cleaned and correct addresses appended to the bounce-back files.

The e-mail mentioned that the sender had already filled in part of the form for the recipient. This is done by prepopulating fields in the form for which the sender already has the data (name, address, company, and so on).

Tip: One of the problems with e-mail, as opposed to paper communication, is that you can't get a handwritten signature on it—and circulation qualification forms must be signed. *Electronic Products* got around this by asking in their response form a personal question that only the subscriber would know. This can be something like the last four digits of the social security number or the month and day of birth. This technique is also used in telephone selling, such as when you activate a credit card by calling a toll-free number.

—— Original Message ——

FROM: ELECTRONIC PRODUCTS Circulation <ep@mail8.enlist.com>
TO: <mfeit@ix.netcom.com>
SENT: Tuesday, August 03, 1999 8:15 PM
SUBJECT: Subscription Requalification

Michelle Feit
ePostDirect Inc.
Reader Number: 12345678

Dear Michelle,

It's time to renew your free subscription to ELECTRONIC PRODUCTS. We hope you've enjoyed your subscription—each issue is a great resource for engineers seeking the latest information on electronic components and their manufacturers.

Visit your personal renewal form at: http://www.enlist.com/cgi-bin/eps2?e=mfeit @ix.netcom.com&r=12345678

Thanks again for your interest in ELECTRONIC PRODUCTS, the Engineer's magazine of Product Technology.

Regards,

Barry Green
VP, Circulation
ELECTRONIC PRODUCTS

Online Subscriber Qualification Controlled circulation subscribers have to be periodically requalified by filling out a qualification card. This e-mail enabled current subscribers to save time and eliminate paperwork by requalifying online.

Here is an e-mail sent to people who filled out a qualification card to receive the magazine. It gets them to give the publisher their e-mail addresses by offering a bribe. A special drawing is a good way to get people to opt in, since you only have to give one prize instead of a bribe to everyone.

FROM: ELECTRONIC PRODUCTS Circulation <ep@mail8.enlist.com>
TO: <michelle.feit@epostdirect.com>
SENT: Tuesday, August 03, 1999 8:14 PM
SUBJECT: Sony Discman Drawing

Michelle Feit
ePostDirect Inc.
Reader Number: 12345678

Dear Michelle,

Thanks for requesting your free subscription to
ELECTRONIC PRODUCTS. To show our appreciation,
we'd like to enter you in a special drawing for a
FREE SONY DISCMAN. Please submit your entry at:

http://www.enlist.com/cgi-bin/eps1?e=mfeit@ix.netcom.com&r=12345678
Thanks again for your interest in our magazine,
and good luck in the drawing!

Regards,

Barry Green
VP, Circulation
ELECTRONIC PRODUCTS

This message is brought to you on behalf of ELECTRONIC PRODUCTS in an effort to simplify the renewal process for you and to keep your FREE subscription coming to you. Any feedback you have on this type of notice is welcome.

If you wish to stop receiving such messages, please click on this link: <INSERT OPT-OUT LINK FOR EP CAMPAIGNS>

Or, reply to this e-mail with the word "remove" in the subject line. For better service, please be sure to include the following information in your reply:

Name: <INDIVIDUAL NAME>
Your ELECTRONIC PRODUCTS Account #: <ACCOUNT NUMBER>

New Subscriber Acquisition Mailing The next two messages were sent to potential subscribers. Barry Green, vice president of circulation for the publisher, described the results from these efforts as "marginal" but would not release specific numbers.

SUBJECT: Electronic Products Magazine
DATE: 26 Mar 1999 00:54:49 -0000
FROM: Electronic Products Magazine <ep@mail5.enlist.com>
TO: mfeit@ix.netcom.com

Dear Michelle,
My records indicate a colleague at Motorola is reading ELECTRONIC PRODUCTS magazine and thought I'd contact you regarding a project I'm working on.

My publication, ELECTRONIC PRODUCTS magazine, is forming a network of industry professionals we can contact and interview for stories we're researching for publication. The goal would be to include feedback from more practicing engineers in our stories. If you'd like to participate, please fill out the Web form at:

http://www.reference.com/~david/epmag/ep_form.html

As a token of our thanks, I'd like to offer you a free subscription to ELECTRONIC PRODUCTS. And feel free to forward this message on to colleagues at Motorola who might have an interest in participating. We're always looking for readers at companies pushing the envelope of electronic design.

Regards,

Barry Green
VP, Circulation
ELECTRONIC PRODUCTS Magazine

————— Original Message —————

SUBJECT: ELECTRONIC PRODUCTS Magazine
DATE: 29 Mar 1999 20:14:28 -0000
FROM: Electronic Products Magazine <ep@mail5.enlist.com>
TO: mfeit@ix.netcom.com

Dear Michelle,

My records indicate a colleague at Motorola is reading ELECTRONIC PRODUCTS magazine, and I'd like to offer you a free subscription as well. ELECTRONIC PRODUCTS is a resource for engineers seeking the latest information on electronic components and their manufacturers.

If you'd like a free subscription, just fill out the online subscription form at:

http://www.enlist.com/cgi-bin/eps4

And feel free to forward this message on to colleagues at Motorola who might have an interest in the magazine. We're always looking for readers at companies pushing the envelope of electronic design.

Regards,

Barry Green
VP, Circulation
ELECTRONIC PRODUCTS Magazine

E-Advertorial/Special Report These are e-mails written like a cross between an advertisement and an article. They are similar to what copywriters call *editorial style ads*—copy-heavy print ads designed to look like an article in the magazine or paper rather than a paid message. This is a popular format and works well because it fits in with the Internet's focus on information and news. Here is a sample written to sell an information report on privacy:

ARE YOU BEING INVESTIGATED????

Learn the Internet tools that are used to investigate you, your friends, neighbors, enemies, employees, or anyone else! My huge report SNOOPING THE INTERNET of Internet sites will give you . . .

Thousands of Internet locations to look up people, credit, social security, current or past employment, driving records, medical information, addresses, phone numbers, maps to city locations . . .

Every day the media (television, radio, and newspapers) are full of stories about PERSONAL INFORMATION being used, traded, and sold over the Internet . . . usually without your permission or knowledge.

With my report I show you HOW IT'S DONE!!!

It's amazing . . .

- Locate a debtor who is hiding, or get help in finding hidden assets.
- Find that old romantic interest.
- Find e-mail, telephone, or address information on just about anyone! Unlisted phone numbers can often be found through some of these sites!!

Perhaps you're working on a family "tree" or history. The Internet turns what once was years of work into hours of DISCOVERY and INFORMATION. Check birth, death, adoption, or social security records.

MILITARY
Check service records of Army, Navy, Air Force, or Marine Corps. Find out who's been telling the truth and who's been lying. Perhaps you can uncover the next lying politician!!!

FELLOW EMPLOYEES
Find out if your fellow employee was jailed on sex charges, or has other skeletons in the closet!!

PERFORM BACKGROUND CHECKS
Check credit, driving, or criminal records, verify income or educational claims, find out military history and discipline, previous political affiliations, and so on.

YOUR KIDS' FRIENDS
Find out the background of your children's friends and dates.

WHAT'S THE LAW? STOP GUESSING!!
Look up laws, direct from law libraries around the world. Is that new business plan legal??

NEW JOB? NEW TOWN? NEW LIFE?
Employment ads from around the world can be found on the Internet. Get a new job and disappear!

The Internet can tell you just about ANYTHING, if you know WHERE to look. BONUS REPORT!!!!

Check your credit report and use the Internet to force credit bureaus to remove derogatory information. My special BONUS REPORT included as part of the

SNOOPING THE INTERNET collection reveals all sorts of credit tricks, both legal and—for "information purposes only"—some of the ILLEGAL tricks.

Research YOURSELF first!

What you find will scare you.

If you believe that the information that is compiled on you should be as easily available to you as it is to those who compile it, then . . .

You want to order the SNOOPING THE INTERNET report I've put together.

This huge report is WHERE YOU START! Once you locate these FREE private, college, and government websites, you'll find even MORE links to information search engines!

YOU CAN FIND OUT ANYTHING ABOUT ANYBODY ANY TIME using the Internet!!!!

1) WE TAKE: AMERICAN EXPRESS   VISA   MASTERCARD
   TYPE OF CARD AMX/VISA/MC??_____
   NAME ON CREDIT CARD_____
   CREDIT CARD #_____
   BILLING ADDRESS _____
   CITY_____
   STATE_____ ZIP_____
   PHONE (INCLUDE AREA CODE)_____
   WE WILL BILL $39.95 to your account
   SALES TAX ($2.90) added to CA residents

   Send $39.95 ($42.85 in CA) cash, check, or money order to:
   CASINO CHICO
   Background Investigations Division
   305 Nord Ave.
   P.O. Box 4191
   Chico, CA 95927-4191

2) Send the same above requested credit card information to above address.

3) Fax the same above credit card information to 916-895-8470.

4) Call 916-876-4285. This is a 24-hour phone number to place a
   CREDIT CARD order.

I will RUSH back to you SAME DAY my SNOOPING THE INTERNET report!

Log on to the Internet and in moments you will fully understand . . .

What information is available—and exact Internet sites to get there!

2nd BONUS!!!!

Along with the report we will send a $3\frac{1}{2}$" disk with sites already
"HOTLINKED." No need to type in those addresses. Simply click on the URL
address and PRESTO you are at the website!!!

Personal ads, logs of personal e-mail, mention of individuals anywhere on the
Internet are "yours for the taking" with this report.

- Lists of resources to find even more information (private investigation
  companies, for example)
- Order surveillance equipment (if legal in your state)
- Send anonymous e-mail
- Research companies
- Research technology
- Locate military records
- Find information on criminals
- Find wanted fugitives—perhaps even a close associate!

ABSOLUTE SATISFACTION GUARANTEED

Your satisfaction is 100% guaranteed, just return the material for a full refund
within 30 days if you aren't 100% satisfied.

Jon Scott Hall Publications

To Sum It All Up

- Internet direct mail is not a completely separate discipline from conventional direct mail. Many of the sales dynamics for both forms are similar.
- The main difference in Internet versus printed direct mail seems to be the length of copy that prospects are willing to read. Evidence indicates that people are more inclined to read and respond to long copy in printed direct mail than in Internet direct mail. People seem more willing to flip and scan printed pages than they are to scroll through a long e-mail message. If you have a lot to say, you might put part of your message in your e-mail and the rest on a Web page the recipient can click through to for more information.
- Another difference between Internet and print direct mail is the position of the offer. In printed direct mail, the offer is traditionally made at the close of the letter. In Internet direct mail, it is made both in the opening and the close of the e-mail. This allows interested parties to respond immediately by clicking on a link without having to read the entire message.

Getting and Using Internet Mailing Lists

Unless you live in a cave, you know that Internet marketing is growing in popularity almost exponentially. In a recent online survey, more than 50 percent of direct marketers polled by Edith Roman Associates said they now use the Internet as a marketing tool.

More and more e-mail lists—*e-lists*—are emerging on the market today. Availability of e-lists is growing rapidly, from 300 six months ago to more than 1,000 as of this writing. The number of marketers using e-mail lists is growing just as rapidly.

E-mail marketing is getting positive results. Barry Green, vice president of circulation for Hearst Publishing, has successfully integrated e-mail into his circulation efforts, as well as made his house opt-in e-list available for rent. He reports response rates to e-mails sent to subscribers of 20 percent and better.

Ivan O'Sullivan, president of Elron Software, claims, "I can get the same results from e-mail as postal mail, but quicker." Sue Butler, president of KIDASA Software, says, "We got a 10 percent response rate from *Electronic Products'* e-list and no complaints." This makes it the top-performing list—conventional or Internet—used by her firm.

The biggest hurdle in e-mail marketing today is finding enough e-mail addresses to support such great results on a large scale. Most companies have only a portion of their databases coded with e-mail addresses—and of those coded, as many as 30 percent are returned as undeliverable. Key-punch errors, which account for many bad addresses, may be reduced by requiring double entry on e-mail addresses.

Converting Your House List to an E-List

To build and update a list of customers and prospects that includes e-mail addresses, many companies have changed their printed forms, computer screens, and operational procedures in order to capture e-mail addresses. These measures will give a return on investment as companies gain an easier, faster, and less expensive way to communicate with customers and prospects. Figure 4.1 shows a letter, sent via traditional mail, used to successfully collect e-mail addresses from current customers.

When Xerox wanted to build a customer e-list, they didn't have the e-mail addresses of their 140,000 existing customers—but they did have the e-mail addresses of the 4,000 sales reps who serve them. So they sent an e-mail to the reps announcing a contest encouraging them to give Xerox the e-mail addresses of customers. The reps who gave the most e-mail addresses won Rolex watches and other valuable prizes.

Internet copywriter Scott Smith suggests giving customers and prospects an extra incentive for responding to ads, press releases, and other promotions online rather than offline. Incentives Smith recommends include a free special report or other inexpensive gift, free online newsletter, special discount, free software downloads, or special priority handling of their orders.

These efforts will help you gather e-mail addresses. But not every customer will reply. Then what?

E-list brokers and other e-marketing service firms offer "e-mail address data appending services." These services take a standard mailing address and add the individual's e-mail address, immediately increasing e-mail potential. Depending on your customers, where you got their names, how many are online, and the type of Internet

Dear Customer:

"The net is our future," writes Kevin Kelly, editor of *Wired* magazine. And we're moving into that future—full speed ahead!

To serve you better, we will shortly be doing a number of our communications with our customers online.

To do that, we need your e-mail address. Could you take a moment to jot it on the enclosed postage-paid reply card and drop it in the mail to us?

In return, you will receive timely new product announcements and special offers available *only* online. They will NOT be offered in our regular paper mailings.

Our first special e-mail offer has a retail value of $50! To qualify for your FREE $50, just fill in and mail the enclosed card today. You have lots to gain, and nothing to lose. There's no obligation of any kind.

Sincerely,

John E. Smith, CEO

P.S. If you prefer, phone in your e-mail address by calling toll-free—800-XXX-XXXX. Or send us an e-mail—webmaster@ABCD.com.

☐ YES, ADD ME TO YOUR E-LIST.

Name_____
Title _____
Company _____
Address_____
City_____ State_____ Zip_____
Phone_____ E-mail_____

4 ways to reply
Mail this card today (the postage is already paid!)
E-mail webmaster@ABCD.com
Fax 516-XXX-XXXX
Call toll-free 800-XXX-XXXX

Figure 4.1
Traditional paper letter mailed to customers to collect e-mail addresses

access they have, running your names through an e-mail address data appending service will probably attach e-mail addresses to between 20 and 30 percent of your records.

Once gathered, e-mail addresses can become a new source of profit as list owners create opt-in programs and rent their e-list to approved partners and advertisers. There is some hesitancy about renting e-mail lists, but complaints have not increased and response rates prove these e-lists are working. List owners who have chosen to rent or share their e-mail addresses are doing so in a variety of ways. Some are selling sponsorships on electronic newsletters; others are personally endorsing the advertiser's e-mail message. Most are controlling their own transmissions, but this will change as more e-lists come on the market and mailers' concerns for duplication increase.

Interestingly, the anonymity of the list owner in traditional postal mailings has not translated to the Internet: recipients of the e-mail messages know who sent the message, why they were sent the message, and, if they choose, how to be removed from the list. Promoting awareness of the list owner gives credibility to the message, which may be one reason these e-lists are getting such good results.

Here are some rules for getting the most out of your house e-list.

- Only send to people who have opted to receive e-mail messages.
- Personalize your e-mail (as much as possible).
- Reestablish your relationship with the recipients in the message. (How did you get their names?)
- Always make it easy for them to remove themselves from the list.
- Honor all removals immediately.
- Keep the message brief.

A good way to accomplish many of these things is to put a generic paragraph at the beginning of your message, such as:

This is a message about discount golf supplies. You are receiving this message as an opt-in subscriber to the golfer's e-mail list. If you would like to be removed from this list, please respond to this message with the word "remove" in the body of your e-mail.

There are a number of ways to build an e-mail list on your own. One way is to provide useful content, such as an e-mail newsletter. Companies like Revnet (www.messagemedia.com), SparkLIST.com (www.sparklist.com), and L-Soft (www.lsoft.com) specialize in building, managing, and transmitting large-scale lists. Check their websites for available e-list software and services.

Other services like WebPromote's Engage (www.webpromote .com) and OakNet Publishing (www.oaknetpub.com) are great for smaller businesses because they take care of all the technical headaches, allowing the marketer to simply write the messages and hit the "Send" button. Another way to gather e-mail addresses is through your own company database. Give your current client base an incentive to provide their e-mail addresses. Companies like Digital Impact (www.digitalimpact.com), e-PostDirect (www.epostdi rect.com), or eGain (www.egain.com) will help you build your e-mail database and then show you how to use it. More information on these companies may be found in Appendix A.

Renting E-Lists That Work

There are more than a thousand e-lists on the market today, but how do you tell which ones are the quality e-lists? Ask your e-list broker these six questions. The answers can help you determine which lists can produce profitable results for your product or service. E-list brokers are listed in Appendix A.

What Is the Website's Method for Opting in the People on Its List?

There are dozens of databases of Internet addresses with fancy names and big descriptions, but after digging through the promotional information, they turn out to be nothing much. Prospects who have not requested anything rarely remember how or when they got on the list and probably will not respond. These lists might have a chance with all those free offers that have been circulating on the Web, but serious direct marketers are looking for genuine Internet buyers.

For promotional e-mail, response lists are generally superior to compiled lists. In e-mail, there are numerous lists on the market compiled from InterNIC, which is the organization with which all Web advertisers must register their domain names. Other compiled lists consist of Internet addresses of people who visit Usenet groups.

Response lists, by comparison, consist of Internet-enabled prospects who have either responded to an e-mail offer or registered at a particular website. By doing so, they have actively indicated interest in a particular subject area. Another plus is that, in addition to just the Internet address, the list contains additional information, such as name, address, phone number, and sometimes even buying preferences and demographics.

Early results from Internet marketing programs indicate that the best response is obtained using opt-in lists. The true definition of *opt-in* is that people on an e-list have (a) registered at the website or through some other electronic or paper form and (b) checked the option requesting additional e-mail information from other companies.

Today customer privacy is a key concern both on the Internet and in traditional direct marketing. Opt-in ensures privacy and prevents spamming by giving people control over whether they receive e-mail marketing messages. According to a survey by IMT Strategies, more than half of all e-mail users feel positive about e-mail marketing when opt-in lists are used, and three-quarters respond to e-marketing messages with some frequency.

Sending unsolicited e-mails to people who are not opted in usually does not work. Spamming is illegal, and such blind e-mailings usually get terrible results. Opt-in lists clearly are the better way to go.

Different list owners use different definitions of "opt-in," resulting in lists of varying quality. When you visit websites and fill in guest pages, note that some websites have prechecked the "Yes, I want to receive e-mail from other companies" option. So when you complete and submit the guest form, you opt in automatically. Increasingly, the term *permission-based* is being used to replace *opt-in*.

Other websites require the registrant to proactively check "yes" to the opt-in option. This is indicative of a more responsive, qualified e-list.

Make sure the opt-in language explains clearly that other companies will be e-mailing the Internet user. If Web surfers visiting the site are not presented with the choice to opt in, they may respond negatively to receiving e-mail from direct marketers, including you.

How can you find out what *opt-in* means to the e-list you are considering testing? Ask for their opt-in language. Or go to their website and register. If an e-list owner won't give you their opt-in language or the URL address of their website, question the integrity of their list.

A number of lists use a form of "reverse opt-in." They broadcast e-mails to Internet addresses with an advertising message that includes the promise of future promotional e-mails. They state that if the recipients don't want to receive future e-mails, they must click on "Unsubscribe" (or a link appearing immediately after the word) to remove themselves from the list.

Therefore, these so-called opt-in lists are in reality "opt-out," and prospects who take no action are considered to have given their permission to send them e-mail. (This is the electronic equivalent of mailing qualification cards for a controlled circulation publication, and considering anyone who does *not* send in the qualification card with a note saying "I don't want to subscribe" as a qualified subscriber.)

What Type of Relationship Does the Site Have with the People on Its List?

The most responsive lists have ongoing relationships between site and registrant. Whether customers are receiving a monthly magazine or weekly newsletter, or are purchasing products from the company, look for lists of people who have an ongoing relationship with the site and are not just surfers. You want to know how often the people are returning to the site, how often the site is contacting them, and the last contact date.

How Old Are the Names?

In traditional direct mail, mailers pay a premium to rent newer, fresher names. Known as *hotline* names, these are people who have ordered from a catalog or direct mail piece within the past three, six, or twelve months. Why?

In traditional direct marketing, lists are judged by recency, frequency, and monetary. *Monetary* is how much money a customer on a mail-order buyer list spent. Given as a dollar amount, this represents the average size of the mail-order purchase made by the buyers on the list. Average size of order is a good indication of whether people on this list might be willing to pay your price.

Frequency refers to how often the customer places an order. *Recency* refers to how recently the customer placed an order. Experience proves that the more recent the order, the more likely the customer is to buy again. This is why mailers pay extra for hotline names.

In contrast to the demand for hotline names in paper direct mail, Internet marketers are finding that older lists sometimes pull better than newer lists! One reason may be that people who want to receive e-mail offers stay on such lists, while people who don't, opt out— meaning they asked to be removed from the list.

How Is the E-List Maintained?

Well-maintained lists add new names, match e-list names to e-mail preference files, update address corrections, and remove bouncebacks and opt-outs. Thanks to the speed of the Internet, there is a lot of activity on e-lists. A dirty file can decrease response and increase flaming, bounce-backs, and costs. Look for e-lists that are updated monthly or more frequently and guarantee 100 percent delivery.

When you rent a quality response e-list, don't be surprised when the list owner refuses to transmit the names to you and instead insists on transmitting your e-mail, for a fee, themselves. This is standard practice among owners of quality lists. It's the electronic equivalent of a conventional list owner who won't send his or her list directly to mailers but ships only to bonded letter shops.

In a recent survey of list owners, we found that 56 percent insist on doing the transmission themselves, while the others will release their e-mail lists to mailers. Research shows that most of the firms that release their e-mail addresses have inferior compiled lists.

Why do owners of quality opt-in lists insist on controlling their lists so closely? One reason is to ensure the integrity of the list by eliminating tampering. More important, it prevents the people on the list—whose trust the owner values—from receiving unwanted offers. And it ensures that Internet users get only offers of interest . . . including yours.

What Selections Are Available on the E-List?

Selections are essential for target marketing. E-lists have two types of selections: website data and individual data.

Website data are generated from log reports, and a quality e-list will have them available. Examples of site data are original registration date, last time visited, and number of times visited.

Individual units of data are gathered directly from the registrant or by list enhancement through demographic overlays. Examples of individual data units are consumer versus business, age, gender, job title, industry, and special interests. Selections allow you to target only those Internet prospects most likely to respond to your offer.

Some e-lists offer significant selectivity. Catelogs.com, an e-mail list of people who have requested online merchandise catalogs, allows selection by age, income, and a multitude of product interests, including clothing, electronics, food, travel, books, and magazines. Versions! E-Mail, an e-list of computer prospects, lets you select names by application and operating systems used.

Other selections typically available include the following.

Geographic Some e-lists can be segmented by location: state, SCF, ZIP code, county, and metropolitan area. (Note: SCF refers to Sectional Center Facility. All ZIP codes included under a given SCF share the same first three digits.) If you are planning a mailing designed to get businesspeople to attend a conference in New York City, you might mail only to executives located within a 100-mile radius of midtown Manhattan.

Remember that the Internet and e-lists are worldwide. Therefore, when renting e-lists, be sure to specify the geographic area—region, country, or state—you want to target. Don't send e-mails to Europe or Asia if you can't handle leads or orders from overseas.

Demographic Some lists provide quantitative characteristics of a given population: age, sex, income level, wealth, race, and other vital statistics of a personal nature. A great many mailing lists, for instance, allow selection by sex (male or female).

Psychographic This segmentation refers to the psychological make-up of your target audience and is more difficult to identify. A mailer sponsoring a seminar on "How to Become a Published Author," for example, might mail seminar invitations to members of the AARP (American Association for Retired Persons) on the assumption that many retirees are looking for something to occupy their time and might consider writing for publication. The premise is unproven, however, and a test mailing to this list might fail to generate sufficient response. A better choice might be the *Writer's Digest* subscription list, where people have indicated their interest in writing by buying a magazine on the subject.

Buying Patterns   As discussed, three important selection criteria for mail-order buyers are frequency (how often they buy through the mail), recency (the date of their last purchase), and amount (how much they spent). Many list descriptions provide a dollar amount for average order, representing the average amount spent by people on the list.

Experience proves that buyers who buy often and spend more are better prospects than those who buy infrequently and spend less. In conventional direct mail, those persons most likely to respond to a new mail-order offer are those who have recently responded to a previous mail-order offer! This is why hotlines—the segment of a list composed of the most recent buyers—are priced higher than the rest of the list.

E-lists seem to reverse this last rule. The longer one appears on an e-list, the more likely they are to respond. One reason might be that those who were added to the e-list more recently may be newer to the Internet—and therefore less confident about transacting online.

Business Lists   Selection criteria include job function, title, plant size, industry (often specified by SIC code), number of employees, annual sales, and types of products purchased.

Does the E-List Owner Offer Any Value-Added Services?

Some e-lists offer value-added services that can increase the effectiveness of your marketing. An e-mail message can be personalized by putting the person's name in the body of the copy. Immediate click-through reports show how many people took the next action by clicking through to a website.

Other value-added services available include split tests for multiple messages, list owner endorsements, address corrections, e-mail address appending, data enhancements, and e-mails with graphics and rich media, to name a few. Many of these services can increase response and reduce cost per order.

Growing Acceptance of E-Mail Marketing

For many companies, e-mail marketing represents one of the most cost-effective, efficient, and compelling forms of direct marketing. It is currently the only medium that can effectively fulfill the promise of one-to-one marketing.

So why does there seem to be so many negative reactions to company-distributed e-mails? Actually, there are probably fewer than many people believe. Times Direct Marketing Inc. has found the negative response rate or flame rate to be $\frac{1}{1,000}$th of a percent. At that rate, if you send a million e-marketing messages, you could expect about ten flames—negative and critical e-mail replies from people on the list complaining that you have spammed them or that they are annoyed to receive your e-mail.

> **Tip:** If possible, when ordering opt-in e-lists, omit ZIP code 90210. Reason: Most website guest pages require filling in a ZIP code field to complete the registration process. This creates a problem in foreign countries that don't use ZIP codes. The best-known U.S. ZIP code to foreigners is 90210, from the TV show "Beverly Hills 90210." Many use this ZIP code in filling in Web registration forms, and as a result, we have discovered that many e-lists have huge quantities in 90210—most of them foreign!

Traditional direct marketing vehicles such as direct mail or business reply cards can generate a much higher rate of negative responses. The difference is that it's easier to ignore negative messages written on reply cards, although the dollars-and-cents cost is much higher.

For one of the major Internet search engines, TDMI performed an outbound e-mail campaign to promote a new section of the search engine's website. TDMI sent out 2.5 million e-mail messages, generating a 4.4 percent response rate. The cost per response was $0.32. If the same campaign had included direct mail, the cost per response would probably have been greater than $10. In addition to cost-per-response metrics, TDMI measured negative reaction in two ways: (a) "take me off your list" or unsubscribe rate and (b) negative responses. The unsubscribe rate was approximately 3.4 percent, and the negative response rate was only 0.002 percent.

This campaign mirrors the results of other programs. When evaluating whether to include direct e-mails as part of an overall direct marketing program, companies must consider the benefits (very low cost per response rates and high return on investment) and weigh them against the costs (an occasional flame-o-gram and possibly a loss of some consumer goodwill).

In another campaign, TDMI tested the effectiveness of e-mail against online banners and traditional direct mail. Targeting software developers, the test campaign consisted of sending out 15,000 e-mails and 30,000 direct mailers, and placing banners on five websites. The results show that the cost per response from direct mail was ten times more expensive when compared against e-mail, and the cost per response from banners was twice as high when compared against e-mail.

In reviewing the results of twenty-three campaigns, TDMI learned that the most effective way to use e-mail marketing is as an announcement medium, not a sales medium. Companies that successfully implement e-mail marketing programs use them to simply "announce" the availability of an offer on a website and point people to that site.

The content and length of e-mail messages are also important to the success of a campaign. In tests of e-mail copy length and content, an offering that is brief and simply stated proved to be the most effective way to achieve a high response rate in an e-mail. In several tests, TDMI has earned responses rates that are 30 percent higher when an e-mail consists of no more than four sentences and a URL, when tested against e-mails that contained seven to eight sentences and a series of promotional bullet points. But don't take this as a hard and fast rule; we've seen a number of e-campaigns where long-form e-mail significantly outpulled short form.

Modeling Your E-List

Modeling techniques used to refine traditional lists can also be used to improve the response performance of e-lists, especially with your house file of customers and prospects.

By modeling a prospecting list, you can turn unprofitable lists into profitable ones, and profitable lists into stellar performers. You can segment and then select good prospects versus mediocre prospects, mailing more frequently to the former and less frequently to the latter. You can further segment inactive accounts, expired subscriptions, and other marginal customer files in a data archive.

Many different modeling techniques are available, and some are better than others for specific business objectives. You also need to know the lingo so that you can speak with the statistician in his or her own language.

Analysis begins with a definition of the business challenges or objectives. In direct mail, that's usually (but not always) increased response.

The statistician then determines, based upon the objectives, which analytical methods are most appropriate for the job.

In many ways, the statistician's role is similar to that of a physician diagnosing a patient. The physician must evaluate the situation and subsequently prescribe the most effective remedy. The statistician must evaluate business objectives, as well as the information available, and prescribe a correct methodology for achieving these objectives. An incorrect technique, much like an incorrect prescription, can lead to ineffective or even disastrous results.

Creating a good model starts with an exploratory data analysis (EDA). The EDA helps the statistician understand the "personality" of the data to be modeled (in this example, the responses).

Comparing the customers generated by your mailing against the lists mailed, for instance, tells you who responded. Matching records mailed and the responses to demographics and transactional/promotional information, and examining the interplay between variables that give you the greatest lift in response, further enhances understanding of who's responding to what.

To gain knowledge about your customers' demographic profiles, and what variables are important in predicting response, a good statistician will use some combination of the following EDA techniques in developing a model for you.

Univariate Analysis

This technique measures the effect of single variables (such as age, income, employee size, SIC) on the target variable—response. For example, as income increases, does response increase or decrease? How about size of order?

Other key factors to evaluate include whether the predictor variable contains enough data to be statistically valid, contains valid information or garbage values, or needs to be transformed into a more "modeler friendly" format. Your statistician may do a frequency distribution and other descriptive measures to see whether patterns in the data emerge.

Bivariate Analysis

This is similar to univariate analysis, except that you are doing cross tabulations of two variables (for example, SIC by employee size) to see whether more complex patterns emerge. This type of analysis may reveal relationships not detectable through univariate analysis.

For example, univariate analysis may reveal that SIC is not predictive of response, and number of employees at a site is not predictive of response either. However, viewing SIC and employee size simultaneously with respect to response may indeed reveal a relationship. It may turn out that SIC 80 (health-care professionals) with fewer than five employees in their offices are extremely predictive of response. However, health-care professionals by themselves (without the presence of less than five employees) are not predictive of response.

Factor Analysis

Sometimes referred to as *dimensionality reduction analysis,* factor analysis helps to group similar variables such as home value and income to determine whether they are statistically redundant. Redundant variables can be eliminated from the analysis or grouped together into composite measures.

An exaggerated example of redundant variables are age and date of birth. Factor analysis helps to identify the true number of independent pieces of information by eliminating redundancies in the data, which in turn helps to simplify the analysis process and make your model more intuitive.

Suppose that within your marketing database you have information on product purchases for more than 100 products. You are having a model developed to predict responsiveness to a particular catalog promotion, and you know that product purchase history is likely to be a significant attribute in predicting responsiveness.

In theory, each product purchased could be used as a predictor variable. But this would yield 100 possible predictors, far too many to include in a single model. Also, many of the 100 products may have an affinity to one another and thus be somewhat redundant in predicting response. Factor analysis may help by grouping the products into a smaller number of more manageable categories, thus reducing the number of predictor variables and ultimately leveraging more information than if these product variables were considered separately.

Cluster Analysis

Factor analysis is commonly, though by no means exclusively, used as a precursor to cluster analysis. Cluster analysis evaluates a large, heterogeneous population of businesses or consumers and breaks it down into smaller segments with "like" characteristics. The primary benefit of cluster analysis is that it makes it easier to target these more homogeneous, well-defined universes.

Suppose you profile your customer base in its entirety and learn that the average number of employees at your customer locations is 75. It may be that not one of your customers has 75 or even close to 75 employees. Perhaps roughly half of your customer base consists of smaller businesses with 25 employees on average, and half of your customer base consists of larger businesses with 125 employees on average. Targeting your customer base as a whole would lead you to believe that companies with 75 employees (the overall average across your customer base) are your ideal target, when in fact they are not a core market.

Cluster analysis extracts these submarkets within your database, making it easier to target—both from a modeling perspective as well as a creative marketing perspective—these dynamic groups of customers.

Each submarket may have different performance (response) patterns. Let's say your database pulled a 1 percent response to a particular promotion. But the 25-employee segment pulled a 1.5 percent response, while the 125-employee segment pulled a 0.5 percent response.

In actuality, cluster analysis would use several variables (not just employee size) in determining the various market segments resident within a database. The greater the number of variables to evaluate, the more clusters you are likely to find.

Discriminant Analysis

Often referred to as *cross-validation analysis*, discriminant analysis tests whether groups being used are valid discriminators.

For instance, a university uses a formula for its entering freshmen to determine in which level of a foreign language they are to be placed. If the freshmen completed one to two years of high school Spanish, they are classified as level A. If they completed two to three years, they are classified as level B.

Next, the university administers a test to the incoming students already preclassified into levels and finds that the scores were very similar. The determination was made that the number of years of a foreign language taken in high school was not a sufficient discriminator to determine a freshman's knowledge.

The idea here is that if the groups perform the same, there is no reason to keep them apart. Discriminant analysis is often used to cross-validate cluster groupings identified within a database or assign new customers into such clusters identified within the database.

CHAID Analysis

Short for *chi-square interaction detector*, CHAID is a technique used to segment a population with respect to its relationship to a target variable, such as response. Responders are compared with nonresponders for various attributes to determine whether a statistically valid difference exists.

CHAID can be likened to a tree with branches. The trunk is usually a variable within the database found to have the greatest impact on the target variable. The branches are different variables—and combinations of variables—that produce an even greater impact on response. As you move up the branches, the impact on response intensifies.

For example, within the database, the trunk is made up of individuals with incomes exceeding $100,000. This group responds 1 out of every 100 times mailed. Farther up the tree, the first branch consists of a group of individuals with incomes exceeding $100,000 and ages thirty-five to forty-five. This group responds 5 out of every 100 times mailed.

A second branch is composed of a group of individuals with incomes exceeding $100,000, ages thirty-five to forty-five, and females, who respond 10 out of every 100 times mailed. Climbing of the tree stops when the desired lift in relation to the potential universe is maximized.

Selecting Your Modeling Method

Now that you've done your exploratory data analysis, it's time to pick a modeling methodology.

It is theoretically possible to get to a model that predicts a fantastic result but does not provide you with sufficient quantity to justify a mailing. This is why you must get involved in the modeling process. You must examine the interplay among variables that gives you the greatest lift for the quantity you must mail to have a profitable business. If you can't scale up your mailings, it won't matter that you've gotten the best response anyone ever had on the list.

There are three basic multivariate modeling techniques commonly used in direct marketing: *linear regression, logistic regression,* and *neural net.*

Linear regression, also known as *least squares estimation,* seeks to find the smallest variance between points. Linear regression can be used on anything that can be averaged (such as dollars, lifetime value, or average order size).

Logistic regression uses a technique called *maximum likelihood estimation,* which seeks to find a model that gives you the greatest proportion of successes. Use logistic regression in situations whose outcomes are characterized as a yes or no; response or nonresponse; or better, same, or worse.

Neural net is a technique that is good for finding patterns in the data that are nonlinear. Its strength is that it can test for all the combinations of variables, not easily detectable through traditional statistical methods, to find positive and negative patterns that determine response.

A few software programs on the market claim to do all the different types of regression modeling automatically. The problem with this is that the model can only be effective if you understand the data, their relationships to each other, and the type of methodology to use for the information to be discovered.

For example, using linear regression to answer a yes-or-no type of question will probably give poor results. Yet these programs could and do sometimes show the best results using the wrong methodology.

So be careful, and remember to clearly communicate your business objectives or challenges. Only then can your statistician prescribe the appropriate medicine for your marketing challenges.

Merge-Purge

In traditional direct mail, through a process called *merge-purge,* different mailing lists can be merged together on the computer and the duplicate names eliminated. This is usually cost-effective only in larger mailings—say thirty thousand to fifty thousand names or more.

When you rent a conventional mailing list, the list broker or manager sends it to your letter shop or data processing bureau—which, with all the lists in hand, can perform this merge-purge for you.

As of this writing, most e-list owners prefer to do the transmission in-house and do not release their e-lists to outside service bureaus. Since they won't share e-lists, the lists remain isolated, and no merge-purge is possible.

As a result, many duplicates are probably being e-mailed. The duplication rate on e-lists is unknown. As more e-list owners release their lists to outside transmission bureaus, merge-purge of e-lists will become more prevalent, duplicates eliminated, and the duplication rate known.

"The e-mail marketing industry is going to run into a major merge-purge problem," says Rosalind Resnick, CEO of NetCreations. "Nobody ever ships their list to an outside letter shop for merge-purge."

Co-Ops

Some e-list brokers are considering offering co-op mailings. In a co-op, a single e-mail would contain advertising messages and response links to separate URLs for multiple advertisers. This is the online equivalent of insert programs.

Having three, four, or more advertisers split the list rental and transmission costs makes Internet direct mail extremely cheap. The question is whether the response would decline in proportion or less sharply. If a co-op is a quarter of the cost of a solo e-mail but generates half the usual response, then it can pay off.

Endorsed Exchanges

We mentioned earlier that some e-list owners will endorse the e-mailer's product or service. This is called an *endorsed e-mailing*. Others will swap lists with other e-marketers, and each endorses the other's product. This is an *endorsed exchange*.

Endorsed mailings are not new in direct marketing; they have been used with success for many years in traditional direct mail. In online marketing, where Internet users are much more receptive to e-mail from companies they have a relationship with, endorsed mailings overcome the perception of spam that is sometimes associated even with legitimate opt-in e-marketing. We recommend you look for and test endorsed mailings when available. Even if the e-list owner doesn't offer it as a standard selection, you might be able to get the endorsed mailing simply by asking.

Deliverability

In traditional direct marketing, most list sources guarantee deliverability of 93 percent or somewhere in that range: If you mail 100 pieces and more than 7 come back as undeliverable, the list company pays a penalty to you.

Many e-list brokers guarantee 100 percent deliverability. That doesn't mean there are no bad e-mail addresses on the list. It just means any that bounce back and cannot be delivered will be replaced with other e-mail addresses from the list rented.

In Chapter 7 (page 127), we talk about *click-through reports* e-list brokers provide to show you how many recipients of your e-mail got it and how many responded by clicking on the URL in the message. These reports typically show bounce-backs or undeliverables as well.

Depending on the list, bounce-backs are typically in the neighborhood of 8 to 10 percent. Using the same address matching techniques used in e-appending services, correct e-mail addresses for many of these undeliverables can be found and the e-mail forwarded to the new, correct address.

Collaborative Filtering and Closed-Loop Marketing

Two other e-marketing techniques worth considering are collaborative filtering and closed-loop marketing. Both of these techniques take e-marketing beyond the model of traditional direct mail and closer to the ideal of one-on-one "relationship marketing."

The company DoubleClick invented the term *closed-loop mar-keting*. They use cookies to track people in their network. Whenever a person logs on to one of the many sites within the DoubleClick network, DoubleClick can serve up a predetermined banner ad based on the type of site visited. Alternatively, if DoubleClick has the person's e-mail address, they can send him or her an e-mail message instead of serving a banner.

Early research indicates this kind of highly targeted, one-on-one personalized e-marketing message—as opposed to an e-marketing message mass broadcast to an entire e-list—generates higher click-through and sales rates. As of this writing, however, it's uncertain as to whether the greater sales are enough to offset closed-loop marketing's considerably higher costs. If you test this approach, keep a close eye on your cost per order.

Collaborative filtering, pioneered by Macromedia, is based on the premise that people who behave like your prospect are good predictors for what your prospect will do. Macromedia offers several software programs, such as LikeMinds, that enable e-marketers to do collaborative filtering.

First the software measures the prospect's Internet activity, demographics, buying habits, and other data. Then, based on the behavior of people who have characteristics similar to the prospect, it allows you to target personalized e-mail offers—with different products—he or she is most likely to respond to.

For example, a bookseller fulfills an order for a John Grisham novel. After a week, the bookseller sends an e-mail to the buyer saying, "We hope you liked the Grisham novel. Our customers who read this novel also enjoy novels by Scott Turow. If you purchase a Scott Turow novel today, we're offering a special discount of 5 percent. Click here to order: www.bookseller.com/turow/." The link takes the prospect to the Turow selections available on the bookseller's website.

In one collaborative filtering program, a jeans manufacturer found a close correlation between taste in fashion and taste in music. This makes sense, if you think about it: punk rockers seldom wear three-piece suits, and not too many senior citizens like Smash Mouth. E-mails targeted to different prospects, based on music preferences, with different styles, pulled a high response.

The Future of E-Lists

E-technology and e-marketing are changing at lightning speed. What is in store for the future?

To begin with, more names. As of this writing, there are more than ten million permission-based names available on various e-lists. As the use of the Internet continues to climb, and online shopping grows in popularity, this universe will likely expand to many more names.

As of this writing, there are three basic types of lists. The first, which all legitimate marketers avoid, are the "spam lists"—Internet addresses collected off the Internet. We might consider these the Internet equivalent of traditional compiled mailing lists, in which names are taken from phone directories and other public sources. Mailing Internet users unsolicited e-marketing messages can in many instances be illegal, as explained in Chapter 8.

One step up from the spam lists are the legitimate opt-in e-lists. Most e-marketing is currently targeted at these lists. These are the Internet equivalent of traditional controlled circulation subscription lists. The individuals on them have qualified themselves but haven't actually bought anything.

Most traditional direct marketers find that, in conventional direct mail, the best response comes from response lists—lists of people who have bought something through the mail. We are only starting to see true response lists in e-marketing, mostly from online catalogs. As tracking capabilities improve, we can increasingly measure not just click-throughs but also online purchases. As e-list owners capture purchasing activity, they will begin to add "mail order buyer" as an e-list selection. When that happens, direct marketers will benefit by e-mailing to a growing universe of Internet users who have identified themselves as online buyers, not just browsers or shoppers. Keith Wardell, president of Shop2u.com, says in an article in *Target Marketing* that people who shop from catalogs are four times more likely to shop on the Internet than people who are on opt-in lists of noncatalog shoppers.

Since more and more data are being tracked and measured, selectivity on e-lists will rapidly expand. You will be able to select names on e-lists according to type of computer, type of modem, ISP used, even type of access—56K, ISDN, DSL, T-1, dial-up. You will be able to select prospects to mail not only based on the websites they visited, but also the pages they browsed and how much time they spent on each. Other Internet selections include communities of interests or newsgroups the prospect belongs to, banner ads clicked on, topics searched on through search engines, or even how long the person has been using the Internet.

Through data overlays, offline and online data are being merged and enhancements to e-lists are adding a wide range of demographic and psychographic *selects* or *selections*. For business e-lists, these selections include number of employees, annual sales, industry, and job title. For consumer e-lists, you can select by age, income, lifestyle, marital status, presence of children in household, annual household income, hobbies, and areas of product interests.

One selection that is just becoming available, "intenders," will also grow in usage because of its potential for high response. A leader in this field is MatchLogic. By using cookies to track user activity, they accurately monitor, for a large database of online users, the websites visited, banner ads clicked on, and key words searched on. So, for example, if you visited a lot of automobile sites and reviewed pages on new models, and searched the Internet for websites on cars, MatchLogic could identify you as someone intending to or thinking about buying a new car.

Obviously, auto dealers would be more likely to get a response on a new car promotion from this group rather than other e-lists. In fact, one major auto maker routinely gets 15 to 22 percent click-throughs to e-mails inviting car owners and *auto intenders* to visit its website and register for a discount on the new model.

In one e-campaign, the auto company invited owners of a particular luxury auto model to a free dinner introducing the new year's model. The response rate was more than 70 percent.

Auto intenders are just one of many intender selections available from MatchLogic. Others include intent to purchase online and intent to have children.

As competition grows, lists become commodities, and mailers can more easily access mailing lists directly, list brokers have to add more value to their clients—or they will perish. And marketers will want to get faster service on list recommendations, delivery, and transmission to speed campaign cycle time. One solution is to increase efficiency through automation.

A decade ago, the only available technology for automation was electronic data interchange (EDI), which was rejected because of cost and implementation issues. But now, the Internet makes automation not only possible but also affordable.

What list functions could we automate to increase efficiency? Here are six potential areas for improvement.

• **Online usage.** Instead of people calling the list managers and owners to find out tests and continuations on lists, it would be great to get this information from a centralized database. This would free brokers to spend more time analyzing lists to improve their recommendations, and not on the logistics of getting the information in the first place.

• **Online list counts.** Nothing is as frustrating as planning a mailing at 2 A.M. for a 9 A.M. presentation to your client or boss and not having access to list counts because the list broker is at home sleeping. After all, how can you plan a campaign—or even know whether sufficient names are available—if you don't have the counts?

With automation, direct marketers would not have to wait for a list manager or owner to return their calls; they could access list counts online from a central source. (Some list brokers already offer instant online list counts with round-the-clock access through their websites.)

• **Online status reports.** To make sure your list order is filled, you pick up the phone, call the list manager, and ask for confirmation. This is time-consuming, frustrating (voice mail and phone tag), and wasteful. According to the DMA's *List Metrics Report* published in August 1999, more than 90 percent of the list brokerage community has access to e-mail. Why can't the list managers or their service bureaus automatically update a centralized server with order status as soon as the list is run and shipped? The broker could either log on to a password-protected Web page that would give the shipping information or, better yet, receive a confirming e-mail. The confirmation would include quantity shipped, shipping date, methods of shipment, and any tracking number.

• **Data transmission.** Over the Internet, electronic information can be sent anywhere in the world, at any time, for free. So why is anybody still shipping files on magnetic tape? Transmitting all data to the service bureau electronically would cut a full day off the order fulfillment and shipping process. This is a significant time savings, especially on three- to five-day orders, where it might literally mean the difference between getting a file into the merge-purge or not mailing it at all. Electronics transmission would also save money on tapes and delivery charges.

• **Online ordering.** To ensure accuracy and timeliness of data—including usage, counts, and status—all orders ideally should feed into a centralized online ordering system. Universal product codes to identify list name, mailer name, broker, and manager can be used to ensure that all systems are talking the same language.

• **Electronic approvals.** Bill Gates has observed that the amount of paper consumed doubles every two years. Once upon a time, the computer industry predicted a paperless office. Instead, the usage of paper is increasing geometrically. Every list order needs to be approved by the list owner. This includes approval of a sample mailing piece. To create an electronic approval system, these samples would need to be supplied in digital form. Direct mail pieces created on the computer are already available as digital files, and those created manually can easily be scanned into digital format. For automated approvals, the digital files are simply attached to an e-mail and sent to the manager or owner for review.

To Sum It All Up

• The list universe for conventional direct mail is larger than the e-list universe, with many more lists and selections to choose from. But the universe of Internet addresses is rapidly catching up with the offline list world in size, quality, and selectivity.

Tip: Online prospects who have opted in and voluntarily given their e-mail addresses are ten times more likely to respond than people whose e-mail addresses were appended to their files in an existing list via an e-address appending service.

- Never mail to a compiled list of Internet addresses. Only mail to opt-in lists of Internet users who have agreed to receive unsolicited promotional e-mails.
- As with traditional direct mail, Internet direct mail seems to generate a higher response when the list is well matched with the product or offer. If you are selling a subscription to a computer magazine, for example, use opt-in lists from computer-related websites.

5

BROADCASTING THE E-MAIL MESSAGE

IN CONVENTIONAL MAIL, a letter is written, inserted in an addressed envelope, and placed in a mailbox. The letter is collected and taken to the local post office by a postal worker, where it is forwarded to a larger substation for processing. One substation passes the letter to another until the letter finds its way to the delivery postman of the receiver, who delivers it.

This process is similar to information transfer on the Internet. This temporary store-and-forward method for moving letters is exactly how electronic mail, or e-mail, is transported in an automated network.

The main differences between traditional mail and e-mail are as follows:

- Instead of transmitting written documents in addressed envelopes, the system moves text-based electronic messages with attached files.
- E-mail can be delivered much more quickly.
- E-mail processing carries little or no expense.

Almost as easy as stamping a letter and dropping it in a mailbox, e-mail requires that the user establish an e-mail account and learn how to compose a message. E-mail hardware includes a computer and a modem (or alternate network connection).

The modem is needed to access the network over a telephone line. The modem converts the language of the computer to an audio signal that can be transmitted through standard telephone equipment. The e-mail software required to accomplish this is available through network service providers.

Users who subscribe to AOL or another online service typically receive e-mail service as part of the subscription rate. Users who opt to connect through an Internet service provider (ISP) need to install e-mail software (or a Web-enabled browser) for e-mail service.

Once an e-mail account is established, a message can be created, addressed, and sent across the network. Clicking the "Send" button in an e-mail application initiates the packet-switching process used to transmit the message.

The data in an e-mail message are broken into small bits of information called *packets* (typically no more than 1,500 characters per packet) and assigned a destination and forwarded with error protection identification. The error detection coding is to ensure that messages arrive with some degree of reliability.

Upon arrival at its destination, the e-mail data packets are reassembled into the original message. Packet switching is accomplished automatically, without human intervention.

E-mail was one of the original uses of the Internet and is still probably its most popular. E-mail is often the first thing a user experiments with when going online.

E-mail messages can be sent through a private network, an online service, or an ISP. E-mail can also be used to move file attachments effectively across the network. This procedure is as simple as choosing the menu option "Attach file" and navigating to find the file to be sent.

The rules responsible for executing packet-switching actions are labeled transmission control protocol/Internet protocol (TCP/IP). TCP/IP is the Internet standard for routing packets of data through powerful computers known as *nodes* or *routers*.

TCP/IP ensures that all the computers connected to the Internet are capable of communicating in the same language. In addition to directing data packets across the network, TCP/IP is responsible for collecting and assembling data on the receiving end back into the original message.

Data packets do not move in sequential order, one after another, along a single path. Each data packet is assigned the quickest route available, and since routing is done on the fly (as the situation changes), the best route may change in a fraction of a second. Consequently, the last packet sent from a sender's node might be the first to arrive at the receiver's computer.

TCP/IP takes responsibility for placing the data packets in the correct order so the intended message is delivered to the receiver. For example, suppose the message "This is to confirm, do not cancel my reservation!" is received and the packets are incorrectly reassembled like this: "This is to cancel my reservation, do not confirm!" You can imagine tha problems it would cause!

Just as a handwritten letter needs the protection of an envelope, e-mail needs protection. The simple mail transfer protocol (SMTP) provides a preliminary clearance for e-mail to be sent from sender to receiver.

The sending computer notifies the intended receiver that a message is to be sent. The receiving computer can then acknowledge the forthcoming e-mail or can notify the sender of an error prior to the message being transmitted.

For example, if the intended recipient is not at the receiving address, or an invalid address is posted, or some other error is detected, the SMTP can help control the flow of legitimate e-mail. Once approval is established, SMTP lets the receiver know that a message is being sent.

To do direct mail on the Internet, you need an effective e-mail message and a list of e-mail addresses. But how do you distribute your message to these prospects? There are two basic options: with a listserver or through a service bureau.

Listservers

A listserver is a software program that sends e-mail messages to Internet mailing lists. When you rent names from an e-list broker, the e-list owner will transmit your e-mail message to his e-list for you. But what about e-mailing to your house file? That's where a listserver can help.

When you use a listserver you put yourself on the cutting edge of marketing and give yourself an astonishing competitive advantage. This is easy to understand when you think about how much a business spends to mail or fax its marketing offers versus how little it costs to send the same messages over the Internet.

Appendix A lists several listservers. You can get an adequate listserver for a purchase price (actually an annual license fee) of around $300 to $600.

What advantages can a listserver give a business in its Internet marketing program? A listserver enables your Internet mailing list to grow itself. Prospects can place themselves on your Internet mailing list by filling in a reply form on your website. You do nothing! They simply click on "Submit" and are added to the list. The listserver will send a note out to the address that was added, confirming acceptance. It can also attach a separate welcome note. This confirms for the person that he or she subscribed and is now on the list. And it provides instructions on how to remove himself or herself.

The listserver program will remove bad e-mail addresses instantly. If you mail your information out to, say, five thousand people, the odds are that about fifty addresses will not work anymore. This is due to people switching their addresses or just ending their service.

The listserver handles these bad addresses with no effort on your part. It will delete the bad addresses and even send you a note letting you know which addresses were removed and why.

Removal of an address from the listserver is as easy as putting it on in the first place. Say you send out a note to that list of five thousand, and twenty-five people want off the list. If you used a manual bulk e-mail program (described a little later in this chapter) to send to the list, you would need to look up the addresses and remove them one at a time, which could take more than an hour. No need to do this with the listserver.

With a listserver, people have two ways of removing themselves from your list. They can visit your Web page to remove their address. Or, they can send a note to the listserver with the word "Remove" in the body of the message. You have a template ready that requires you to "clip and paste" the address for removal.

The average amount of people who are not able to follow instructions and remove themselves from a list of five thousand names is about five people. It takes about five seconds per address to remove them, since the listserver just needs the address for removal. It does the lookup and deletion automatically.

Posting (sending) a message to your entire list is as quick and easy as sending an individual e-mail to a single person! You simply send a note to the listserver and include a special password that tells the program you are posting. The listserver understands the password and instantly sends the message to the entire list. Then it e-mails you a confirmation letting you know what the message was and how many people on the list it is being mailed to.

You can access and examine your list anytime. All you do is send a message to the listserver with the same password for posting, but you include the command "List" and then the name of your list. You will then instantly receive an e-mail message including all of the names on the list. This allows you to monitor the list's growth.

By using a series of simple password-protected commands you can manage a list of twenty as easily as twenty thousand via e-mail. No fancy UNIX code or need to connect with the server to remove or send to the list. Listservers are perhaps the most advanced service on the Internet today, since they have been around even longer than the World Wide Web and newsgroups.

Think of the listserver as a minibroadcast center you control from your desktop. It builds its own list and takes care of posting, just as a microphone allows a disk jockey to broadcast to listeners of a radio station. Therefore, you need to figure out what content to send to people so that they will keep reading. Remember, it is just as easy to lose an e-mail prospect as it is to gain one, so you must spend the time to craft messages of interest.

Here are some useful guidelines for material content for publishing to your list.

• Make sure that you never just send ads to the list. Always have something in your message that will benefit the audience. There is no faster way to lose readers than to overstuff your message with ads.

• You will need someone in your organization to produce the content for your message. Some companies, like magazine publishers, have it easy here. They can have one of their editors make up an e-mail newsletter from their print materials. Minimal modification is required to get the material Internet-ready.

- Product manufacturers have to do more research. For example, a website that sells ski equipment would need to look into some content regarding the latest ski news, resorts, and so on to include in their message. A hint: visit some newsgroups and websites that are relevant to your business. You will be surprised at how many of these sites have articles and news that you can use for your publication. Just ask for permission to use the information, and you will be on your way to publishing your first Internet newsletter.

- Format of an Internet newsletter is almost as important as the content. Ever picked up a book or magazine without a table of contents? Annoying is an understatement! You must have a few things in your newsletter to make it work. These include:

  - name of the publication
  - date and issue
  - removal information
  - table of contents
  - short intro paragraph
  - publisher, editor names
  - well-defined headers that correspond to the table of contents

Under each major heading you will need to make sure you include a title and any other relevant information. The following sample e-mail shows how CompuServe begins its monthly newsletter.

```
''''''''''''''''''''''''''''''''''''''''''''''''''''''''''''''''''''''''''

"All aBout CompuServe," Vol.1 Issue 2. Sept. 18, 1997
The Companion Newsletter to CSi's Forum and Communities
From CompuServe Interactive Business Partners and Sysops

''''''''''''''''''''''''''''''''''''''''''''''''''''''''''''''''''''''''''

ISSUE HIGHLIGHTS

— Finally, Flat-Rate Pricing Is Here!
— H&R Block Announces CompuServe Sale to WorldCom-AOL
— Personalize Your E-mail Address
```

— Use 5 Megs of Space for Your Web Page

— New Version of Off-Line Navigator: Virtual Access 4.0

— "Kevin and Kell" Cartoons in Funnies Forum

— Microsoft Access Support Live in the Access Forum

— A Handbook for Maturing Hipsters

— Deal With Tough Back-to-School Issues in ADD Forum

— Screen Saver Salutes Princess Diana

— See How Versace Dressed the Supermodels

— Need Help Ferreting Out Those E-Mail Addresses?

— Go Winsupport for Windows 95 Patches, Updates on CSi

— Screamin' Guitars in Rock Forum

— Help Is Here for Cranky Electronic Gadgets!

— Headache Support Group Launches in Good Health

— Real Estate Forum

— Can We Talk? Try the Internet Chat Relay Forum

```
````````````````````````````````````
```

FROM THE EDITORS' KEYBOARD

```
````````````````````````````````````
```

Two big decisions last week had us sitting on the edge of our chairs. First, CompuServe announced a landmark decision to let members choose flat-rate pricing if they wished. On its heels came the announcement that telecommunications giant WorldCom agreed to buy CompuServe Inc.—and that a complex swap would allow America Online to assume control . . .

Order information is also critical to the success of your Internet newsletter. You don't need an order form in the newsletter since you can just refer people to a URL or e-mail address.

You must be careful when shopping for a listserver. Many companies will set a very low monthly or yearly license fee but then charge you for the amount of times you use the listserver and for the amount of names you have. This will only lead to a situation where you keep getting bills every time you mail out to your list. Over a year this can get very expensive, especially as your business grows.

A good listserver vendor will charge you a flat fee and state clearly any extra costs. You should look to pay in the neighborhood of $300 to $600 per year for your own listserver.

# Bulk E-Mail Programs

Why won't a cheaper bulk e-mail program do as well as a listserver? Most bulk e-mail programs are designed to send e-mail to a list of people that you manually input onto the list. Bulk e-mail programs have many major drawbacks, including the following:

- E-mail addresses must be manually added or removed. This means that people must send you their addresses and then you must retype them onto the list. Also, removal takes more time since you have to do a lookup and then delete.
- Bulk e-mail programs offer no way for the person receiving the message you send to get off the list automatically. This leads to administration problems if you forget to remove half a dozen people. The next time you mail to the list you can expect some spam complaints to your Internet service provider.
- Bulk mailings to a list are often a one-time event and are considered spam. This is the real purpose of most bulk e-mail programs on the market today. They are designed to strip e-mail addresses from newsgroups and websites for a single purpose: spam!
- The worst part of bulk e-mail is that it is a program used on your local computer. It is not a mail server program. In fact, it needs to send mail through your ISP's server.

Most ISPs have made it so that bulk e-mail programs can't send through their mail server. A listserver, on the other hand, brings the benefit of a high-speed connection to the Internet rather than a 56K connection from a regular computer modem.

A listserver is like a broadcast tool to be used as you see fit for solo Internet e-mail or in coordination with your website. It keeps your current customers and prospects updated on your business in a timely manner and costs pennies a day to maintain. With the elimination of administration, your business does not need to hire a person to handle your e-mail list. This represents a very large savings and more money in your pocket!

# Service Bureaus

Service bureaus are third-party service firms that, for a fee, transmit your e-marketing message to Internet lists—your own, rented, or both.

In the early days of Internet direct mail (about a year or so ago!), you rented e-lists from a list broker for a fee—typically $100 to $200 per thousand names. Then you paid an additional fee, usually around $100 per thousand names, to transmit your e-mail.

Today most e-list brokers offer transmission, and there are stand-alone service bureaus that offer it as well. You might work with one of the latter for transmission of your house file. Some are listed in Appendix A.

Some e-list firms that also offer transmission now throw it in at no charge. If you rent a list from them, the transmission is included in the price.

Ask the service bureau what type of technology it is using to transmit your e-mail. Does it have a lot of bandwidth to handle large volume? A dedicated T1 line is better than a 56K line, and a dedicated T3 is even better.

## Timing of Transmission

Direct marketers have long tried to formulate rules on timing of direct mail. Some conclusions have been reached for conventional direct mail, and you may want to consider these when timing your Internet direct mail.

Marketers of information products, especially business improvement, how-to, and self-help, find the best months to mail are January, February, October, and November.

January is overall considered the best month for mail-order marketing, with July and August generating the lowest response rates, approximately 10 to 20 percent less than other months.

Holiday offers work best from September through December. E-commerce websites that sell gift merchandise experience their peak traffic around the Christmas holiday.

Internet marketers are still experimenting with the best time to transmit their marketing e-mails. The online marketing manager for Omaha Steaks has been successful sending e-mail promotions tied to seasonal themes, such as spring and the beginning of the barbecue season. (See Figure 5.1.) They also do well with fourth-quarter e-mails promoting Omaha Steaks products as the perfect holiday gift.

Dear Online Friend,

My favorite time of year is here—grilling season! Since you have requested to receive special information from Omaha Steaks, I want to share my secret for grilling perfect steaks with you. Our Foolproof Steak Cooking Chart will allow you to grill perfect steaks every time. You'll be the hit of every barbecue! To view this chart, go to: http://omahasteaks.m0.net/m/s.asp?H302578543X80390

Tips:
- To cook perfect steaks every time, check out our Foolproof Steak Cooking Chart.
- Filet mignons will take 30 seconds to 1 minute less time than shown in chart.
- The cooking times in the chart are for fully thawed steaks.
- All times are approximate.

Sincerely,
Frederick J. Simon, Owner
Omaha Steaks

P.S. Take advantage of our Buy 1, Get 1 FREE offer! Now order 6 (5 oz.) top sirloins and get 6 more for FREE! This offer is only available through this e-mail. Order today!
http://omahasteaks.m0.net/m/s.asp?H302578543X80391

If you feel you have received this message in error or you wish to be removed from our list, please go to:

http://omahasteaks.m0.net/m/u/oma/o.asp?e=steve_roberts%40edithroman.com


**FROM: Omaha Steaks[SMTP:newsletter@omahasteaks1.m0.net]**
**SENT: Friday, July 09, 1999 1:01 PM**

*Figure 5.1. Omaha Steaks e-mails*

**SUBJECT: Great Grilling Recipe from Omaha Steaks!**

Dear Online Friend,

Omaha Steaks wants to help you make great meals at a moment's notice.

Good food - and time spent sharing it with people you love - is one
of life's greatest pleasures. So today, I want to share a delicious
pork chop recipe with you!

6 boneless pork chops, thawed
1 cup orange juice
⅓ cup soy sauce
¼ cup olive oil

Marinate chops for 1½ hours in the refrigerator.
Broil or grill over medium heat for approximately 7 minutes per side.
Makes enough for 6 chops.

Enjoy!

Sincerely,
Frederick J. Simon
Omaha Steaks

P.S. Right now you can enjoy 12 (4 oz) boneless pork chops for
only $29.00 or any of our great monthly specials and we'll also
send 6 burgers or a computer game FREE to each shipping address!
Go to:
http://omahasteaks.m0.net/m/s.asp?H249500569X179576

If you feel you have received this message in error
or you wish to be removed from the list, you can unsubscribe by going to:

*Figure 5.1. Omaha Steaks e-mails (continued)*

## Frequency

Another issue is frequency: How often should you send promotional e-mail to your customers?

With e-mail, especially to your own house file, the cost of printing and postage is eliminated. You could literally send an e-mail to your customers every day, if you wanted to. But should you? Probably not.

If you e-mail too frequently, you risk bothering your customers. In very few businesses do the customers want or need to hear from the marketer every day, or even every week.

What's the optimum frequency? Twice a month seems to work well in e-mail marketing. To prevent oversaturation with promotional mails, we recommend making one of these communications your monthly e-mail newsletter or e-zine (see Chapter 9, page 185), alternating with a promotional mail.

Omaha Steaks also e-mails its customers twice a month. As you can see from the samples we just reviewed, one of the e-mails each month is purely promotional, such as a sale or gift offer. The other is informational, usually a recipe.

Our research indicates that the optimum frequency is one e-mail to your e-list every two to three weeks. The maximum advisable frequency is weekly. However, this doesn't include thank-you e-mails, which should be sent immediately to customers whenever they place orders.

## Day and Time

Unlike third-class bulk rate traditional mail, which might arrive on the prospect's desk or in his or her company's mail room anywhere from two days to three weeks after you mail it, e-mail delivery can be timed almost to the minute (or at least to the hour).

Does it matter when you send an e-mail? Again, different Internet marketers have different theories.

Omaha Steaks doesn't think timing makes much of a difference, but they do have some preferences. They typically send e-mail marketing messages during the middle of the week. Their reasoning?

On Monday people go through their e-mail quickly because they have so many from the weekend; on Friday they are getting ready for the weekend and so want to get rid of their e-mails quickly.

Other e-mailers have also found midweek is best, particularly Tuesday and Wednesday. Many avoid Monday and Friday.

However, it depends on the audience and the offer. For example, late Friday night and early Saturday morning work well when e-mailing to small businesses. These people often respond to Friday night mailings during the weekends, as many are working from home offices.

Michelle Lux, a vice president of marketing at Doubleday Interactive, has even tested time of day. In one test, she found that click-through response to her e-zine increased 5 to 12 percent when it was e-mailed at noon.

Her best mailing time and day for the Doubleday Book Club e-zine is Monday at noon. For business-to-business offers, Lux suggests mailing Tuesday or Wednesday.

Gaming and entertainment offers should be e-mailed on Thursday, says Lux. An e-campaign from a newspaper publisher offering a sweepstakes for a free trip to Florida was deliberately e-mailed on the weekend to get traffic to come in over the weekend. It did not work, says Lux.

She advises e-marketers to monitor website traffic to determine peak periods. E-mail should then be transmitted to arrive slightly earlier than this peak website period. "The Web traffic pattern shows the way customers like to look at you online," explains Lux. "Be there with an e-mail an hour earlier to market and feature items you have for them." If there is a day of the week when Web traffic is at its lowest, do not e-mail on that day.

Writing in *DM News* (December 13, 1999, p. 32), Al DiBlasi suggests that e-mailing Tuesday through Thursday is best because it avoids the "Friday afternoon mail purge" as well as the Monday morning mail purge from messages accumulated over the weekend. He suggests not mailing on holidays for similar reasons. However, he says, there are no absolute rules.

The bottom line? Test to determine the best months, days, and times to maximize response to your e-mail marketing messages.

## Case Study: Ticketmaster Online/E-Dialog Springsteen Campaign

Ticketmaster engaged e-Dialog to conduct an event-driven e-mail marketing campaign with the Ticketmaster customers who purchased their tickets for the New Jersey leg of the Bruce Springsteen tour online. Ticketmaster is the first online ticket company to engage in building one-to-one relationships with its customers through this form of targeted digital direct marketing.

The campaign consisted of three separate mailings, spanning the full cycle of direct marketing objectives, from initial contact, to personalized, service-oriented messaging and targeted purchase opportunities. The first mailing was sent after customers purchased tickets online and was used to verify their e-mail addresses. The mailing also included HTMLDetect, e-Dialog's tool to detect which recipients are able to view HTML-based e-mails.

Having established the digital dialog with Ticketmaster's customers, the second mailing, which was sent three or four days prior to the concert, was a service-oriented, customer-driven message. It provided details such as seating charts and directions to the arena, and was sent in either HTML or plain text format, depending on the findings from the first mailing.

The third mailing featured targeted purchase opportunities and demonstrates the value of e-Dialog's digital direct approach, as traditional direct marketing mediums cannot provide this combination of speed and personalization. Sent the morning after the recipient attended the show, the message contained a play list from the concert, including links associated with each song that enabled the recipient to purchase the album that song appears on. In addition, the message included discounted purchase opportunities for tour T-shirts and other memorabilia.

The campaign generated a 47 percent response rate and a 20 percent conversion rate (customers choosing to purchase an item as a result of the third mailing), all with a less than 1 percent opt-out rate.

As a result of the campaign, Ticketmaster is considering additional one-to-one digital direct marketing initiatives, such as maintaining a list of Springsteen fans or working with bands to deliver messages from the artists to customers.

## Special Considerations for Sending E-Marketing Messages to AOL Accounts

In 1992, Prodigy was the number-one online service with two million subscribers. America Online (AOL) was a distant fourth, with two hundred thousand.

Today AOL has emerged as the leading online service. According to research from Simba Information, AOL's twenty-two million subscribers is almost double the total subscriber base of the next nine largest online services combined.

Based on the amount of spam some America Online subscribers receive, you might think AOL allows spamming. But it does not. Its policy clearly states its antispamming position: "You may not use the AOL Service to send unsolicited advertising, promotional material, or other forms of solicitation to other Members except in those specified areas that are designated for such a purpose (e.g. the classified area)." Transmission of chain letters and pyramid schemes of any kind is also not allowed on the AOL service.

You can only send e-mail marketing messages to people with AOL accounts if they are on an opt-in list or are part of your own customer file. But even then there are several other problems with e-mailing to AOL accounts.

Recall from Chapter 4 our discussion of e-mail appending services (page 70). For a fee, you can have e-mail addresses attached to existing customer records, allowing you to communicate with your customers via broadcasted mass e-mail.

In e-mail appending, such services can generally find e-mail addresses for approximately 20 to 30 percent of the files they run. One reason is that e-mail addresses in companies usually follow a common naming convention.

For instance, at Edith Roman Associates, the naming convention is the person's first name, an underscore, last name, and then "@edithroman.com." So Steve Roberts is steve_roberts@edithro man.com.

Many companies use a variation of the company name after the *at* sign (@), and then the person's name before it. So if you can figure out a company's convention, you can get the e-mail addresses of everyone who works there.

**For your information:** According to an article in *Investment News* (December 6, 1999), both the House and Senate recently passed different versions of legislation that would give electronic signatures over the Internet the same legal weight as a signed paper document. This could potentially help increase Internet business for online brokers, business-to-business marketers, and others who require a signed contract, agreement, or purchase order as part of the purchase transaction.

But if a lot of your customers are AOL users, that match rate will likely be lower. The reason is that the appending process is not as effective in finding AOL addresses as it is with non-AOL addresses, based on the format of the addressing. Since all AOL addresses end with "@aol.com," and the alphanumeric characters before the *at* sign rarely match the name, they are almost impossible to find.

Another problem is that for most e-mail marketing messages, the standard response mechanism is to embed a unique URL address in the e-mail. The customer clicks on this address to link directly to a Web page or other online response device.

In regular e-mail boxes, the link becomes live as soon as they e-mail is received. But in AOL, this does not happen—in effect, the response mechanism does not work. Special programming must be used to make the embedded link "hot" in the AOL-received message, so that the AOL customer can click and respond.

Without the live hot link, the AOL receipt has to cut and paste the URL address into a separate file. This process is cumbersome and results in depressed response, with click-through rates below 1 percent. Special coding for AOL e-mail accounts can overcome this problem, but many e-list vendors do not offer this service.

A new version of AOL, 5.0, was being released as this book went to press, and it supposedly lets you embed URLs in e-mails. But that does not solve the problem for the many users running earlier versions.

## To Sum It All Up

- When you rent an e-list, the list broker will give your e-mail message to the list owner, who will transmit it for you to his or her list.
- You need a listserver, bulk e-mail program, or other software or service bureau to transmit e-mail marketing messages to your house file of Internet addresses.
- Doing Internet direct mail to AOL users is more difficult because most versions of AOL do not allow you to embed a URL link in the e-mail message, and embedded links are the most effective response mechanism for Internet direct mail.

# 6

# REPLY OPTIONS AND MECHANISMS

OK. SOMEONE GETS your e-mail and is interested. How does he or she reply? What kinds of response options do you build into the e-mail? More than one? What if you don't have a website that can capture the response? This chapter examines the response options you can build into your e-mail message.

## Web Response Forms

Every company that does Internet direct mail should have a website. The website is typically the primary response mechanism for e-campaigns. Why is this so?

Internet users who are on the Internet like to stay there. They don't want to jump back and forth between Internet, mail, phone, and fax, if they can avoid it. Allowing them to get an e-mail and then click to a website for more information is convenient and quick for them.

The most popular response mechanism for Internet direct mail is to send the prospect to a Web page where they can fill out a form and then submit it via your website. Just write within your e-mail message a link to your Web page address. It will automatically be highlighted in blue, indicating that it is interactive.

Ask the prospect to click on the website link appearing directly in your e-mail message. This will send him or her directly to the desired Web page where the prospect can interact with and respond to your site.

You can send prospects to your home page or to any other page on your website. You can also send the prospect to a custom response form posted on your website or on your server. We find it is most effective to send the prospect to a reply form created specifically as a response mechanism for the e-mail marketing campaign. For instance, if the e-mail promises a 10 percent discount, the form the prospect goes to should have the headline, "Register here for your 10 percent discount!" Copy at the beginning of the Web form should refer back to the e-mail and link logically with it. If you send the prospect from your e-mail to your regular home page, the special offer made in the e-mail might not be apparent or easy to find, and the prospect may lose interest and leave.

When sending the prospect to your website, always send him or her to a page specifically designed as a response mechanism to the e-mail offer. Do not merely send the prospect to your home page. Sending the prospect to the home page instead of a specific customized response page is akin to handing a prospect the phone book when he or she asks you for your phone number. Do not make the prospect work to figure out how to respond or find the right path. You should construct the transaction so it is impossible for the prospect to not respond quickly and easily.

Since many Internet users have multiple e-mail addresses—typically one for business and another for personal use—ask for the preferred e-mail address on your registration form. Web marketing consultant Glen Fleishman says you can increase the likelihood of getting prospects to put a valid snail mail and e-mail address on the registration form by offering them a discount coupon for their first order, a free gift, or some other incentive. They, of course, won't get the incentive unless they give you the correct address.

Fleishman also suggests avoiding the assignment of custom account numbers, user IDs, passwords, or other codes specifically required for the user to revisit or order from your site. People forget these rapidly, and if they forget and are rejected by your site, they will leave and not come back.

## Other Internet Direct Mail Response Options

A hot (interactive) link within the body of your e-mail marketing message to a specifically designed Web page or form should be the primary response mechanism. But you can and should offer other options.

Some people, although surely a minority, may want to call, write, or fax. Complete contact information for their use—including the marketer's address, phone number, and fax number—should be included in the e-mail sig file, as discussed in Chapter 3 (page 56). If for some reason you want to encourage offline response, put your toll-free phone number in the body of the e-mail several times and, if you are using HTML graphics, highlight it by using color or by making it bold and large.

There are other ways for the prospects to respond online aside from the conventional method of clicking an embedded link in the e-mail text. Consider these especially for mailings primarily to AOL lists where embedded links often cannot be used.

One option is to have the prospects respond directly via e-mail. Your e-mail copy instructs them to click on the "Reply" button, type a response, and "Send" it to you—just like replying to any regular e-mail. The disadvantage of this is that it doesn't bring them to the Web form or page you want them to see. This response method can be valuable when e-mailing prospects a follow-up or keep-in-touch type of reminder. "If a prospect has been meaning to contact you but hasn't because he or she has been busy with everything else, your e-mail message provides an opportunity to reach out with only as much effort as it takes to click," writes self-promotion consultant Ilise Benun.

Another option is to include a short response form or reply section within the body of the e-mail marketing message. Prospects can check off the appropriate boxes to indicate their interest, then click on "Reply" and hit "Send" to respond. They can also print the reply form, complete it by hand, and fax or mail it to the marketer, as long as a response address and fax number are provided.

In addition to online response, give offline response options for prospects who are new to the Internet and prefer to respond the old-fashioned way. The easiest is to include your toll-free phone number in your e-mail. You can also incorporate a fax-back form into your message, then suggest that they print out the form, complete it, and fax it to the number indicated.

## Web Forms and Prepopulated Forms

In regular direct mail, filling out the reply card or form for the prospect—instead of making him or her do it—has been found to boost response. The same can be done in Internet direct mail.

In conventional direct mail, the mailer can inkjet or apply a label to a reply form that shows through a window in the envelope. When the prospect removes the form from the envelope, it is already filled out.

In Internet direct mail, the Web-based reply form can be "prepopulated" too. The recipient's name and address are already filled in. This is done automatically by importing the appropriate information from the e-list or e-database. A sample is shown in Figure 6.1. As with printed direct mail, the prospect can make any corrections before submitting his or her order.

## Personalized URLs

At least one company, Quest, now offers a set of methods and tools that enable e-marketers to mass produce websites and to personalize each one with the recipient's name in the domain name as well as personalizing the content. Example: You send an e-mail to Joan Harris. The e-mail says, "We have a special offer on a Web page just for you! To see it, click www.onlinemarketer.com/joanharris."

The technology guarantees name uniqueness, enabling Internet marketers to handle, for example, multiple John Smiths. The only limits to content personalization are the data available in the database and imagination. Each could have completely unique content. (Business methods and many technology elements are proprietary to Quest Systems Group Inc. U.S. and international patents are pending.)

**Prepopulated data**

Last Name

August

First Name

Sam

Address 1

533 Waterdale Rd

Address 2

Apartment 3G

E-mail

Sam@zelco.com

City

Savannah

State

New York

Telephone

914-945-2638

THANKS!

| Submit | Reset |

*confidential*

*Figure 6.1. Prepopulated response form*

There are no practical limits to the number of promotional web-sites that can be created. Theoretically, if a database containing the names of every person on the planet existed, individual websites could be generated for all five billion of them.

This capability to give each prospect a URL with his or her own name built into it is the electronic equivalent of ink-jet and laser personalized direct mail reply forms.

The recipients are notified of the existence of their personal sites either by e-mail or by a letter or postcard.

One test for a catalog marketer generated more than 3.5 percent response in four days, with an average order of more than $200. This compares extremely favorably with the total response of 1 percent typically generated from a conventional mailing. Even better, all of the buyers are new customers! All had failed to respond to a number of prior mailings.

Seeing one's name in a domain name is a real attention-getter that motivates people to check out the site. Because all content is generated programmatically, each site can be highly personalized.

Marketers can measure when the recipients visit their sites and how often they come back. Knowing which "envelopes" have been opened, when, and how often allows the marketers to generate follow-up ticklers that boost response. Although the custom personalized sites are typically planned to be live for only two to three weeks, they are persistent as compared to direct mail, which is frequently trashed. Many customers will come back to their sites several times before buying. Users of this method have received e-mail from customers saying that this is the most interesting promotion they have ever seen and thanking the mailer for including them.

In addition to consumer-targeted applications, the use of business-to-business direct mail applications is obviously an area of intense interest. Personalized websites may prove to be highly effective in any business situation in which it is important to deliver a message to a specific individual or to a select group of people, and there is a need to drive action or establish a relationship. Examples include:

- requesting a key executive appointment
- special promotions
- seminar invitations
- product announcements
- lead generation programs
- delivery of a proposal
- conference invitations
- testing direct marketing messages
- high-value information delivery
- market research
- announcements to a sales force

## Basic Internet Response Models

There are several e-campaign models currently in use. These include:

- retail impulse purchase
- retail considered purchase
- mail-order considered purchase
- customer-service-assisted purchase

The first two are proven; the latter two are in the developmental stages. Let us take a quick look at each of the four.

*Retail impulse purchase* means making a relatively small purchase directly online, with the entire transaction being conducted on an e-commerce website. A classic example is Amazon.com. Say you need a book on raising teenagers. You log on to Amazon.com, search book topics by "parenting, teenagers," review the descriptions of available books, and order one or more. The Internet direct mail, if used, drives people to the site or to a specific page on the site describing the current offer.

*Retail considered purchase* is similar, except the consumer needs more information before making a purchase decision—that's why it's called a *considered* purchase. Websites selling nutritional supplements are good examples. Many offer considerable research material on the nutrients, searchable, readable, and even downloadable free of charge, to help people decide which if any supplements they should be taking. Again, the Internet direct mail drives people to a Web page or form offering the product being advertised.

A *mail-order considered purchase* is the attempt to sell a product that is traditionally marketed through long copy mail order—a direct mail package, magalog, minilog, or catalog—over the Internet.

The model for this mode is less clear than the others, since there is fear and hesitation about translating traditional long copy direct mail packages to long copy e-mails. The fear, of course, is that long copy—which is proven to work in traditional direct marketing, especially for newsletters and other information products—is not proven to work in e-marketing messages.

The e-mail message does not have to contain all the sales copy, of course; it can send the recipient to a Web page or form with a lot more sales copy. But how much should be in the e-mail itself? How much on the Web page the recipient clicks through to? Should it be as extensive as a traditional direct mail package? These are unanswered questions we are just beginning to test.

Dani Levinas of Georgetown Publishing warns direct marketers, "Unless you have a great Web page that sells, don't send them [prospects] there." He also warns that including a website URL in a traditional direct mail package can, for selling information products, actually depress response.

He recently did a split test to promote a printed subscription publication. The conventional mailing, which did not list the Georgetown website URL, produced 170 orders. In a test cell in which the URL was added to the address line of the order form, the mailing pulled only 110 orders. Adding the website actually decreased response 35 percent!

In another test cell, the traditional order card was replaced with a page that said "To save 25 percent of your time, go visit this website" and listed the URL. Georgetown got 2,200 hits, but only seven paid orders! "Just mentioning the Web page address distracted the people from buying directly [from the mailing piece]," Levinas concludes.

## Human Response for E-Marketing Inquiries

The fourth model is *customer-service-assisted online purchasing*. This is used for more complex and expensive consumer offers as well as a lot of business offers.

With the emergence of e-commerce, customer service is rapidly being recognized as the key to improving online sales, customer loyalty, and brand equity. While much of the focus has been on e-mail management systems, many Internet companies are now recognizing the need for immediate service. Hence, the emergence of live text-based customer service.

A good example is the site for Lands' End, where you can have an audio conversation over the phone with a customer service rep while viewing merchandise on the online catalog at the website. Other such sites let you communicate with customer service reps by typing in an on-screen window, similar to a chat group.

Providing live customer service, however, presents a different set of challenges versus fielding e-mail inquiries. Robert LaCasclo, an expert in live Web response, offers ten tips your customer service staff should follow when addressing live text-based inquiries via the

Web. His firm, LivePerson, makes software to enable this type of online interaction with Web visitors. (See Appendix A.)

**1. One or two typos per conversation are OK.** It's all right to make a couple of mistakes while typing a response. It lets people know you're real and not an automated response. But be careful. Too many errors will make you look sloppy and unprofessional.

**2. Type as you speak.** Type in a conversational manner. Unlike a more formal letter or memorandum, this is a real-time dialogue. Be wary of using tone in your message, as this is difficult to detect in a text-based conversation.

**3. Keep the conversation moving.** If necessary, break long responses into two or three separate blocks. This avoids long pauses (see number 8) and allows your visitor to begin reading the first part of your response while you are completing it.

**4. Get straight to the point.** Typing and reading a conversation takes longer than actually speaking to someone. A general rule of thumb is no more than thirty words in each response block. This will keep the conversation flowing smoothly.

**5. Avoid yes/no answers.** Your customer's question is important; don't shortchange your answer. The customer may have spent a couple of minutes typing a question to you. A one-word response does not convey similar effort or thought on your part. Consequently, this type of response can often be interpreted as cold and impersonal.

**6. Use preformatted responses.** As much as 70 to 80 percent of all inquiries received by a site generally fall under the category of frequently asked questions. By anticipating these questions and developing preformatted responses, you will not only save time when responding, but you will help to ensure consistency in your answers. (Caveat: If you overuse preformatted responses, you may alienate customers. Be sure your operators customize or personalize preformatted responses as needed.)

**7. Get personal.** Leading customer service companies generally have a common characteristic: they treat each customer individually. Live customer-service solutions help websites achieve this by providing a true one-to-one marketing experience. Address your customers by name, reply to their specific questions, and be there for them. Your customers will appreciate the attentiveness and personal service.

**8. Avoid the awkward pause.** You know the feeling. You're in the middle of a conversation with someone and then suddenly there's silence. Not only can that silence be discomforting, but you'll be more likely to shift your attention elsewhere. The same thing can happen during a live-text conversation. You'll have a little more time between pauses in a text conversation versus a spoken one, but the general rule is no more than forty-five seconds between responses.

**9. Solve problems.** Have operators ready to answer questions as they occur. A real-time service solution only works when there are people on your end to take calls. Train your operators sufficiently so they can resolve most inquiries without requiring additional assistance. Make sure they follow up at the end of each conversation to ensure the customer's questions have been answered satisfactorily. If an operator doesn't have an immediate answer for a customer, the operator should say so and get back to the customer promptly. It's the follow-up and effort that the customer will ultimately remember.

**10. Close sales.** Many questions occur at that critical point of sale. Consequently, it's imperative that your operators recognize this and make the most of their contact with your customers. Anticipate and answer common questions that may arise during the checkout process. Lead them through the sale.

If you are unable to offer the product a customer is looking for, use it as a chance to cross-sell and make other recommendations. Once confident they are intent on making a purchase, you can then use this opportunity to upsell. Suggest a complementary product or add-on, or recommend the next model up or a higher level of service. But don't get pushy. Remember that the customer is typing, and this requires greater effort than speaking. Once they say no, then move on. If done well, nothing sells like a live person.

## Affiliate Programs

One of us, Bob, has a website, www.bly.com, which he uses to promote his direct marketing copywriting services. One of the pages, "Publications," highlights books Bob has written. Although www.bly.com is not an e-commerce site, Bob wanted to offer visitors the convenience of ordering the books online from his site, if they wished to do so. The solution? He established an affiliate program with Amazon.com.

With an affiliate program, you can link your site to others offering such a program. For instance, an author can link to Amazon.com. A software company that did not want to offer hardware could link to Dell, allowing its online customers to order PC equipment directly from Dell.

There is no cost for the link. In a typical affiliate program, the website to which you link will pay you 10 to 15 percent of the cash price of the initial order they get from any customer who goes to their site directly from yours. It's a nice way to provide your online visitors with extra service and convenience, while making a few dollars in the process.

## To Sum It All Up

- The primary response mechanism for Internet direct mail is to encourage the readers to click on an interactive link within the e-mail message that takes them to a website or form.
- Your response device for this method can be any website, page, or form, but as a rule a Web page or form designed specifically as a reply device for that particular e-mail message will generate more sales results than just sending prospects to your website's home page.
- Although 99 percent or more of recipients will respond via the interactive Web link embedded in your e-mail message, provide alternative response options—especially toll-free telephone numbers—for those who prefer to respond offline.

# 7

# TRACKING AND
# MEASURING RESULTS

DIRECT MARKETING IS perhaps the only form of marketing in which the results can be meaningfully and accurately tracked and measured. Since Internet marketing is the next stage in direct marketing's evolution, it is only logical that it, too, can be precisely tracked and measured. This includes banner ads, websites, and, of course, Internet direct mail.

According to Cahners Advertising Research:

- Eight out of ten manufacturing professionals have requested further information on a product after seeing something on the Internet about it.
- Use of the World Wide Web among manufacturing professionals increased 15 percent from 1996 to 1998.
- Purchase of business products on the Internet increased 13 percent from 1997 to 1998.

"Two years ago, if someone proposed sending out a million pieces of information to a million customers within two hours—using messages personalized to particular tastes and interests, and at a price of less than five cents each—you probably would have thought that person was crazy," writes Bridget McCrea in *Web Merchant* magazine (summer 1999). "And if they promised you a 15 percent response rate and a guarantee that the majority of those responses would be received within twenty-four hours, you would have certainly had a good guffaw and walked away. E-mail is currently fulfilling that promise."

## Response Speed

One of the biggest advantages in measuring online direct marketing response versus conventional direct marketing response is that replies to transmitting a message to an e-mail list are almost instant. The e-campaign can be set up and mailed in as little as a few days. This allows you to test creative messaging and different offers and lists inexpensively.

A good way to approach a first-time mailing is to narrow it down to about five different list selections and mail to each of them in small quantities. Based on the results, you can continually optimize the campaign by mailing only to the lists that are working.

You can also test sales appeals, offers, and copy to see what works best. Zelco sent one hundred thousand e-mails consisting of ten different messages. Within one week, 85 percent of the responses were in. Tabulating the results, three of the messages were identified as controls.

In another test, Bruce Dietzen, director of corporate sales for ichat, Inc. (www.ichat.com), a leading supplier of Web-based real-time communications software, sent an e-marketing message to PostMasterDirect.com's thirty thousand–member web design and promotion list. Ichat's sales quadrupled. (See Appendix A for contact information.)

"We sent out e-mail at 10 A.M. one day, and by 3:00, we had hundreds of visitors on our site, where we interacted with them directly via our software and then called them immediately afterwards," Dietzen says. "In five hours' time, we closed $50,000 in sales, including a single order for $20,000." Response rate was 7 percent.

"At fifteen cents a name, this is the best price/performance tool that I have ever encountered," Dietzen says. "There's another benefit, too. The time it takes to cycle a targeted e-mail marketing campaign is only two days. I was used to print marketing campaigns that took two months!" Now, ichat can create a campaign one day and book orders the next.

"Faster cycles at lower costs means a lot more campaigns are possible," Dietzen says. "That's what drives sales growth."

## Measuring Online Response

In this new age of information, it is impossible to focus on each piece of incoming data. One of the challenges to an online marketer, therefore, is to determine which metrics are the best gauges of site performance.

The basic building blocks of Internet metrics are impressions and clicks. They can help indicate how a campaign is performing, particularly branding campaigns, where impression levels give a measure of advertising reach.

The simplest metric to calculate is the click rate, which indicates how inviting your e-message is and how well the banner ad placement is performing. Though the average response to banner ads is 0.5 percent to 1 percent, click rates vary by product segment. Click rates are best used when the site or advertising campaign is fairly new and for those sites whose primary purpose is information.

For content websites, the most important metrics are those that show how many people get to the site and how long they stay. A low visit rate indicates that surfers are either aborting the load process (hitting the stop button or linking elsewhere) or repeatedly clicking the creative unit because the page is taking too long to load.

Then there is how well the website is pulling orders. Orders per million impressions tells how many impressions are needed with a particular Web page to get an order.

However, there must be sufficient order data to take action on this metric, and the number of orders it takes to reach valid conclusions will vary according to your product and industry.

If the primary goal of the site is to sell, the ultimate metric is cost per action (order, subscription, new member, e-mail opt-in, and so on). To get this metric, divide the number of actions into the cost of running the banner ad on the site (which may include agency and central serving costs).

Because advertising-site traffic fluctuates weekly delivery, it is sometimes difficult to correctly tell the true cost per action until the end of a buy period. As with orders per million impressions, there must be enough orders or time to make an informed, statistically significant decision. And sometimes maximizing efficiency may go against your volume goals.

For e-commerce sites, orders per million impressions and cost per action are the best gauges of performance and productivity.

Beyond the basics, there is a plethora of other information available for a price. New vendors appear daily willing to track everyone who ever got to your site. While this information may be good for some markets, it is not for everyone. You need to find the right person at the right time and give that person the right message to entice him or her to your site.

## Types of E-Mail Responders

Internet direct mail respondents can be classified into three categories: hot, warm, and cold. Each category, based on promptness of response to the marketing message, brings a different kind of online prospect.

*Hot* responders are those who click through within twenty-four hours. E-mail is easy to share with a click, and hot responders are the most likely to send your message to other people—ten, on average. These hot prospects are interested in the next and best thing, and are not strong on brand loyalty. Their behavior is difficult to predict, and they frequently bounce from site to site. They prefer short e-mails—sixty words or less.

*Warm* responders click through within three days. They will often read several paragraphs of copy, and they are solid prospects.

*Cold* responders take more than three days to respond. They are not as e-mail responsive as hot or warm responders and are a tough sell. You can get through to them in a number of ways, such as with free trials offers or a strong online community on your website.

Response rates to e-marketing messages range from 4 to 10 percent, with 10 percent being an optimistic target. The real question is how to go back to the 90 percent who didn't respond with another e-mail and bring back another 10 percent—and then another, and another, again and again. This is why an increasing number of mar-keters do e-campaigns instead of one-shot e-mails.

## E-Campaign Response Analysis

But what about specific responses to promotional e-mails? There are three main measurements currently used.

The first is click-throughs. This tells you how many people who received the message clicked on a link in the e-mail to a specific site, page, or form on the Web.

The second is replies. Of the people who clicked through to a response form, how many completed the form and submitted it to you?

The third measurement is sales or inquiries. How many people who completed the form actually ordered a product or requested more information, such as product literature or a price quote? This information can and should be tracked in your customer database.

As we've mentioned, the two basic online reply mechanisms for Internet direct mail are a click-through link embedded in the mes-sage and a reply form included in the body of the e-mail. The prospect either clicks on the link to go to a particular Web page or response form, or fills out the reply form in the e-mail received and clicks on "Reply" to submit it to the mailer.

You can increase response to Internet direct mail by making a special offer available only over the Internet. Tell customers that they will get free shipping, 10 percent off, a free gift, or some other special, and that this is being offered only to online customers receiv-ing this e-mail. Be sure to put a code (such as "Ask for Betty" or "Request extension 123") for those who respond offline via a call to a toll-free number, and let them know they will receive the spe-cial offer whether they respond online or offline.

Your e-list manager, database manager, or transmission bureau should provide log reports that summarize the results. (See Figure 7.1.) Such a report should include the date of transmission, number of promotional e-mails transmitted, click-through response rate, undeliverable messages (bounce-backs), and opt-outs. The opt-out rate is the number of people receiving the message who asked to be removed from the e-list.

> **Tip:** Make sure the forms you're asking e-mail recipients to click through to actually work. Few things are more frustrating than filling out a form online, only to have it wiped out or not accepted. Forms processing programs should save all information that users key in, writes Scott Kirsner in *CIO WebBusiness* (September 1, 1999). And they should be intelligent enough to correct minor errors, such as when users deploy dashes instead of spaces in a credit card number, or use 9 instead of 09 to represent September in a date field.

## Measuring E-Campaign Results

Let's analyze a hypothetical campaign in which an e-mail marketing message is sent to your house file and generates a 5 percent click-through response rate. The results are shown in Table 7.1.

Say the up-front cost to set up your list for e-mail transmission and create the first message is $5,000. The result is a list of one hundred thousand customer files for which you have e-mail addresses to which you can broadcast e-mail messages, assuming the appending results in a one hundred percent match rate. Actually, e-appending services usually find Internet addresses for 30 percent of the records you submit, maximum.

Since you own the list, there is no list rental cost. Transmission is $100 per thousand for service bureau charges, so it costs $10,000 to send e-mail to the whole list of one hundred thousand.

In traditional third-class bulk mail, mailings that are undeliverable are simply thrown away and never reach their prospect.

In Internet direct mail, however, you are instantly alerted when you e-mail to a bad address; the e-mail bounces back to you, indicating that you do not have a valid address. You can use e-mail appending to get correct addresses for these customers, then retransmit your e-mail message to reach them.

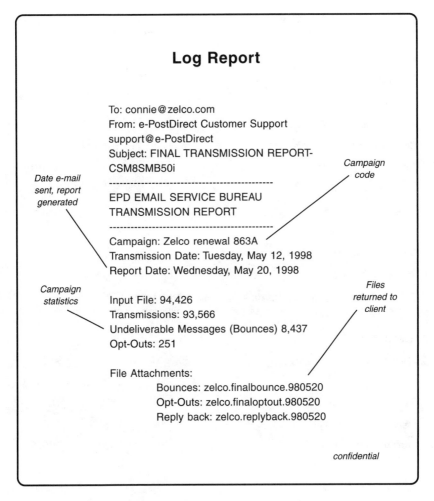

**Log Report**

To: connie@zelco.com
From: e-PostDirect Customer Support
support@e-PostDirect
Subject: FINAL TRANSMISSION REPORT-
CSM8SMB50i
-----------------------------------------------
EPD EMAIL SERVICE BUREAU
TRANSMISSION REPORT
-----------------------------------------------
Campaign: Zelco renewal 863A
Transmission Date: Tuesday, May 12, 1998
Report Date: Wednesday, May 20, 1998

Input File: 94,426
Transmissions: 93,566
Undeliverable Messages (Bounces) 8,437
Opt-Outs: 251

File Attachments:
        Bounces: zelco.finalbounce.980520
        Opt-Outs: zelco.finaloptout.980520
        Reply back: zelco.replyback.980520

*confidential*

*Date e-mail sent, report generated*

*Campaign code*

*Campaign statistics*

*Files returned to client*

**Figure 7.1. Sample transmission report**

In the previous example, we assumed you started with a customer list that contained no e-mail addresses and to which you had to append the addresses. Generally e-mail address appending costs $250 to $1,000 per thousand names. By the way, in all these examples, we assume a 5 percent click-through rate.

### Table 7.1 House File Campaign Without E-Mail Addresses

| | | | |
|---|---|---|---|
| Response rate | 5% | | |
| Initial costs | $5,000 | | $5,000 |
| Pass to match house records | 100,000 | $50 | $5,000 |
| Append and transmit addresses | 30,000 | $250 | $7,500 |
| Capture and transmit order | 1,500 | $300 | $450 |
| Total cost of the effort | | | $17,950 |
| Total records e-mailed | | | 30,000 |
| Responses expected | | | 1,500 |
| Cost per response—initial campaign | | | $11.97 |
| Cost per response—additional campaigns | | | $2.30 |

### Table 7.2 House File Campaign With E-Mail Addresses

| | | | |
|---|---|---|---|
| Response rate | 5% | | |
| Initial costs | $5,000 | | $5,000 |
| E-mail transmission | 100,000 | $100 | $10,000 |
| Pass to correct bounce-backs | 20,000 | $50 | $1,000 |
| Append and transmit corrected addresses | 6,000 | $250 | $1,500 |
| Capture and transmit order | 5,300 | $300 | $1,590 |
| Total cost of the effort | | | $19,090 |
| Total records e-mailed | | | 106,000 |
| Responses expected | | | 5,300 |
| Cost per response—initial campaign | | | $3.60 |
| Cost per response—additional campaigns | | | $2.66 |

If you already had the e-mail addresses, you would have no appending expense, and your bottom-line cost per response would be significantly lower, as shown in Table 7.2.

Now let's take a look at an e-mailing to a rented e-list. As with traditional direct marketing, it costs much more to get a response

**Table 7.3 New Business Campaign**

| | | | |
|---|---|---|---|
| Response rate | 5% | | |
| Cost to create form | $5,000 | | $5,000 |
| Purchase e-mail list* | 50,000 | $175 | $8,750 |
| E-mail transmission | 50,000 | $100 | $5,000 |
| Capture and transmit order | 2,500 | $300 | $750 |
| Total cost of the effort | | | $19,500 |
| Total records e-mailed | | | 50,000 |
| Responses expected | | | 2,500 |
| Cost per response—initial campaign | | | $7.80 |
| Cost per response—additional campaigns | | | $5.80 |

*$120 to $400 per thousand names based on list quality, size, selects, and type (business versus consumer)

from a stranger than from customers who already know you, as shown in Table 7.3.

# E-Mail Testing Strategies

E-mail marketing has significantly different fundamentals than paper direct mail, and e-mail marketers should create strategies that are different from those of paper mail campaigns. There are several infrastructure differences.

- E-mail campaigns require Web pages and tracking processes. These form the basis of large fixed costs. And as smart managers demand more sophisticated programs, fixed costs will get higher.
- E-mail variable costs are practically nil. It costs pennies rather than the fifty cents to one dollar it costs for paper, package, and postage.
- The technologies are new and are quickly evolving. E-mails are made up of lots of little technologies linked together.

These enable content, delivery, response handling, tracking, and reporting.

- Campaigns are quick but not simple. Today most e-mail programs are deliverable in five to seven days (one to three days on a rush basis)—much faster than the four to twenty or more weeks for direct mail. But it's a new game everyone is learning to play.

Then there are program limitations:

- Few e-mail names exist. Maybe 10 percent of customer databases list e-mail addresses.
- Limited data means weak segmentations. Today, e-mail names don't have much descriptive data tied to them.
- E-mail has high additional costs that marketers don't want right now. These include transmission and list rental fees (which are dropping rapidly), as well as creative costs—copy, design, HTML programming. Of course, these are a drop in the bucket when compared with the creative costs of doing a traditional paper direct mail package.

Finally, the guideposts are different:

- Marketers are racing for new revenues. Marketers are impatient to show success on first-time mailings. They seek sales revenues, early cash flows, and return on investment measurements to justify the new channel. Doing smaller e-mailings doesn't help save costs.
- While direct mail has a long history, e-mail marketing is new. There are no established models or segmentations that have captured past learning, so no one knows how a list or creative response rate will pan out. Anyone who predicts hard numbers is fooling himself.

So how do you leverage this learning to create your e-mail strategy? First, manage for the big picture:

- Focus on developing your experience base. Prove that the channel works, the fulfillment process works, and the reports show what you want them to show. Build your internal learning.

- Manage your boss's expectations. Don't try to break even on the first few tests. Invest in the mailings as learning for the future.
- When it comes to quality of names, recipient consumers are all over the map. Consumers are still getting used to habits of reading and replying to e-mail. Some opt-in lists have strong, loyal relationships with the source website. On others, the people on the e-list don't remember opting in, where they registered, or what the site is about.
- Tracking results to customers is tough. Tracking sounds easy, but this often involves gathering as much information as possible on as many names as you can right away. And have confidence in your test offer if it provides relevant value to your target base.
- Mail your best customers first and frequently. Build a critical volume of mail results and extrapolate from there.
- Mail to addresses that hit your website. These prospects and customers often will be your best source of names.
- Keep the creative variations to a minimum. But do HTML and text simultaneously to optimize responses. Focus on big-impact levers like different offers.
- Spend money on building your own segmentations on the back end. Overlay as much information as you can from your marketing database and outside sources. For instance, you can overlay your customer file with a selection for credit card holders. Then your response to offers where a credit card can be used for payment will increase when you e-mail only to this segment of the list.
- Interpret the results with perspective. Be realistic about what you can measure with statistical confidence. Look for the hint of opportunity in the list or creative for the next mailing. Don't throw out the medium because the click-through rate is low. In this stage of evolution, it will require four to five mailings over a number of months before you can see clear, predictable results.

E-mail is already starting to incorporate advanced digital techniques in videos, streaming banners, rich text, personalized content, even music via MP3. Do these techniques work, and are they worth the extra cost and trouble?

We recommended A/B splits as the best way to determine the answer. Let's say you are selling a subscription to a magazine. You can do an A/B split with straight ASCII text as opposed to the same message enhanced with HTML images of magazine covers and pages. If the HTML version wins, you can go further and then split test it against a more elaborate rich-media presentation—for example, one incorporating movement or sound.

Following is a nice example of a graphic e-mail from iPrint, the leading online print shop. The animation is simple but effective: It alternates between a picture of the product (greeting cards) and the message "20% off" set in stylized type with a drawing of holly.

5 - S E C O N D   S P E C I A L

Holiday greeting cards in October?

[GRAPHIC SWITCHES BETWEEN PICTURE OF PRODUCT AND "20% OFF" ILLUSTRATION]

Not a bad idea if you like saving time and money!

Impress customers and colleagues with professionally printed greeting cards now 20% off the regular price.

This early bird special won't last long, so visit iPrint.com today.

You have received this message because you are on iPrint.com's mailing list. If you do not wish to remain on iPrint.com's e-mail list, simply forward this message to: unsubscribe-iPrint9@msi.iPrint.com. You are on the mailing list as [Royal@iPrint.com].

If you have been forwarded this message by a friend and would like to subscribe to future mailings from iPrint.com, simply send an e-mail to subscribe-iPrint9@msi.iPrint.com.

# Tracking E-Marketing Activities to Bottom-Line Sales Results

"Over the past three years, the online sales channel has become the most important retailing revolution since the 1960s shopping-mall boom," says e-commerce consultant Jim D'Arcangelo. For instance, the number of online shoppers increased more than 15 percent from December 1998 to fall 1999, the opposite of what has been the rule of thumb for traditional brick-and-mortar shops during typically slow summer months.

J.C. Whitney, an automotive cataloger, has gotten click-through rates of more than 40 percent, with 5 percent of the click-throughs ordering a product online. One campaign produced twelve hundred orders at a mailing cost of only $500.

Just as in traditional direct marketing, everything in Internet direct marketing is subject to testing, and the only meaningful answer to whether something will work is a test result. For instance, iPrint.com gets new customers with loss-leader offers. (A loss leader is an initial order for free or a nominal fee designed to acquire a customer.)

Royal Farros, president of iPrint.com, says he has tested offering 300 custom labels completely free versus asking for $1.45 for the labels for shipping and handling. His finding: asking for money cuts the up-front response by 50 percent or more. On the other hand, offering the labels completely free attracts freebie seekers rather than customers: those who pay the small shipping charge are two to four times more likely than the pure freebie seekers to become ongoing iPrint.com customers. We find a similar dynamic in traditional print mail-order selling: charging a dollar or two for a product sample attracts a more qualified respondent—one who is more likely to order a full-size container of vitamins, adhesive, oil, or whatever—than offering the sample totally free.

Retailers interested in capturing the growing online consumer audience are embracing e-commerce. This rapidly developing market has dramatically changed the way many product categories are branded and will continue to do so. Marketers and retailers are already facing considerable challenges as they attempt to transfer retailing concepts—assortment, merchandising, pricing, and pro-motion—to the world of online commerce.

On the Internet, the competitive landscape is dramatically dif-ferent and consumers shop in different ways. For example, con-sumers can comparison shop among different merchants with the click of a button and may be more price-sensitive than the tradi-tional shopper. Shoppers also can make purchases around the clock instead of during store hours, which increases demand on order pro-cessing but creates a more satisfied, less harried customer.

The most distinct advantage is that each consumer can be cap-tured. And while the most important metric for any retailer will always be sales, the ability to analyze each stage of online consumer behavior with audience tracking capabilities gives the savvy online retailer an advantage over traditional retailers.

Data sources and analytical tools for competitive intelligence, performance measurement, and consumer behavior tracking now available to online marketers are far more sophisticated than what is available to traditional merchants. A person browsing through a traditional store is not likely to be shadowed from the housewares department to women's shoes to the toy department, where a sale is finally made. Online marketers have access to very granular pur-chase data, enabling them to understand the behavior of consumers in a way that brick-and-mortar retailers can't.

## Customer Acquisition

This metric helps e-commerce merchants understand how success-fully they are converting their engaged shoppers to buyers. In this framework, some companies are converting engaged shoppers to buyers but could use a higher number of shoppers. These companies should focus marketing efforts on generating traffic. Others have the traffic but are not motivating shoppers to buy.

## Customer Retention: Repeat/Loyalty and Competitive Analysis

Both brick-and-mortar and online marketers and retailers know that the best way to increase loyalty and retention is a customer focus.

For some customer segments, the deciding factor will be price sensitivity; for others, it will be customer service.

Competitive analysis is critical to both online and offline marketers and retailers. The data allow savvy online marketers and retailers to determine whether their customers are just visitors, engaged shoppers, or actual buyers. The data, available in real time, are invaluable to online merchants as they build their businesses.

## Customer Conversion

The next metric to consider is the conversion of qualified shoppers to buyers. This metric, called *conversion rate* or *look-to-book*, is as important to online marketers as it is to offline merchants. Again, online merchants have an advantage over their brick-and-mortar counterparts because they can monitor the shopping behavior of all online shoppers as they migrate toward a transaction. This capability enables the online marketer or retailer to clearly identify:

- the pages that motivate qualified shoppers to buy
- which prices and promotional activities work
- at which places consumers drop out

**Testing rule:** In direct marketing, online or offline, you can only get a valid result by testing one variable at a time. If you test "free" vs. "$1.45 shipping and handling," everything else in the e-marketing message—copy, design, list, time of transmission—must be the same. If you were to vary copy for the $1.45 offer, for example, and it did not pull as well as the free offer, how could you know whether the reason was the price or the copy? You could not. That's why testing must always be a scientific A/B split of one variable—price, list, offer, copy, straight ASCII text versus HTML versus visual mail—at a time. As naturalist Aldo Leopold wrote in his essay *The Round River,* "To keep every cog and wheel is the first precaution of intelligent tinkering."

None of this behavioral detail is available to brick-and-mortar marketers and retailers who must make do with anonymous cash register receipts, bump analysis, and mall intercepts.

Monitoring the conversion rate and other behavioral markers at or near the online checkout will help online marketers and retailers understand the rate at which shoppers are moving toward a transaction. For some customer segments the deciding factor will be price sensitivity; for others, it will be customer service.

Competitive analysis is critical to both online and offline merchants. The following questions are important considerations and should be constantly evaluated as sites evolve.

- How does e-commerce traffic compare site by site and to other shopping categories?
- Which e-commerce categories attract the most visitors and shoppers?
- At what rate are visitors being converted to shoppers and to buyers, site by site and by category?
- What is the percentage share of window shoppers versus qualified shoppers by category?
- How many are repeat shoppers? How does that compare to direct competition and the category?
- What is the demographic profile of visitors, shoppers, and buyers? How does this compare to the Web-using population and direct competitors?

The goal of in-depth third-party measurement in e-commerce is to gain a complete picture of online shopping behavior, information that should help Web marketers and retailers attract more shoppers, retain loyal customers, and build a thriving e-commerce business.

## To Sum It All Up

- Internet direct mail to rented opt-in lists generally pulls between 4 and 10 percent response as measured in click-through rates. No standard industry statistics regarding conversion of click-throughs to sales have been established that are widely accepted as the norm.

## How Does Your Web Marketing Measure Up?

WebSideStory (www.websidestory.com), a San Diego-based company specializing in Internet technologies, services, and sites, created both of these services for benchmarking your Web marketing results:

### StatMarket.com

*Accurate Internet statistics and user trends in real time.*

Services include e-data mining. StatMarket presents raw data computed from millions of daily Internet visitors to websites monitored by WebSideStory technology. StatMarket .com is the most accurate source of data on Internet user trends.

### Hitbox.com

*Website traffic counter and analysis tool.*

HitBox (and its high-end counterpart StatMarket eData Mining) remotely and anonymously collects and warehouses data from visitors to websites. In other words, it monitors the "who, what, when, and where" of every visit.

Hundreds of thousands of websites analyze their traffic with HitBox technology. Through the company's massive in-house network operating center, WebSideStory analyzes and stores data from billions of visitors to these sites every month. This has created an immense warehouse of data on Internet users—the largest of its kind. WebSideStory converts the massive amounts of raw Internet user data it collects into usable information.

HitBox is the most popular and comprehensive Web traffic analysis service. It also is the largest community of independent websites ranked by traffic.

- Graphic and animation techniques have in many instances increased Internet direct mail response rates and should be tested in A/B splits with straight text e-mails.
- Conventional direct response offers—including free gifts, discounts, and free shipping and handling—work extremely well in Internet direct mail. If you have such an offer, put it up front in your e-mail message; do not bury it.

# AVOIDING SPAM, FLAMING, AND OTHER UNIQUE INTERNET MARKETING PROBLEMS

MANY E-MARKETERS worry about spamming—sending illegal and unwanted e-mail. This chapter deals with how to create promotions that achieve your sales objectives without violating Internet etiquette, angering Internet users, or causing your ISP to disconnect you.

## Internet Users Are Sensitive to Spam

Internet users as a group do not like unsolicited e-mail. The Internet culture still views it as an unwelcome commercialization of the medium. Users have even developed the term *spam* as a pejorative reference to this type of e-mail. Furthermore, the Net is a community. Recipients of e-mail perceived as spam can vent their opposition to thousands of users in public newsgroup forums, thereby quickly generating negative publicity for the organization. The Nike Corporation is so sensitive to spam that it publishes an antispam policy right on its home page, which reads as follows:

> OK, so you're on your computer minding your own business and you get an e-mail telling you about a special offer from Nike for free shoes, or some other golden opportunity. Don't believe it. It's

143

not real. For the record, Nike doesn't send out unsolicited e-mails. From time to time we'll notify consumers who let us know they want to hear from us. Otherwise, any information on the Internet from Nike to the public comes on www.nike.com or www.nike biz.com.

Spammers routinely harvest e-mail addresses from newsgroup postings and then spam all the newsgroup members. Spam lists can also be generated from public directories, such as those provided by many universities in order to look up student e-mail addresses.

Spammers often hide their return e-mail addresses so that the recipients cannot reply to the spammer. Other unscrupulous tactics include spamming through a legitimate organization's e-mail server so that the message appears to come from an employee of that organization.

Some measures have been put in place to limit spam. Deja.com filters spam postings from its Usenet archives (www.deja.com). Many moderated newsgroups also filter spam. Some e-mail programs offer users the option to filter spam as well. There have also been a number of suits filed by ISPs seeking to recover costs from spammers for the load put on their systems by the tremendous number of messages. It is important to remember that all unsolicited e-mail is considered spam, but just as with direct mail, when the e-mail is appropriate and useful to the recipient, it is welcomed, unsolicited or not.

The Council for Responsible E-mail (CRE), a part of the Interactive Media Association, set guidelines for Internet marketing at its February 2000 meeting. The key considerations for Internet direct mailers:

- Marketers must inform Internet users, upon collection of the user's Internet address, of the marketing purposes for which the respondent's e-mail address will be used.
- Marketers cannot collect e-mail addresses with the intent of sending bulk unsolicited commercial e-mail without the Internet user's consent or knowledge.
- Marketers should not use subject lines that are deceiving and mislead readers as to what the content of the e-mail is really about.

- All Internet direct mail must include either an option for the recipient to unsubscribe from receiving future messages from that sender, list owner, or list manager, or provide valid and responsive contact information for the sender, list manager, or list owner.
- The CRE opposes sending bulk unsolicited commercial e-mail to an e-mail address without a prior business or personal relationship. Online transaction activity, such as opting in at a website, satisfies the requirement of a prior business relationship.

## To Spam or Not to Spam?

What is "spam"? It is unsolicited e-mail, usually promotional, sent out to multiple recipients.

Professional spammers use special "spamware" programs designed to harvest e-mail addresses from public places, such as Web pages and Usenet newsgroups. The software can scan a text document, recognize an e-mail address, and add it to a database. It's possible to buy an e-mail list compiled in this way or to have a bulk e-mail company send out your ad to their proprietary list.

So should you try it? Should you join the legions of multilevel marketers and chain-letter writers now sending out their offers to millions of Internet users?

Spamming is against longtime Internet standards of "netiquette," and for that reason it is considered unethical by many Internet users, both veterans and novices. Although this fact is not to be discounted, it is not necessarily the primary issue from a marketing standpoint. Does the marketer care about courtesy? Some do, some don't. A sense of decency will not prevent all marketers from spamming. Neither will ethics or morality.

If e-mail is done legally, does it still annoy people? Initial results from e-campaigns indicate that it does not. The proof is that opt-out rates—the number of people who reply and ask not to receive further e-mail marketing messages—are low. If people hated e-mail marketing messages, they'd opt out by the carload, or the response rates would be miniscule—and they are not.

**Warning:** The Internet is considered by many to be an untouchable forum for the free exchange of ideas and opinions, but watch out. What you say on the Internet can be held against you in a court of law. M. H. Meyerson, a securities firm in Jersey City, New Jersey, has filed a lawsuit alleging that individuals posting defamatory messages about the company on an Internet bulletin board knowingly distributed false information to drive down the company's share price. More recently, First Union Bank fired seven employees in a Charlotte, North Carolina area office for sending pornographic and other inappropriate e-mail. In the fall of 1999, the *New York Times* fired twenty-three employees for sending e-mail that was "inappropriate and offensive."

Is e-mail advertising the same as direct mail? As telemarketing? Some argue that it is not, because the *recipient* bears the cost of e-mail. By the very nature of the Internet, electronic mail arrives "postage due." The e-mail user or that user's employer pays a provider for Internet access. That provider incurs cost for all traffic received on its network. So the spammer is actually forcing the recipient to pay the cost of his advertising. Direct (postal) mail advertisers, on the other hand, pay the cost of their own advertising and, in fact, subsidize the postal system. And how many telemarketers would get a listening ear if they called collect?

A more critical issue is: how does the recipient view the advertising message? Spam is widely hated on the Internet. A Harris poll of computer users reveals that, out of those who are receiving unsolicited bulk e-mail, 42 percent want to stop receiving it.

Granted, some portion of the public hates all advertising and would stop receiving direct mail, telemarketing calls, newspaper and magazine advertising, and television commercials, if they could. However, Internet users are able to retaliate in ways other consumers can't. And the widespread hatred of spamming can be damaging to the image of the company that uses it.

We are now seeing a deluge of spam. How much? According to *Time* magazine, "Unsolicited junk e-mail now accounts for 10 percent of all Internet traffic and up to 30 percent of the 26 million daily messages on America Online."

The longer you use the Net for business or other purposes, the more likely you are to dislike spam because of the intensity and volume of the onslaught, as well as the unwanted intrusion in your inbox.

## Crime and Punishment for Spammers

The risks of spamming can be considerable. Here are some compelling reasons to avoid spamming:

• **Technological retaliation.** Some antispammers will send e-mail bombs, huge messages that can clog Internet servers or crash them. Other spam haters have been known to send continuous faxes to spammers' fax machines in the middle of the night. After one company sent out a spam message, someone rigged up a robot that called their toll-free number over and over for three days.

• **Loss of Internet service.** More than likely, your Internet service provider prohibits spamming and will terminate your account if it receives complaints. If you become known as a spammer, Internet service providers will set up blocks so that no e-mail from your domain can be delivered to their systems. In some cases your mail will be bounced back to you, but in many cases your mail will just be rejected and you'll never know.

• **Reputation of the company.** Internet users can have a surprisingly strong voice. If your company becomes labeled as a spam advertiser, you may need to launch some serious PR damage control.

• **Public and legal action.** The public, especially in Western lands, is becoming increasingly concerned with privacy. If you're a database marketer or direct marketer, you're no doubt already aware of this issue. If the public begins to feel invaded, it will take action, either in the form of restrictive laws or court action. In fact, this is already taking place with regard to bulk e-mail advertising. Self-regulation is in the interest of all responsible advertisers.

## How to Spot Spam Instantly

Here is a spam received by one of the authors. Can you spot clues that tell you it's a spam?

- You can't tell who it is from.
- The headline uses all caps (it shouts).
- Legitimate e-mail opt-in lists cost $100 to $250 per thousand. This list is one million names for $200.
- "Enterprise" or "enterprises" usually indicates a small-time Internet operator looking to make a quick buck.
- There's no mention of where they got the recipient's name.
- You aren't given a website to click through to.
- There's no opportunity to opt out and be taken off the list.

—— Original Message ——

**FROM: <678&^(*(44@mail.com>**
**TO: <dkLLN4355.com@uunet.uu.net>**
**SENT: Saturday, September 11, 2000 3:31 AM**
**SUBJECT: MAKE MONEY AND GET RICH ON THE INTERNET!!!**

This is Cyberslush Enterprise and we are sending you this e-mail to let you in on some of the best prices in bulk e-mailing. If you are interested in more information, please call anytime—555-555-5555.

Prices:

$200.00 For 1 Million E-Mails Sent

$400.00 For 3 Million E-Mails Sent

$600.00 For 5 Million E-Mails Sent

$800.00 For 7 Million E-Mails Sent

$1000.00 For 10 Million E-Mails Sent

We also have target lists. Just call and ask!

P.S. I am able to send you proof of your mailings. I will send you via e-mail, uploaded mail-log files of the actual sendings so you can know first-hand exactly what I'm doing for you.

IT REALLY DOES WORK!! I made this ad short so call for more info.
CALL NOW FOR INFO . . . 555-555-5555

cybersmuch101@mail.com. If link fails, please call anytime.

## The Golden Rule of E-Marketing

The golden rule for preventing spam and complaints is: *Opt out for customers, opt in for acquisitions.*

If you're going to send promotional e-mail messages to your customers, ask them if it's OK. In every message, give them a reminder that they can opt out of receiving future e-mail marketing messages at any time, and give them an easy way to do so—usually by clicking on "Reply" and typing "Unsubscribe" or "Remove."

When a new prospect visits your website, ask the person to opt in when he or she gives you a name and address. On the registration form, add a box that says something like: "From time to time we send our customers messages from other companies we deem to be of interest. If you are willing to receive such messages via e-mail, click here." When the visitor checks the box and submits the form, he or she she becomes an opt-in name—and you can send promotional e-mails without fear of spamming.

## Opt-In E-Mail

Nearly everyone agrees that spam is bad, but hardly anyone will admit to doing it. In the clamor to avoid the dreaded tag of "spammer," nearly every e-mail marketer claims the mantle of being an "opt-in" marketer. Indeed, on the Internet, the magic word isn't "please" but "opt-in."

Regardless of the terminology, the e-mail marketing field is growing. Forrester Research predicts that e-mail marketing will top $1 billion in four years, taking its part alongside banner ads as a potent legal weapon in the e-marketing arsenal.

What really is opt-in? Until recently, the term has been somewhat loosely defined. But in December 1998, antispam advocates and the Direct Marketing Association held a summit in Washington, D.C., to sort out the definition. After five hours, the participants hammered out areas of agreement regarding unsolicited e-mail ads. Together they laid the groundwork to try to reduce abuse of the Internet by senders of unsolicited bulk e-mail. Participants agreed to:

1. Support legislation that, at a minimum, prohibits false identification in commercial e-mail.

2. Acknowledge opt-in (defined by the group as "the recipient has stated and not rescinded his or her desire to receive the type of mail which you are sending") as the most successful targeting method for online marketers.

3. Work to create a nonprofit global opt-out list similar to the DMA's Mail Preference and Telephone Preference services supported by marketers and free to consumers, which allows both business entities and individuals to perform a one-time global opt-out from unsolicited commercial bulk e-mail.

While the summit was a start (and a welcome sign of cooperation between direct marketers and notoriously confrontational Internet activists), there is still a great deal of room for interpretation within that definition.

Luckily, that's a healthy thing for the nascent industry. The flexibility of the resolution leaves plenty of room for companies to develop a wide variety of business models, some of which have counterparts in traditional direct marketing, and some of which don't.

The top point of debate is over what it really means to opt in: At what point do consumers give permission to receive e-mail messages, and how do they control what they do and don't receive and from whom?

Some companies take a hard line, only allowing the company that collects an e-mail address to use it. One marketer holding this view is Berkeley-based MarketHome, which serves clients such as Coach and Park Seed. "We are relationship builders, not prospectors," says MarketHome CEO/president Jim Williams. "If someone buys a product from a company and signs up for our e-mail, that is the beginning of a relationship that is carried out over the channel of e-mail. It's nothing to do with this one-time offer."

Instead, MarketHome manages proprietary lists for in-house purposes, such as database marketing, one to-one offers, and loyalty programs. Explains Williams, "What we do is help clients market to their existing customer base for retention, loyalty, and remarketing.

We send information, announcements, and sales information to people who already have a business relationship with that company."

MarketHome's competitors include CMG Direct's PermissionPlus and NetCreations' PostMasterDirect services, both of which convert anonymous Web traffic into registered customers and solicit approval from users to send additional targeted messages from the company. However, both NetCreations and CMG offer additional direct marketing programs that take this model a step further. NetCreations and CMG ExpressNet build databases by asking users to tell them what kind of mail they'd like to receive. E-PostDirect also builds custom e-mail opt-in prospecting databases for direct marketing clients.

On January 10, 2000, the Direct Marketing Association (DMA) launched its e-Mail Preference Service, which allows consumers to register for free at www.e-mps.org for an opt-out list indicating that they don't want to receive promotional e-mails. Marketers can download the list online, then purge the opt-out names from their own e-lists.

## E-Mail Etiquette

While we're discussing Internet direct mail, let's review some dos and don'ts that apply to any electronic business messages you may send.

• **Don't pester people.** Sending e-mail, it seems, is so easy that some people overdo it. If you call a prospect every day, that's pestering, and the same goes for e-mail. Respect people's time and privacy. Don't use the technology to excess just because it's there.

• **Don't be devious.** Remember, CRE prohibits e-mail marketing messages that are deceiving or misleading. The subject line should not make the recipient think he's getting something he's not. Obviously, determining what's misleading is a judgment call, so use your best judgment. If you dislike getting direct mail that looks suspiciously like a bill or an IRS notice, avoid using similar deceptive tactics in your e-mail marketing.

• **Don't overburden your recipient.** E-mail that goes on and on is tiring to read on the computer and taxing on the attention span. Huge files that take a long time to download are also an annoyance to many recipients, especially those with older, slower PCs. When sending rich-media and graphic e-mail, keep file size to a maximum of 400 to 500K, and preferably 200K or less.

**Warning:** As this book goes to press, two states—Virginia and California—are considering proposals to tighten restrictions on commercial e-mail. If the Virginia proposal passes, it could be devastating to e-marketers. The reason: through the World Wide Web network and AOL, virtually all e-mail passes through Virginia on its way to its final destinations, and because of this route, the Virginia laws apply.

- **Do use discretion with multiple addressees.** Someone who doesn't reveal his or her e-mail address to every Dick, Jane, and Sally may not appreciate your listing it visibly when you send a single message to many people at once. Most e-mail systems have separate procedures for "carbon copies" where the list of recipients appears along with the message, and "blind carbon copies," where the list is nowhere to be seen. Take care to send the "blind" kind of message to a list, especially where those on the list really deserve to remain anonymous to each other, as with people answering classified ads.

"Play it safe," advises Barbara Kaplowitz, editor of *The DeLay Letter*. "Consider e-mailing only to those with whom you have a prior relationship. If you must send bulk e-mail, try to avoid those states with existing laws." Figures 8.1 and 8.2 summarize major legislation affecting Internet direct mail. Figure 8.3 on page 158 offers antispam addresses for reporting complaints.

## To Sum It All Up

- Only send Internet direct mail to rented opt-in lists or your own customer and prospect files.
- Every e-mail marketing message you send should give the recipient an easy way to opt out of receiving future e-mails from you. And you must honor all such requests.

- Do not try to deceive or fool prospects into thinking your e-mail marketing message is not a promotional message or that it is not from a marketer. Do not be misleading or unethical in any of your Internet communications.

---

## LEGISLATION

S. 771—Senator Murkowski—Unsolicited Electronic Mail Choice Act
Requires correct header information, valid origination address, and telephone numbers, and "remove me" requests honored.
*Passed August 1998, amendment to S. 1618 antislamming bill.*

H.R. 2368—Representative Tauzin—Data Privacy Act of 1997
Proposes voluntary guidelines concerning the collection and use of personal information. Prohibits marketing use of government data without individuals' consent, including the displays of social security numbers.
*Pending in House.*

S. 875—Senator Torricelli—Electronic Mailbox Protection Act of 1997
Proposes valid origination address, "do not e-mail" requests must be honored and not distributed to other parties who intend to send unsolicited email.
*Pending in Senate.*

H.R. 1748—Representative Smith—Netizens Protection Act of 1997
Propose preexisting and ongoing relationship or permission from the recipient. Proper headings with date and time sent, identity of the business sending the message, valid return e-mail address and telephone number.
*Pending in House.*

---

*Figure 8.1 Legislation regarding Internet direct mail*

---

### E-Mail User Protection Act (Introduced in the House)

HR 1910 IH

### 106th CONGRESS

### 1st Session

### H. R. 1910

To prohibit abuses in the use of unsolicited bulk electronic mail, and for other purposes.

### IN THE HOUSE OF REPRESENTATIVES

May 24, 1999

Mr. GREEN of Texas introduced the following bill; which was referred to the Committee on Commerce, and in addition to the Committee on the Judiciary, for a period to be subsequently determined by the Speaker, in each case for consideration of such provisions as fall within the jurisdiction of the committee concerned

A BILL

To prohibit abuses in the use of unsolicited bulk electronic mail, and for other purposes.

*Be it enacted by the Senate and House of Representatives of the United States of America in Congress assembled,*

SECTION. 1. SHORT TITLE

This Act may be cited as the 'E-Mail User Protection Act'.

SEC. 2. LIMITATIONS ON THE USE OF UNSOLICITED BULK E-MAIL.

(a) PROHIBITION- It shall be unlawful for any person, using any means or instrumentality of, or affecting, interstate or foreign commerce—

(1) to initiate the transmission of an unsolicited bulk electronic mail message that contains a false, fictitious, or misappropriated name of the sender, electronic mail return address, or name and phone number of a telephone contact person;

---

*Figure 8.2 Complete text of e-mail user protection act currently in force.*

(2) to initiate the transmission of an unsolicited bulk electronic mail message to an interactive computer service with knowledge that such message falsifies an Internet domain, header information, date or time stamp, originating e-mail address or other identifier;

(3) to initiate the transmission of an unsolicited bulk electronic mail message and to fail to comply with the request of the recipient of the message, delivered to the sender's electronic mail address, that the recipient does not wish to receive such messages;

(4) to use, create, sell, or distribute any computer software that is primarily designed to create, on an electronic mail message, false Internet domain, header information, date or time stamp, originating e-mail address or other identifier.

(b) VIOLATIONS-

(1) CIVIL FINES- Whoever knowingly violates subsection (a) shall be fined not more than the greater of (1) $50 for each message delivered in violation of such subsection, or (2) $10,000 for each day the violation continues.

(2) CRIMINAL SANCTIONS- Whoever—

(A) intentionally violates subsection (a)(1) by misappropriating the name or electronic mail return address of another person; or

(B) intentionally violates subsection (a)(3) by initiating the transmission of unsolicited electronic mail to an individual who has specifically communicated to the violator that individual's desire not to receive such mail;

shall be fined under title 18, United States Code, or imprisoned not more than one year, or both.

SEC. 3. ENFORCEMENT

The Federal Trade Commission shall have the power to enforce a violation of section 2 as an unfair or deceptive act or practice prescribed under section 18(a)(1)(B) of the Federal Trade Commission Act (15 U.S.C. 57(a)(1)(13)).

SEC. 4. RIGHT OF ACTION AND RECOVERY OF CIVIL DAMAGES.

*Figure 8.2 Complete text of e-mail user protection act currently in force (continued)*

(a) RIGHT OF ACTION-

(1) ACTIONS BY INTERACTIVE COMPUTER SERVICES- Any interactive computer service that has been adversely affected by a violation of section 2(a)(2) may recover in a civil action from the person or entity that engaged in such violation such relief as may be appropriate.

(2) ACTIONS BY RECIPIENTS- Any person or entity that has received an unsolicited bulk e-mail and been adversely affected by a violation of section 2 may recover in a civil action from the person or entity that engaged in such violation such relief as may be appropriate.

(b) RELIEF-

(1) ACTIONS BY INTERACTIVE COMPUTER SERVICES- In an action under subsection (a)(1), appropriate relief includes—

(A) such preliminary and other equitable or declaratory relief as may be appropriate, including an injunction against future violations;

(B) actual monetary loss from a violation, statutory damages of not more than the greater of —

(i) $50 for each message delivered in violation of section 2(a)(2); or

(ii) $10,000 for each day during which the violation continues; and

(C) a reasonable attorney's fee and other litigation costs reasonably incurred.

(2) ACTIONS BY RECIPIENTS- In an action under subsection (a)(2), appropriate relief includes-

(A) such preliminary and other equitable or declaratory relief as may be appropriate, including an injunction against future violations;

(B) actual monetary loss from a violation, statutory damages of $50 for each message delivered in violation of section 2(a)(2); and

*Figure 8.2 Complete text of e-mail user protection act currently in force (continued)*

(C) a reasonable attorney's fee and other litigation costs reasonably incurred.

SEC. 5. DEFINITIONS.

For purposes of this Act:

(1) UNSOLICITED BULK ELECTRONIC MAIL MESSAGE- The term 'unsolicited bulk electronic mail message' means any electronic mail message initiated by any person for commercial purposes, except for—

(A) electronic mail sent to others with whom such person has a prior relationship, including a prior business relationship; or

(B) electronic mail sent to a recipient if such recipient, or someone authorized by them, has at any time affirmatively requested to receive communications from that source.

(2) ELECTRONIC MAIL ADDRESS- The term 'electronic mail address' means a destination on the Internet (commonly expressed as a string of characters) to which electronic mail can be sent or delivered.

(3) INTERACTIVE COMPUTER SERVICE- The term 'interactive computer service' has the meaning given that term in section 230(e)(2) of the Communications Act of 1934 (47 U.S.C. 230(e)(2)).

(4) INTERNET DOMAIN- The term 'Internet domain' means a specific computer system (commonly referred to as a 'host') or collection of computer systems that the Internet can reference, that are assigned a specific reference point on the Internet (commonly referred to as an 'Internet domain name'), and that are registered with an organization that the Internet industry recognizes as a registrar of Internet domains.

(5) INITIATES THE TRANSMISSION- The term 'initiates the transmission,' in the case of an electronic mail message, means to originate the electronic mail message, and excludes the actions of any interactive computer service whose facilities or services are used by another person to transmit, relay, or otherwise handle such message.

SEC. 6. EFFECTIVE DATE.

The provisions of this Act shall take effect 45 days after the date of enactment of this Act.

**Figure 8.2 Complete text of e-mail user protection act currently in force (continued)**

Pyramid schemes
E-mail: pyramid@ftc.gov

Stock scams
E-mail: Cyberfraud@nasaa.org and enforcement@sec.gov

Mail fraud
E-mail: fraud@usps.gov

Health products
E-mail: Otcfraud@cder.fda.gov

*Figure 8.3. Antispam e-mail addresses for reporting complaints*

# INTEGRATING INTERNET DM INTO YOUR E-BUSINESS

How can e-marketing and conventional marketing be used together to get greater results than either on its own could achieve?

E-mail marketing has often been referred to in the trade press as the "killer app" (killer application) on the Internet. But it is only part of a total e-campaign, which is in turn only part of an overall marketing program.

In this chapter we look at ways to integrate e-mail marketing with other online marketing, and to integrate online marketing with a total marketing campaign.

## Multimailing: Integrating E-Mail with Postal Mail

E-mail marketing has become widely accepted as a highly responsive direct marketing medium. Some wonder if they should choose e-mail marketing in lieu of postal marketing.

We recommend doing e-mail marketing *in addition to* postal marketing, rather than *instead of* postal marketing. Why? Each method provides marketers with different advantages in reaching their intended targets. By combining the advantages of both, through a process we refer to as *multimailing*, marketers can realize outstanding results.

Postal mail pieces affect the buying process differently than e-mailing does. Postal direct mail, in the form of catalogs, brochures, and circulars, tends to stay on the desk for a while. People can hold it, view it, refer to it, file it, and, hopefully, respond to it.

E-mail is more immediate. It appeals to our impulsive nature. Either the recipient will respond to it, or the recipient won't. By following up your direct mail campaign with e-mail, you can influence the person who is holding on to your brochure and is as yet undecided, or has forgotten about using your product or service.

One thing we have learned is that we should offer people more than one way to respond to us. Targeting with both a postal and e-mail campaign gives your prospect or client two different ways to respond to you in a method and at a time and place of his or her choosing. This makes it easier for the prospect to reply. What's more, sending your offer twice, in two different ways, offers an opportunity to raise the visibility of your company and reinforce its message, making it more likely that prospects will respond.

Aside from higher response, some other benefits of multimailing include timeliness, lower cost, and the ability to do one-to-one personalization.

A case in point: Three months prior to an upcoming event, a conference marketer mailed a brochure to previous conference attendees as well as to the active subscribers of *Electronic Products (EP)* magazine, a highly targeted audience of electronics engineers and managers.

They then followed up with a series of e-mail messages to the same people who received the brochure by transmitting to the opt-in e-mail addresses of the *EP* subscribers. E-mails were sent twelve, six, and two weeks prior to the conference.

During this series, based on results of their tests, the conference promoter was able to change the copy to entice people to sign up for the show, without the long lead time that is required to go back to press for printed brochures or self-mailers.

The conference company also used e-mail to advise prospective attendees of new sessions being offered and the changes that had been made to the keynote speakers scheduled. They personalized their messages with "special one-to-one discounts" for signing up immediately. The attendee was prompted to get the discount by clicking on a link to the conference website and entering a "preferred attendee priority code." The code, which was supplied in the e-mail message, allowed the promoter to track and tabulate the response.

The mailer also asked the recipients to forward the e-mail to a colleague. Asking the recipient to forward the e-mail to other potential buyers is known as *viral marketing.*

The e-mail can be forwarded in an instant with the click of a mouse, making it much easier to send to friends and colleagues than conventional paper mail. Evidence suggests that this approach can be just as effective in consumer e-mailings as well.

There are many commercially available lists that offer you the ability to send your message to both postal and e-mail addresses. But be careful to ask your list broker to verify that the people on these files have given their permission to send them e-mail. Avoid postal lists in which e-mail addresses have been added through e-appending but have not been opted in.

**Message #1:**

**TO: steve_roberts@edithroman.com**

**SUBJECT: Ethernet Networking Conference**

On March 27-29 more than 100 of the sharpest minds in the world of high-speed Ethernet networking will gather at the Gigabit Ethernet Conference 2000 in San Jose to describe where this fast-moving field is heading. http://www.gec2000.com/em/ Please reference Priority Code "EMX."

If you are developing communications equipment, providing components or support tools, integrating or installing systems, or managing networks, it's critical that you be among the participants listening to what these industry leaders have to offer and asking them the questions you need answered.

This 3-day program is packed with practical information on the latest advances in high-speed Ethernet networking plus demonstrations of the hottest new products. Here's your chance to learn about the brand new 10 Gigabit standard, which is about to be certified for development. Also find out about the network processor chips, which look to be among this year's major breakthroughs. Explore such exciting topics as LAN/SAN integration, enterprise IP telephony, high-speed routing, multilayer switching, policy-based network management, long-haul gigabit Ethernet, and achieving quality of service.

You'll come away with knowledge that will be essential for developing new products, identifying new markets, and providing services and support for networking applications. Don't get left behind in this fast-changing business!

Sound interesting? Want to find out more? Go now to http://www.gec2000.com/em/ and reference Priority Code "EMX" for up-to-the-minute program details (speakers, topics, times, sponsors, exhibitors, and an online registration form).

Sign up now and enjoy BIG savings . . . full conference registration is $1,245 at the door but just $995 when you enroll via the special e-mail website. Can't get away for the full three days? Not a problem. Two-day and one-day plans are also available, as is attendance at single tutorials.

But what you get is far more important than what you'll save . . . This is the premier event of its kind in the country. It brings together some of the most influential people in high-speed Ethernet networking under a single roof for three solid days. Nowhere else will you find such easy access to the people and products at the forefront of your industry.

No matter what your role is—network or computer manager, CIO, communications specialist, system/network integrator or analyst, network engineer, hardware/software designer, VAR, OEM, consultant, or marketing manager—you'll come away from GEC2000 equipped with the information, insight, and contacts needed to make your job easier and make you more valuable to your company.

The end of March may seem years away now but you and I know how fast time flies. Why not take a moment today or tomorrow to get back to us and lock in these attractive discounts?

I've made it easy for you to enroll via this e-mail. And if we hear from you soon, you and your company can take advantage of our "early bird" and group discounts on registrations. http://www.gec2000.com/em/ Please reference priority code "EMX."

Dr. Lance Leventhal, Conference Chair

P.S. Not ready to commit? Save this e-mail, and let us know when you're ready. We'll honor the discounts shown here, just so long as it's in reply to this e-mail.

\\\\\\\\\\\\\\\\\\\\\\\\\\\\\\\\\\\\\\\\\\\\\\\\\\\\\\\\\\\\\\\\\\\\\\\\\\\\\\\\\\\\\\\\\\\\\\\\\\\\\\\\\\\\\\\\\\\

For the first time ever Conference Pro will be able to share important product and service information available over the Internet. If you wish to be EXCLUDED from receiving email from third-party advertisers please click here: www.enlist.com/cgi-bin/ch?c=CP&e=steve_roberts@edithroman.com

**Message #2:**
**TO: steve_roberts@edithroman.com**
**SUBJECT: Gigabit Ethernet Conference 2000**

Just a quick but important follow-up to my invitation of a few weeks ago . . .

Are you going to be able to face the upcoming product design, integration, and network management challenges without more understanding of the new 10-Gigabit Ethernet standard, network processors, high-speed routing, policy-based management, LAN/SAN integration, and wide-area Ethernet applications?

On March 27-29 the key players in the high-speed Ethernet networking arena will be in San Jose to discuss those topics and more at the Gigabit Ethernet Conference 2000. www.gec2000.com/em/

That's a mere 60 days from now, and when I last checked your name wasn't among the registered attendees.

I know how everyday pressures can undermine even the best intentions, so I've made it super easy for you to sign up for this don't-miss conference . . .

Simply go to www.gec2000.com/em/ and follow the simple prompts. It will take just a minute or two.

˜˜˜˜˜˜˜˜˜˜˜˜˜˜˜˜˜˜˜˜˜˜˜˜˜˜˜˜˜˜˜˜˜˜˜˜˜˜˜˜˜˜˜˜˜˜˜˜˜˜˜˜˜˜˜˜˜˜˜˜˜˜˜˜˜˜˜˜˜˜˜˜˜˜˜˜˜˜˜˜˜˜˜˜˜˜˜˜˜

We'll take it from there and will have a registration packet waiting for you when you arrive. By registering now via this e-mail you'll qualify for some hefty savings. Look for "early bird" discounts and group savings.

This event is a showcase for EVERYTHING that's happening in our industry. Nowhere else will you find such easy access to the people and products shaping the future of Gigabit Ethernet. There will be tutorials and sessions on performance bottlenecks, LAN/SAN integration, network processors, 10-Gigabit standard (about to be released for development), high-speed routing, multiplayer switching, performance analysis, troubleshooting, policy-based network management, chip sets, long-haul GbE, QoS issues, testing, MAN/WAN applications, cabling/interconnect, and market analysis.

˜˜˜˜˜˜˜˜˜˜˜˜˜˜˜˜˜˜˜˜˜˜˜˜˜˜˜˜˜˜˜˜˜˜˜˜˜˜˜˜˜˜˜˜˜˜˜˜˜˜˜˜˜˜˜˜˜˜˜˜˜˜˜˜˜˜˜˜˜˜˜˜˜˜˜˜˜˜˜˜˜˜˜˜˜˜˜˜˜

I guarantee you'll come away from GEC2000 smarter, savvier, and with more industry contacts than you can fit in your Palm Pilot. Take that as my personal promise, backed by our no-quibble money back guarantee.

But time's getting to be a factor. Take a quick break right now and let us know you're planning to attend.

Again, the website you want to go to is www.gec2000.com/em/.

Dr. Lance Leventhal, Conference Chair

P.S. The website contains all of the information you'll need: presenters, sponsors, exhibitors, session topics . . . where to be when. We plan to update the site daily as this dynamic conference nears its final form.

**Message 3:**

**TO: steve_roberts@edithroman.com**

**SUBJECT: Last Chance to Register—Gigabit Ethernet Conference 2000!**

The time for saving money on your Gigabit Ethernet Conference 2000 registration is running out. Fast.

But it's an easy fix. Here's how:

Go straight to www.gec2000.com/em/

Take a look at the impressive lineup of topics . . . product design, integration, network processors, high-speed routing, policy-based management, LAN/SAN integration . . . I don't think you'll find a more extensive collection of the products shaping the future of Gigabit Ethernet anywhere, any time this year.

GEC2000 takes place March 27-29 in San Jose.

Just follow the prompts at our website, and you'll be duly registered in a matter of seconds.

Seconds. Because in the world of high-speed Ethernet, networking time is money. And I won't take any more of yours. www.gec2000.com/em/

Dr. Lance Leventhal, Conference Chair

P.S. Compare the walk-in registration fee vs. advanced registration tuition. The difference could pay for a night's lodging. Or a very nice dinner. Even a plane ticket. All for less than a minute of your time.

# Banner Ads Versus E-Mail Marketing

As the money devoted to online marketing grows, so does information about what's working and what's not. The latest question:

Is the Internet a better tool for building awareness, or for direct marketing?

The key awareness tool on the Internet, which is also used for direct response, is banner advertising. A banner ad is a small banner or box containing your message that appears periodically on someone else's website.

An article in the *B2B Direct* newsletter predicts spending on banner advertising will exceed $5 billion in 2000. One Web marketing consultant says that banner ads generate a 40 percent recollection rate, which is comparable to TV commercials.

Many Internet marketing agencies now seem to be scoffing at banner advertising, the most common method of building visibility on the Web. The oft-cited statistic of doom is the click-through rates on banner ads averaging .5 percent. A click-through rate of .5 percent means that for every 200 prospects receiving your e-mail message, one clicks on one or more of the Web links embedded in the message.

According to an article in *DM News* (September 20, 1999, p. 26), Estee Lauder gets a 1 percent click-through rate to its banner ads. Of these, 2 percent become customers. The cost per new customer acquired through banner advertising is $175—much more than the $25 to $50 it costs the company to acquire a customer through traditional media.

Another negative statistic is that people who claim they don't look at banners rose from 38 percent to 48 percent in 1999, according to Market Facts. That same year, the number of people who said they often looked at banner ads dropped from 16 percent to 9 percent. Of two thousand people surveyed by Jupiter Communications, 71.4 percent said banner ads need to be more informational, and 33 percent said they needed to be more creative.

A separate survey of 403 Internet users found that 52 percent had not clicked on any banner ad in the past week. Of those who had clicked on a banner ad during that week, four out of ten could not remember any online ad.

Paul Baudisch, president of NetMarquee, a Needham, Massachusetts, marketing agency, says Internet users are visually discounting the presence of banner ads. Increasingly, companies are testing the direct marketing model, sending complex e-mails to highly targeted lists of prospects. This technique works much the same way as offline direct marketing campaigns. Companies build databases of e-mail addresses by enticing customers to register on a site in exchange for information or access to a special offer.

CATeLOG has built an extensive database by posting registration forms on a variety of popular consumer sites. The agency then puts together e-mail campaigns for different clients and sends them to appropriate consumers mined from that database.

For instance, when A&E Television Networks wanted to advertise its *Live by Request* program, they sent an entertaining e-mail to customers that contained music and other audio enhancements. "I don't think there is a better, more concise, less expensive way to get people one on one," says Mike Mohamed, A&E's vice president of marketing.

When companies use their own homegrown lists, online direct marketing works even better. That's the tactic that New England Business Service (NEBS) employs. The Groton, Massachusetts, manufacturer of forms and supplies started an e-mail newsletter last year. Customers register to receive the newsletter, which includes tips for business owners and special offers. Circulation is at six thousand and growing, says Janie Marshall, manager for marketing communications.

But NEBS has also experimented with banner advertising on different sites that small business owners frequent. "Some did very well," Marshall says. "We continued the ones that worked, we're working on the ones that didn't."

This is a wise strategy according to Michele Slack, an analyst in the online advertising group of Jupiter Communications, who warns that rumors of the death of banner advertising have been greatly exaggerated. "The novelty factor is wearing off," Slack says. "When an ad is targeted well, and the creative is good, click-through rates are much higher."

And in time, fancy e-mailed messages might not be opened either. "It's a novelty right now," Slack says. "When people's inboxes get flooded, you'll see a fall-off there too." Her advice? Incorporate both philosophies into a marketing plan. "The Web is one of the few places where you can combine the two [branding and direct marketing]," she says. "To see it as an either/or, you're missing out on what the Web can do."

# Nine Common Banner Ad Mistakes to Avoid

Banner advertising expert Rob Frankel advises e-marketers to avoid the following mistakes when creating their banner ads:

**1. Overloaded.** Too many colors. Too slow to load. Too hard to read. Nobody wants to grow old waiting for your banner ad to load. Frankel advises designing banner ads that will load and view easily with last year's technology. "Personally, I design pages for people running no more than Netscape 2.0 on the equivalent of a 486 running at 66 MHz and 256 colors," says Frankel. "That means your art should still be no deeper than eight bits, unless you're a true minimalist and can bring it in at no more than four."

**2. Unattractive.** People like good-looking stuff. What works for Cindy Crawford can work for you, too. (Her site, by the way, is www.cindy.com.) So if you're not a digital da Vinci, find someone who is and pay him or her a few bucks to make your banner look great.

**3. Too many bells and whistles.** Just because technology offers you bells and whistles doesn't mean you have to use every one of them. Chances are that the average Web surfer has been through several sites before he or she gets to your banner. Give the reader a break. Don't overdo motion, movement, or message changes. And allow some time to digest what you're displaying.

**4. Illiteracy and illegibility.** These are the ads that make you scrunch up your face and twist your head trying to make some sense out of the illegible scrawls that some knucklehead thinks are cool. But prospects don't care how cool you think it looks. If they can't read it, you've lost any chance of their clicking on it.

**5. Missing link.** Your banner looks great but isn't linked to anything. That's a mistake that anyone should be able to detect and prevent with a simple check.

**Note:** New sniffer technology enables the e-mail transmission bureau to determine bandwidth and send a different banner based on download capability. Susan Bratton, a vice president at Excite@home, recommends preparing banner ads in four different sizes: 5, 10, 15, and 20K.

**6. Link errors.** Your banner looks great. The link works . . . directly to a 404 message (meaning the requested Web page was not found). Maybe this one isn't your fault. Maybe your webmaster inadvertently forgot to tell you he or she switched servers. But even if it was the webmaster's fault, who do you think will catch the blame? Keep checking those banner links every few days.

**7. Weak message.** The same things that make good ads make good banners. Unfortunately, the same things that make bad ads make horrible banners. If you don't know how to write and design a clever, compelling message, hire someone who does. Nothing turns off potential prospects more than a really stupid attempt at being clever, an offense usually committed with the aid of a bad pun. Remember that your ad is a representative of you, containing a smattering of your personality and ability. If it looks dopey to a viewer, guess what they're going to think about you? It's better to be clear than clever.

**8. Confusing message.** Your banner looks pretty, but nobody understands what the heck you're talking about. This is the number-one mistake made by do-it-yourselfers.

**9. Boring banners.** One common mistake is that your banner doesn't compel your recipients to respond within a certain time frame. Without a deadline, there is no immediacy to act, which means they scroll away until they forget it.

## Placing Banner Ads

The basic options for banner advertising are a site buy, category buy, or run of network.

**Tip:** Since banner ads are written in HTML, you have flexibility in color and font. Experiment. Mina Lux, a vice president with Doubleday Interactive, found that indenting a banner ad five spaces and using a larger headline increased click-through 184 percent.

A *site buy* refers to placing a banner ad on a specific website. A *category buy* places your banner ad on a selection of websites in a specific category—for example, a group of sites all related to sports, TV, or computer programming. A *run of network buy* places your banner ad on a bunch of unrelated sites all managed by the same hosting service.

In banner advertising, the best media buy is not obvious and is contrary to what works in traditional direct marketing. In traditional direct marketing, targeted media work best. So you want to place your ad in publications where you know the readers are interested in your type of offer. If you are selling fishing lures, for instance, you run in the fishing magazines. If you are selling accounting software for small businesses, run in small business magazines.

Why does this work best? You are targeting a large group of readers you know have an interest in your offer. So your response is high.

Specialized magazines with limited circulations are usually less expensive to advertise in than large-circulation general publications. Also, when you run a specialized offer in a generalized magazine, you are, in essence, paying to reach a lot of people who are not your prospects. So the cost per order is most favorable in the more targeted magazine.

On the Web, the cost difference between a site buy and a run of network buy is not as great as in print. And, although a lot of the people who browse your ad on a run of network buy are not your prospects, enough *are* so that it still pays off. Some early testing suggests that run of network buys are actually more profitable than site or category buys. But it's too early to call this a definitive rule.

# The Ten Commandments of E-Marketing

Catherine Devlin, an e-marketing consultant, gives the following tips for creating and implementing a consistent e-marketing campaign.

## Rule 1: Use Dynamic Creativity in Your E-Marketing Campaign

New media is not just a banner ad or GIF animation. It's full and integrated media impacting the senses with motion and animation. Use voice, music, movies, animation, and sound effects to enhance the impact of your message. It can be all of those, or just one or two, but it's got to be dynamic, not static.

With the integration of truly new media, use all the aspects of media within your budget. If you have a banner ad, add sound to it. If you have an icon, make it work effectively for you by converting the icon into a QuickTime movie. Innovate with the format that you have to work with. Conceive of new ways of doing banner ads. We're talking about integrating all aspects of new media.

## Rule 2: Be Consistent with Your Message Throughout Your Entire Campaign

Your message should be consistent in both your digital marketing campaign and in your campaign across traditional media channels. Often, a client hires a separate online advertising agency to complement its full-service agency. Different agencies pursue different campaigns, some of which could be contradictory or not complementary. A consistent message broadcast throughout the digital marketing campaign reinforces the same message along traditional advertising channels.

## Rule 3: Reinforce the Traditional Branding with a Consistent E-Branding

Whatever branding you are doing, wherever it is, must be consistent in image and tone with the branding throughout your entire campaign. Again, e-branding that differs from, or contradicts, the branding produced by the traditional advertising agency is problematic. A dropped connection between the two may confuse your targeted market. Companies that have embraced e-marketing have taken traditional methodologies and applied them to the e-marketing world. The same tried-and-true methods work, if they're applied properly, in the e-world.

## Rule 4: Follow Through with Consistent and Timely Back-Up E-Campaigns

You don't have a good golf swing unless you have an accurate follow-through. The same is true with e-campaigns. In the digital world, we're moving seven times faster than everybody else. You must have a follow-up planned before you launch the first foray. Launch your first foray in e-marketing and be prepared with your second and third attack.

Your second campaign has to be smart. It must reinforce what the first one said. It has to follow in a timely manner and it should have a back-up campaign. In the traditional advertising world, maybe one full-page ad, each quarter, in a particular trade magazine might have worked for you. Now you need to have more consistent, conscientious, articulate campaigns in phases two, three, and four ready to go before you even bother with phase one. All campaigns should have a consistent key message across all media, both digital and traditional.

## Rule 5: Use Innovative Techniques in Your E-Marketing

Try a cool idea like a virtual postcard. The postcard could be a screen capture of your home page or a more target-specific page on your website. E-mail that postcard to your customer to link the user directly to a particular page on your site.

Virtual postcards are a brand new campaign idea in which you ensure that the message—a specific page link—gets to your users through an e-mail message. It reinforces the visual message. It allows prospects to link directly to a particular page within your site, so it might be the product page for the product you happen to be marketing. Then it allows them to instantly bookmark that page.

You're not giving them the general URL home page. You're linking them directly to some secondary or tertiary page inside your site. The reverse side, just like an ordinary print postcard, contains a written message. It rotates by clicking on "Press here to see the back." That brings us back to Rules 2 and 3, which advise linking your virtual campaign—your e-marketing campaign—to your traditional campaign and ensuring consistency of the branding message.

You can also have a printed postcard mailed to customers. They get the postcard on their desk. The message is reinforced when they receive it by e-mail. You're hitting them with the same message, the same image, in a traditional way, as well as digitally.

## Rule 6: Enhance Your Database So Your Message Reaches Your Target Audience

Ensure that you capture the data to fortify your database. A major problem e-marketers face is maintaining their databases so that they're constantly up to date and properly categorized. This will ensure that your message reflects the interests of your target market.

## Rule 7: Integrate Back-End Database Access into Your E-Marketing

A fully integrated e-marketing program is just that—fully integrated. There is no one pushing paper behind the scenes to ensure follow-through. If you are a recruiter and advertising for people to apply online, invite them to apply inside a banner ad. Have them click their answer inside your banner ad. For example, in box one: "What kind of job are you looking for? Click 1, 2, or 3 to answer the question." In box two: "What salary range?" In box three: "What's your e-mail address?" And so forth.

Allow the banner ad to act as a window into your database. If you're advertising a financial institution, allow your target market to calculate interest on an IRA or home equity loan. If you own a research company, allow prospects to enter an e-mail address to download research papers.

## Rule 8: Reinforce Your E-campaign with Your Existing Customer Service Program

Follow up with voice mail after a customer purchases from you. If you're a true Web person, things that work for you will work with your audience. "For instance, I registered for an online grocery shopping service," says Devlin. "About an hour later, I got a phone call from the online store's customer service representative, who said, 'Hi, Cathy. This is so-and-so at the grocery store. I understand you want to shop online. Do you have any questions?' I couldn't believe that the grocery store called me back to ask me if I had questions— was I ready to go shopping or did I need any help?" Ensure that your existing customer service programs back up your e-campaign.

### Rule 9: Reinforce Your E-Marketing Message Across Your Delivery Channels

Successful e-marketing means that you would have had contact through your website with your customers. Did you send them a parcel? If you did, ensure the packaging reinforces your message and reflects your campaign, and put a reminder inside for them to shop again—or include some gift or direct mail piece to once again reinforce that key message. Amazon.com includes Post-it notes, bookmarks, and other items with each order, reinforcing the Amazon image, look, and brand.

### Rule 10: Think Award-Winning Creative When Designing Your E-Marketing Campaign

As with all new media, one can err in assuming that because it's digital, you can lower your creativity standards. For some reason, many seem to think that e-marketing doesn't have to be brilliant. Award-winning creative is award-winning creative, whether it's on paper or on the Web. The creative must communicate effectively and meet the needs of the client or prospect.

## E-Marketing Versus Conventional Marketing

"The Internet is not just a new marketplace, it's a whole new medium, and strategies that generate high response rates in the postal world often fall flat on the Net. E-mail marketing requires a new approach specifically tailored to the Net's community and culture," says Rosalind Resnick, president of NetCreations, Inc., a New York Internet marketing firm. Here are a few tips from

Resnick for creating e-mail marketing campaigns that generate superior response.

• **Pick a good list from a reputable source.** Don't buy a list based strictly on price. On the Internet, you can buy a list of a million e-mail addresses for as low as $11. That doesn't mean you should. Lists like these are often what's known as spam lists—databases of names harvested without the recipients' knowledge or consent from newsgroups, chat rooms, websites, and member directories. While spam lists may be cheap to rent, the hostile reaction they typically generate among Internet users can be very costly to your company's reputation. Spamming can also result in your corporate mail-server getting bombed (attacked by angry e-mail messages), and the loss of your ISP account. The only legitimate e-mail lists are those that are generated by inviting Internet users to opt in to lists pertaining to topics of interest and by allowing list members to opt out of a list anytime they receive a marketing message.

• **Keep most direct e-mails short.** Don't go on and on for several pages. On the Internet, people want information and they want it now. That's why short, snappy pitches pull better than long-winded appeals that tell a story, paint a picture, tug at heartstrings, or describe your product's amazing bells and whistles in exhaustive detail. If your message exceeds one screen of text, go back and edit it until it fits. And don't try to squeeze in a second offer in order to save money—it will only lower the response to both of your offers! One strategy: send out your offer by postal mail first, then follow up with an e-mail reminder containing a hotlink to the order form on your website. You can also use e-mail lists to test copy; you'll find out in a day or two what works and what doesn't.

• **Include a call to action.** Don't leave recipients wondering what to do. It's not enough to tell recipients to check out your home page. You need to tell them exactly what you want them to do. Should they sign up for a free trial offer? Should they purchase your product today? The strategy that works best is to include in your message a special URL that visitors can click on to go to your site and fill out a form to request additional information. This way, you can accurately measure the response to your mailing and follow up with qualified prospects. One major retailer recently rang up $20,000 in sales in a couple of hours by sending customers an HTML e-mail message encouraging them to click on links embedded in a graphic and to order products from its website.

• **Set reasonable goals.** Don't expect your e-mail campaign to work miracles. In a postal direct marketing campaign, a 2 percent response rate is considered good, and a 1 percent response rate is considered acceptable. Opt-in e-mail lists, by contrast, tend to generate higher response rates because the list members have prequalified themselves by signing up to receive e-mail messages about various targeted topics. For example, a computer magazine publisher generated a 13 percent response rate to its free trial subscription offer. In general, a 5 percent response to an e-mail offer is good; even a 2 percent response is not a disaster. Remember, even the most responsive list won't work miracles if the ad copy and the offer don't sparkle, too.

## More Ways to Make Being Online More Profitable

These tips are from Joe Vitale, Internet marketing consultant and author of the book *Cyberwriting* (Amacom, 1996).

• **You must have a website.** There's no way around this today. You need a site if only for added credibility. But it also enhances customer service and sales. In a recent study conducted by Thomas Register and Visa USA, 30 percent of businesses said their primary reasons for moving to e-commerce were speed and convenience. In addition, the survey respondents indicated by a margin of two to one that they would give preference to a supplier who could accept online purchasing transactions.

"A website establishes instant credibility," comments Ilise Benun, publisher of *The Art of Self Promotion* newsletter. "It provides anytime access to you and the information about your services, which makes life easier for you and your prospects."

• **You must give people a reason to visit your site.** InterNIC reports that there are more than 1.5 million Internet sites. So why in the world should anyone take the time to see yours? If you have your picture there, or your brochure, or a cute saying, who cares? If you don't give people an appealing reason to zip over to your site, why complain if they don't visit it?

The Internet still has a "gift culture" mentality. Internet users expect freebies, and they appreciate information more than anything else. "I load my own site, www.mrfire.com, with special reports, book excerpts, and original articles on marketing, selling, advertising, and publicity," says Vitale. "All of this information is free. It's the bait I lay out to reel in prospects. When they read my articles, they learn about my books and services. If they like what they read, they may buy my books and services. But if I didn't give this information out, I couldn't really expect anyone to visit my site. Why would they?"

• **You must give people options to buy.** If you don't list your products and services at your site, with different ways to make purchases, you will miss sales. Remember that people are still extremely nervous about buying anything online. Be sure to give them both online and offline options to buy, including a toll-free phone number, street address, and fax number.

• **You must constantly change your site.** You may get people to visit your site once, but how will you get them to return? There are millions of sites for them to visit. "I keep adding new articles and special reports to my site, at the rate of about one a week," says Vitale. "Again, these reports are free. And adding new ones keeps people interested in coming back next week. If you don't change your site, why expect anyone to return to it?"

• **You must stop worrying about registering with search engines.** Everyone with a website frantically tries to get registered with every search engine around. As a result, they waste time and money on every offer to "register your site for $49" that comes their way.

Forget it. There are only six to twelve search engines that really count, and virtually all of them use spiders, or robots, that go out and find your site. You can and should manually register your site with Yahoo!, Lycos, AltaVista, Excite, Go, Netscape Search, AOL Search, MSN Search, Snap, HotBot, Google, and Infoseek, but you don't even need to do that. They will eventually find you. Focus more of your energy on creating a website worth visiting.

**Tip:** Do not overdesign your website. The more graphics you put into it, the slower the pages download to the viewer. According to Zona Research, Web pages take anywhere from three to eleven seconds to download, depending on the user's modem and Internet connection. The average viewer will "bail out"—click off the site onto another—if a page takes more than eight seconds to download. Zona estimates these bail-outs cost e-businesses $4.35 billion annually in lost revenue. Speed makes the difference. One site decreased bail-out rate from 30 percent to 8 percent just by reducing its download time by one second per page. One survey found that 84 percent of websites examined downloaded too slowly.

*(Source: Business News, 8/23/99.)*

"If you want your site to be listed with search engines, pay your webmaster to select the best candidates and make the submissions manually," writes Jonathan Ward in *The Business-to-Business Marketer* (August 1999, p. 3). He found that accepting an Internet offer to have his site automatically registered with numerous search engines for a nominal fee generated a flood of poor-quality inquiries and spam.

Ilise Benun comments, "Maintaining a high ranking on search engines is an arduous task that takes full-time, practically religious devotion."

Danny Sullivan, editor of *Search Engine Watch* newsletter, says the key is to provide search engines with ten to twenty keywords you want your site to be listed under, and rank them in importance. When in doubt, it's better to have more keywords rather than fewer. "Hits related to less important terms can add up," says Sullivan.

Another technique is to have content-rich, text-rich pages, not just graphics. Search engine robots find pages by words, not by pictures.

According to an article in *Internet Marketing Report* (July 28, 1999), a new study shows that only 42 percent of today's 800 million Web pages show up on any of the eleven major search engines. That's down from 60 percent of 320 million Web pages in 1997.

Web pages are proliferating more rapidly than the search engines can keep up. The article advises e-marketers not to depend too much on search engines to drive traffic to their sites. Instead, it advises promoting your URL to your offline customers and forging alliances with reciprocal links to websites of companies whose products complement your own.

- **You must use your sig file to promote your website.** Your sig file is that four- to eight-line paragraph at the end of every one of your e-mail messages. The Internet allows you to promote yourself in your sig. It's your opportunity to list your Web address and give people a reason to visit it.

Since your e-mail messages travel the Internet, get seen by potentially thousands of people, and are usually archived at giant databases like Deja.com where they can be retrieved, you never know who will see one of your messages or when. If your sig file has your website address in it, you just promoted your site to them.

- **Print your website address on everything.** Every ad you run, commercial you air, business card you hand out, catalog you mail, and brochure you distribute should contain your website address. Use the offline world to promote your online presence.

- **Participate in online discussion groups.** Join e-mail discussion groups where your target prospects gather. Do a search at www.liszt.com to find the groups for you. Lurk to get a feel for the nature of the group, and then post relevant responses to the list. As you do, you will be promoting yourself and your business. And if your sig has your website address in it, every time you post a message you will be promoting your website in a perfectly acceptable manner in conformance with Internet etiquette.

- **Cross-promote yourself in partnership with related websites.** We call it *networking* and *co-op marketing* offline. You can do the same thing online. Find websites that serve the same market you do and join forces with them. Maybe advertise on their site. Maybe exchange links. Create online allies to help you make money online.

- **Experiment.** The Internet as a vehicle for commerce is relatively new. Most of us are applying everything we have ever learned about marketing to this new medium. We have to think out of the box, stretch our minds, and create new ways of doing business online. We have to be willing to take risks and try new ideas. Some of this may cost money. Or time. But as Flip Wilson said, "You can't expect to hit the jackpot if you don't put a few nickels in the machine."

## How to Drive Traffic to Your Website

According to an article in *DM News* (October 4, 1999, p. 24), successful website owners report that 70 percent of their marketing budget is spent on media outside of the Web to direct prospective customers to their sites. Internet direct mail is a primary tool for driving large volumes of traffic to your website, but there are certainly other ways to do so. Paul Conderino of *Business & Legal Reports* offers the following suggestions:

- Put your URL on all promotions—direct mail, catalogs, card decks, fax marketing, space advertising, press releases, invoices, and renewals.
- Use search engines. Write short, compelling title and description tags for each page. Focus on one keyword phrase and use this keyword phrase in keyword metatag, title tag, description tag, headline, body copy, and alt tags. The keyword makes it more likely that someone doing an Internet search on the subject will be directed to your page.
- Encourage prospects to register with you to build your e-mail database. Offer a resource and document center, free demos, catalogs, samples, drawings, or an e-mail newsletter.
- Consider testing banner ads. Try offering some of your content in exchange for a free banner ad.
- Link your site to other sites. Set a goal of submitting a certain number of link requests per week. Search on your keywords to identify the top-ranking sites and then submit to those. Consider associations, magazines, consultants, and complementary sites.

**Just the FAQs:** In an article in *Opportunity World* magazine (October 1999, p. 24), John Doyle advises all Internet marketers to add a Frequently Asked Questions (FAQ) page to their websites. This is a page listing, in question and answer format, the most common questions prospects ask and a brief answer to each. The benefit? "You will get fewer e-mails asking you the same basic questions if you have the information instantly available online," writes Doyle. "The FAQ page will save you time, keep your customers happy, and your sales will increase."

- Build strategic partnerships and alliances. List your products on another company's site in exchange for a small royalty on any sales (example: a site selling gourmet pancake batter can list another site's maple syrup). Consider submitting articles for an e-mail newsletter in exchange for a Web link and additional promotion.
- Make it "sticky." Offer your prospects a reason to keep coming back. Good content, free resources and tools, and contests and drawings work well.

"If people aren't flocking to your website, do a little active promotion," advises self-promotion consultant Ilise Benun. "For example, get postcards printed introducing your website and send them out to everyone on your mailing list."

Internet direct mail, of course, is a powerful tool for driving people to your website. You can also use e-newsletters, as outlined later in this chapter.

In her book *The Ultimate Guide to Newsletter Publishing* (Newsletter Publishers Association, 1999, pp. 166–167), Patricia M. Wysocki offers additional tips to bring traffic to your website:

- Include your Web address on letters after the signature line.
- Develop a bookmark with your Web address on it and mail it with fulfillment of your products.

- Offer a weekly update of some sort to keep people coming back.
- Write an e-mail newsletter you can push to your prospects to remind them about your website.

## Fine-Tuning Your Internet Direct Mail Campaigns

It's upsetting to send out an e-mail and not get the results you expected. Before you declare that "Internet direct mail doesn't work," it makes more sense to see whether there's something specific about your campaign that can be fixed and retested. Here are some points to consider.

- **Be clear about what you're trying to achieve.** What response do you want from the user who visits your website? Are you looking for direct sales of a product? Or qualified leads? Are you building a database, perhaps the mailing list for your print catalog? Or are you trying to obtain research data?

- **Have a clear, powerful offer.** By knowing what response you're looking for you'll be able to work out an offer and key selling points. Put simply, your "offer" is what you're going to give them and what they're going to give you in exchange. If you're selling a software program, they're going to give you an amount of money and you're going to give them the program. Want to increase response to your offer? Deliver a strong "call to action" and structure the entire presentation around it. For example, if you're selling a motivational seminar on tape, you will probably have an order form somewhere along the line. Make that order form the focal point of the whole presentation. You might even start your design with the order form, rather than the home page. A call to action is a clear, compelling statement of your offer, urging the user to accept it. Let them know what you want them to do, and ask them to do it.

- **If you have an offer and it isn't pulling, figure out a more exciting offer.** Maybe you can sell the program at $50 off for Web customers—or give away a "light" version free. Are you trying to get answers to a survey? Nobody's going to spend ten minutes

**Tip:** Marketing consultant David Wood provides the following suggestions for enhancing your website:

1. Keep it simple. The best pages are organized and uncluttered.

2. Avoid elaborate graphics in the background or large images.

3. Display who you are, what you do, and how to get more information.

4. Give your address and phone number. Some people prefer these to e-mail.

5. Make it easy to contact a person, or provide a link to an instant e-mail form.

6. Content should include the firm's specialties and capabilities, location, key people, and project photos and descriptions.

7. Have articles, news stories, and recent press releases to extend your public relations efforts.

8. Every additional page should have your firm name and a link back to your home page.

9. If one of your pages is still in development, warn visitors so they won't waste time.

10. Update information by adding new items from time to time.

11. Promote the site in directories, in other browsers, and in search engines.

12. Promote your site through traditional print media. Have your Internet address on your business cards and in your brochures, news releases, articles, technical papers, and all advertising.

online filling out your form just for the fun of it. You've got to offer them something. How about a chance to win a prize? The more compelling the offer (and your presentation of it) the better the response will be.

- **Lead with your biggest benefit or most compelling offer.** If you want the user to respond, your entire direct e-mail approach should be built around (and the response you're looking for should determine) how you open. You only have a few seconds to get the user's attention and convince him or her to follow your presentation. That means firing a big gun to open the battle. "Welcome to Plotnick Screws and Bolts!" is not a big gun. Offer a major benefit for continuing on into the site. Try something along the lines of: "Save $100 on your first shipment of Plotnick fasteners!"

- **Break the text up into short, easy-to-read sections.** Want to send users scurrying back where they came from? Just present them with huge blocks of text in long paragraphs. On the other hand, if you want users to stay with you, make your Web pages friendly and easy to follow by breaking up the copy. Use frequent headlines and bulleted lists. Write short words, short sentences, and short paragraphs.

- **Write in a personal one-to-one, natural style.** Imagine yourself having a face-to-face conversation with the other person. Use contractions—*you'll, don't, I'll*. And it's OK to start a sentence with *and* or *but*—and to use sentence fragments. Like so.

- **Be discerning about the use of graphic design, artwork, and Web magic.** Make sure your design and visuals support the marketing purpose of the site. Poor design can interfere with the direct response process. For example, you may have written a killer headline. But if you display that headline in brown lettering on a dark green background, it will be hard to read. It's possible that beautiful pictures, background images, sound or video, or a Java applet will enhance the selling power of your message. But make sure that you're not including them just to satisfy your own (or someone else's) creative urge.

- **Test.** Objective testing and measurement tell you what works. When you change an element, does the response rate go up or down or remain unchanged? You can test many elements of your site— offer, creative concept, headline, graphic design, order form design, or other factors. It's better to test only one element at a time. Testing different offers might be the best place to start. Even the most basic Web provider these days can offer you an access report for your website. Suppose you have a six-page linear Web presentation leading the user from the front page to an order form, one page at a time. Check your access reports. If the number of visitors drops off sharply after page three, that's an indication something's wrong with that page. For a more sophisticated report or for measurements on a large site, it might be good to invest in specialized software or even the services of an outside firm.

• **Make it easy to respond.** I don't know how many times I've searched high and low on a website and been unable to find so much as an e-mail address. The best response now—a button to click, an online form, an e-mail link. A toll-free number, fax number, or postal address is better than nothing. But if you force prospects to wait and contact you later, you risk losing the urgency and excitement you've built up through your Web presentation and call to action. Remember that many people only have one phone line, so they won't be able to call you when they're surfing the Web.

## Marketing Online with E-Zines

In traditional direct mail, the most popular formats are sales letters, direct mail "packages" (sales letters with an order form, reply envelope, and other enclosures such as brochures, lift notes, or buck slips), and self-mailers.

But there are many other formats that work, and some of them are deliberately designed to look like "reading matter" rather than promotional material. A *magalog*, for example, is a direct mail package that looks like a color magazine. Some direct mail pieces are disguised as informational newsletters. Others look like booklets or reports.

An electronic version of this technique, the e-zine, is gaining acceptance in Internet direct mail. An e-zine is a promotional newsletter mailed to an opt-in list on the Internet. Although the content is written in an editorial, informational style, the purpose is to sell.

> **Tip:** Register your Internet domain name early. When in doubt about a name, register it anyway. Registration is cheap when you get the name directly from InterNIC, the governing body that controls these names. But if someone else registers the name you want, you may have to pay dearly to get them to sell it to you. Recently, drugs.com sold for $823,456. And a Texas entrepreneur recently sold business.com to a California company for $7.5 million. Two years earlier, he had bought the name from someone else for $150,000. One of us, Bob Bly, registered bly.com a year or more before he was ready to put up a website, just to secure the name. Sure enough, a number of Blys approached him later to say they wished they had gotten it first!

The typical e-zine (see Figure 9.1) has five to six short (one- or two-paragraph) items, separated by headings or horizontal lines. Within each is a link to a particular Web page where the reader can get more detailed information on the product, idea, or issue summarized in the e-zine abstract.

One way to use e-zines is to create your own and send them periodically to your entire house e-list. If you contact your e-list twice a month, for example, one of these can be a standard e-mail promotional message, and the other can be the e-zine.

Figure 9.2 shows an example of a promotional e-zine. The publisher, David Baker, sends the e-zine monthly to an opt-in house list of 2,000 names. He reports that traffic on his website more than doubles for three straight days after the issue is e-mailed.

A second option, growing in popularity, is to place a banner-type ad on page one of another company's e-zine. When the e-zine is mailed to their list, the recipients see your ad and can click for more information.

A big advantage of advertising in other e-zines is reach: some of them are seen by millions of Internet users. Another is the relatively

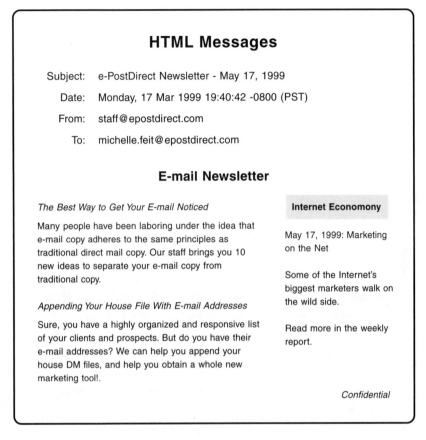

# HTML Messages

Subject: e-PostDirect Newsletter - May 17, 1999

Date: Monday, 17 Mar 1999 19:40:42 -0800 (PST)

From: staff@epostdirect.com

To: michelle.feit@epostdirect.com

## E-mail Newsletter

*The Best Way to Get Your E-mail Noticed*

Many people have been laboring under the idea that e-mail copy adheres to the same principles as traditional direct mail copy. Our staff brings you 10 new ideas to separate your e-mail copy from traditional copy.

*Appending Your House File With E-mail Addresses*

Sure, you have a highly organized and responsive list of your clients and prospects. But do you have their e-mail addresses? We can help you append your house DM files, and help you obtain a whole new marketing tool!.

**Internet Economomy**

May 17, 1999: Marketing on the Net

Some of the Internet's biggest marketers walk on the wild side.

Read more in the weekly report.

*Confidential*

*Figure 9.1. E-PostDirect e-zine*

low cost. Running an ad in an e-zine costs $40 per thousand, versus $150 to $400 per thousand to rent and transmit to an e-list.

Today, advertising with and on e-mail newsletters is becoming one of the most popular forms of online marketing. Why? Because it is inexpensive, highly targeted, and produces results. The media also benefits from low ad clutter, and it seems that that newsletter ads get an implied endorsement from the editors by being inside the content.

In fact, newsletter ads can be one of the most effective marketing investments you can make. For example, there are newsletters where you can reach a targeted audience of thousands of readers, all

From: "David C. Baker" info@recourses.com
To: info@recouses.com
Subject: Management Tools from ReCourses/Persuading
Date: Sat, 6 May 2000 19:26:33 -0500

- - - - - - - - - - - - - - - - - - - - - - - - - - - -

————TABLE OF CONTENTS————

1—What Employees Want
2—Get on the Clue-Train
3—Speaking Engagements
4—Popular White Papers

- - - - - - - - - - - - - - - - - - - - - - - - - - - -

ReCourses is a management consulting firm that works exclusively in the public relations, advertising, interactive, and design fields. Our flagship product is Persuading, a monthly newsletter that provides "Critical Briefings for the Business of Persuasion." See below for information on subscribing.

This free e-mail subscription service offers small nuggets of business advice. You'll also be notified of upcoming roundtables, seminars, key speaking engagements, major site changes, and recent white paper postings. If you have any questions, please contact 888/476-5884. To remove or add subscriptions, go to http://www.recourses.com/ and choose the "subscribe" option from the menu at the left.

- - - - - - - - - - - - - - - - - - - - - - - - - - - -

1—What Employees Want

- - - - - - - - - - - - - - - - - - - - - - - - - - - -

There are certain environments in which employees thrive. If you aren't managing, or if you just aren't suited for it, the evidence will be all over your firm. Based on more than 3,000 surveys and follow-up interviews, we recently completed a study of the type of management environment

*Figure 9.2 Promotional e-zine. Reprinted courtesy of David C. Baker, editor of* Persuading, *www.persuading.com, 888-478-8940.*

employees prefer. The study provided 75 suggestions about what employees appreciate in the working environment, organized into categories: hiring, integration, structure, performance, workload, environment, personal, support, communications, conflicts of interest, external respect, and exiting.

Managing people is the most personally painful thing you do. Sure, establishing systems is perplexing, but the implications of failure are more mental and financial, not personal or ethical. The management environment, though, is a complex task always out of reach. And worst of all, it seldom moves from gray into black and white. It's hard to know that you've done the right thing and doing the right thing is a deeper concern in this arena than your other areas of responsibility. Or at least it should be.

We thought you might benefit from seeing just a few of the 75 suggestions we've gathered about how employees want to be managed:

- I want to respect you as a person of integrity. This is fundamental. Any time you spend planning the course of this business will be welcome. If you are Doing more than Managing, I'm worried about who's steering this ship.
- Keep your emotional and sexual attractions in check. It will cloud the management environment and destroy the fabric of how we relate to each other.
- Follow the policies yourself so that I can see how serious you are about system-wide institutionalization.
- Don't cling to your own status, but don't work too hard at artificially leveling your position, either. In other words, if you need a private office, I'll understand. You aren't one of us and shouldn't try to act like it.
- Don't be afraid of us lest we lose respect for you. We are okay with your making mistakes, but we are not okay with your not taking risks.
- Don't be afraid of conflict or sweep it under the rug. Conflict is inevitable and that's when we need you the most.
- Have a life outside work and don't be embarrassed about it.
- Don't expect me to be as committed as a shareholder would be. I don't have as much as stake as you do, and I want a life outside work, too. That's why I'm working for you and not myself.

*Figure 9.2 Promotional e-zine (continued)*

- Don't avoid management decisions by enacting extensive regulations (e.g., in a handbook that attempts to address every possible situation).
- Quit waffling—just go ahead and fire that person. We all know it needs to happen.
- And go ahead and tell them when you've made the decision (instead of just not looking at them anymore)!
- Don't appeal to loyalty when you want me to stay late or turn down that job offer. Let's keep our accounts short: you pay me fairly and I'll give you value. We should both be able to walk away from this without owing each other anything.
- Take extended time off so that we can show you how much we really don't need you around to run this place well.
- Separate the business from yourself, giving both you and me freedom to critique it meaningfully without defensiveness on your part.

There are more than 60 additional summary points that were gleaned from our 3,000 interviews. They are published in the May issue of Persuading, which is a print-based, web-enabled monthly newsletter that consists of "Critical Briefings for the Business of Persuasion." The publication is written for those who do the persuading (public relations, advertising, interactive, and design) and who want help with internal business issues. The cross-disciplined approach is intentional. Not only are the lines between these disciplines blurring, but each has core strengths that benefit the other.

Every issue consists of hard hitting, useful information of a thematic, archival nature. In other words, it will be relevant now and relevant for years to come (updated articles will be posted on the site, and your subscription will include access to them). Where appropriate, interactive illustrations/expansions of the topics covered in each issue will also be published online. For example, the May issue also includes access to the survey we used.

The subscription price is $360/year for new and renewal subscriptions. It is a limited circulation publication in that the subscriber base will not exceed 3,000 members. Once that number is reached, new subscribers will be

*Figure 9.2 Promotional e-zine (continued)*

allowed to join only when a subscription slot becomes available. We would invite you to the website (http://www.persuading.com) for more information on the publication, upcoming issues, and our philosophy.

Every issue is written for you. Our mission is to make your life easier by providing critical guidelines on how to run your firm even smarter than you are now. That will ensure that your business does not become stagnant, unprofitable, or consuming.

The issues published so far this year are entitled as follows:

01/2000—Positioning Part 1: Specialization
02/2000—Positioning Part 2: Proprietary Process
03/2000—Using Positioning Briefs Effectively
04/2000—The Components of Interactive Work
05/2000—An Environment Where Employees Want to Be

Back issues are available only to subscribers.

Download a sample issue of this new publication at:
(http://www.recourses.com/pdfs/SAMPLE.PDF)

::::::::::::::::::::::::::::::::
2—Get the Clue-Train
::::::::::::::::::::::::::::::::

This weekend I read a book that had been sitting on my shelf for six weeks. It's written by Rick Levine et al., and is entitled "The Clue-Train Manifesto: The End of Business as Usual." It emerged from a website (http://www.cluetrain.com) that posted 95 theses, making hash of corporate assumptions and the impact of the online world.

The foreword sums the book up by noting that "Business, at bottom, is fundamentally human. Engineering remains second-rate without aesthetics. Natural, human conversation is the true language of commerce.

*Figure 9.2 Promotional e-zine (continued)*

Corporations work best when the people on the inside have the fullest contact possible with people on the outside."

The theses themselves, in fact, set the tone for the underlying principles espoused in the book. Here are the first five:

1/Markets are conversations.

2/Markets consist of human beings, not demographic sectors.

3/Conversations among human beings sound human. They are conducted in a human voice.

4/Whether delivering information, opinions, perspectives, dissenting arguments, or humorous asides, the human voice is typically open, natural, uncontrived.

5/People recognize each other as such from the sound of this voice.

I vividly remember attending an AdWeek-sponsored conference in San Francisco in late 1997. The authors of "Under the Radar" were presenting their solutions to breaking through consumer defenses, and a thought hit me: at some point consumers will only listen to people they trust, which means that we need to be good, trustworthy people or our messages will not get through.

That's not to say that studying demographics is evil. It's just that in the end, it will not be enough in this marketing-cluttered universe. Hired pitchmen (that's what we are) will need integrity to craft messages that cause the consumer to pause, raise his/her eye, and pick out that simple voice in the din.

What a great tie-in to the opening segment of this e-mail. How do your employees policies read? Are they human, or are they contrived? How about your mission statement? Marketing materials?

You might want to read this book!

*Figure 9.2 Promotional e-zine (continued)*

```
: : : : : : : : : : : : : : : : : : : : : : : : : : : :
```

3—Speaking Engagements

```
: : : : : : : : : : : : : : : : : : : : : : : : : : : :
```

05/09—Session on "Sustainable Staffing: Legitimate Clones or Functional Experts" at the national spring conference of the Counselor's Academy, part of the Public Relations Society of America.

05/16—Four-hour seminar for studio principals challenged with growing their business. Learn the best role for principals, the necessary systems needed to be profitable, and the best way to position your firm during growth. The seminar is from 5:00-6:30p. Presented by the Portland chapter of AIGA (American Institute of Graphic Arts), the Oregon chapter of ASMP (American Society of Media Photographers), and the GAG (Graphic Artists Guild).

05/17—Preconference session for the national SEGD conference in Portland, OR, entitled "Making Your Firm Distinctive, Inside and Out."

05/24—Keynote presentation on managing the public relations function for the Denver Chapter of PRSA.

06/12—Workshop on "12 Common Business Questions" at the national How conference in Atlanta.

06/16—Panel presentation at the annual conference of Promax/BDA with Clive Burcham (of iDeutsch), moderated by Patricia Spellman (of ABC), entitled "Getting Back Your Mojo."

10/17—Several presentations at the "Mind Your Own Business" conference (cosponsored with How) in Cancun, Mexico, 17-20 October. Keynotes are Bill Taylor (editor of "Fast Company"), Michael Gerber (author of "The E-Myth"), and Jay Shelov (sales guru). Other speakers include Rick Gould, Joan Gladstone, Roz Goldfarb, Caryn Leland, Shel Perkins, Cam Foote, Dave Wood, David Goodman, Charles Collie, and Sheila Campbell. Go to the website to learn more or preregister. The conference is limited to roughly 300 participants.
(http://www.howbusinessconference.com)

*Figure 9.2 Promotional e-zine (continued)*

of whom have opted in to receive the publication for the newsletter that carries the advertisement, at one-and-a-half cents to three cents per reader or less. This is permission marketing at its very best.

- **What is an e-newsletter?** An e-newsletter is simply a newsletter that is created on a computer and is e-mailed to a publisher's subscriber list. E-mail newsletters are sent daily to millions of subscribers in many different categories of interest.

- **Why use newsletter advertising?** Many Internet marketing strategies depend on visitors voluntarily coming back to a website. By itself, this strategy will not work. No Internet marketing plan is complete unless it incorporates both an inbound and outbound strategy. Drawing customers to your website is inbound. Sending messages out includes the use of e-mail and newsletter advertising. A web marketer must use both strategies to have an effective website.

- **What are the advantages of newsletter advertising?** One advantage is a better response rate as compared to banner ads, which makes it a more cost-effective medium. Another is transferability, a fairly unique e-commerce concept. When a person receives a newsletter of high interest, he or she often sends it to a friend or coworker. This pass-along readership is free advertising and is highly encouraged.

- **How do I select the right audience?** Like all other advertising, you must select the newsletter with the right audience. You must also select a newsletter with good content, that is, one that people will read and that has few ads. Most newsletters are fun, enjoyable, readable, and contain about three ads.

- **What will my ad look like?** Most newsletter ads are currently text only. They consist of about fifty words and compare to a short e-mail message ad. Each ad contains a URL that directs the reader to your website where your marketing action takes place. Make sure that the URL does not wrap and works well prior to ad placement.

- **What should I test?** Newsletter ads contain some basic parts just like any other ad and can be changed to fit your needs. But primarily the ad will contain a "From" section, a subject line or teaser copy and a header, creative copy, and a URL to which prospects respond. You can also change and test the length of the message and the creative style.

In addition to format and copy tests, you should constantly test offers. We feel that the basic offers that have been used in direct marketing are applicable on the Web. As in traditional marketing, event marketing is an extremely effective tool in e-commerce. Special offers for Father's Day, Mother's Day, and other holidays can be put together quickly and inexpensively to maximize your website's return on investment.

As you prepare your next e-mail promotion to your house list, consider testing with a few outside e-mail lists and some newsletter sponsorship ads. As you would in any test, vary copy format, offer, and placement. You will be pleased with the results.

When you advertise on e-zines, you pay to have your promotional message included in other companies' e-zines, particularly those with large circulations.

A good example is the e-zine published by Egghead.com. With the Egghead.com E-Mail Newsletter Program, you can prominently display your personalized text message in their daily e-mail newsletter with a hyperlink to your web page or order form.

If you get good results advertising in a company's e-newsletter, you may want to test an e-mail to their e-list as well. Foofoo.com, a website that bills itself as "the definitive authority on the Internet for fun and the finer things in life," sent a separate e-mail to one million people receiving the Egghead.com e-zine. They received twenty thousand replies, which is a decent 2 percent response rate.

Egghead.com's three commerce sites were ranked seventh in at-home reach and sixth in at-work reach among the shopping sites on the Internet by Media Metrix. Putting a message in their e-zine enables you to send it instantly to millions of credit card enabled active buyers of PCs and laptops, Mac or Windows based software, electronics, financial investments, musical CDs, education, clothing, travel, books, magazines, flowers, online services, membership and continuity programs, and more.

When deciding whether to advertise on someone's e-zine, get full details on their subscribers or recipients. The Egghead.com customer, for example, is an educated, affluent thirty-five- to fifty-four-year-old male homeowner in the prime of his earning years. Approximately 15 percent are women. Their relatively high median earnings of $65,000 ensures the disposable income to buy what they want.

With an ad in an e-zine, you can sell a product or service, link to an e-catalog, direct people to your website, create an affinity program, make an announcement, offer an upgrade, conduct a survey, or ask for a charitable donation.

The low-cost distribution can substantially reduce your cost for acquiring new customers by eliminating printing, postage, and list costs. This form of marketing increases response rates by making the purchase easy, fast, and at a time and place where they are ready to buy.

Format for your e-zine ad will vary with the publisher. For Egghead.com, for example, the format is as follows:

*Headline in caps*
GET 5 CDs FREE—JOIN THE CBA MUSIC CLUB

*3 lines of advertising copy (60 characters per line including spaces)*
Select 5 FREE CDs from our huge inventory of
classical, R&B, country, rap, and popular artist
CDs. Click here to order your favorite CDs online!

*1 line optional hyperlink*
www.cdbmusic.com/egghead1.html

This ad in the Egghead e-zine costs $40 per thousand, including the transmission fee.

Each e-zine will have its own advertising requirements and rates. Typically the sponsored ads range from a few words and a link to a URL to around 100 words plus a headline and link. Figure 9.3 shows the ad format requirements for advertising in *ENT Newsline*, an e-zine sent to Windows professionals.

## E-Mail Surveys

Surveys that ask the opinions of customers or prospects, allowing them to respond simply by copying and answering the survey questions, can be as effective as surveys conducted via mail, phone, and fax—maybe more so. E-mail surveys are easier to respond to and less

# ENT *Newsline*

The Independent Newsletter For Windows NT Enterprise Computing

Dear Valued Newsline Sponsor:

We have created the following guidelines to help you format your advertisement so that it fits into our Newsline requirements. Using this template to format your ad ensures it will look the way you intend for it to when sent out to Newsline subscribers.

**Newsline Advertising Guidelines**

- Copy length: 100 words maximum
- Line count: 13 maximum (not including "*" delimiters)
- Maximum line length: Approximate maximum of 60 characters per line (including spaces)
- Special restrictions: Maximum number of random words in upper-case type: 2 (excluding first line)
- No special font formatting (bold, italics, etc.) is supported
- Other special characters: subject to publisher approval

**How to use this template:**

1. Insert your copy into the space below.
2. Highlight your copy and change the text selection to 10 point "plain text" using the copy style drop-down box (not the font selection box).
3. While your text is still highlighted, check the word count by clicking on "tools" followed by "word count." Total should be 100 words or less. Total number of lines should be 13 or less.
4. Adjust line breaks as you see fit to adjust readability, keeping within the 13-line maximum.
5. When satisfied, save the file as a Word document, send it as an e-mail attachment to your sales representative.

*************** SPONSORED BY: **************
Insert up to 13 lines of advertising copy here
****************************************************

*Figure 9.3. Ad requirements for an e-zine*

intrusive than phone surveys, so they may ultimately generate a higher level of response. People like giving their opinions and do so willingly, especially if they believe the end result will benefit them. It is always a good idea to offer survey respondents a compilation of the final survey results.

Customer surveys that use traditional media such as direct mail and the telephone are known to generate response rates as high as 20 percent or more. E-mail surveys should have the potential to do the same if they are used appropriately.

In an article in *DM News*, Jody Dodson gives the following tips for increasing response rates to online surveys:

- **The fewer the better.** Surveying response strategy runs opposite to marketing response strategy. The fewer total customer contacts, the better. You don't want to broadcast your marketing plans, intentions, and ideas to a wide audience. People do talk, so try to expose the smallest number of site visitors to your interview process.

- **Humanize your interactions.** Most people would choose to communicate with other people before they'd volunteer to interact with computers or faceless companies. Show site visitors the actual people behind your data-collection efforts. Try using photos or a short personal message with a signature in the survey invitation.

- **Inform your visitors what they're getting into before they even begin the survey.** Creating realistic expectations will prevent respondent frustration. Make sure you describe the purpose of the research, the time required to complete the survey, and any incentives that are being offered.

- **Brand your interview tools.** Your customers probably like dealing with your company. Don't let them feel like they're interacting with anyone but your company, even if you're using an outside vendor to conduct the research.

- **Be proactive.** Your visitors should never have to work to provide feedback that's going to make your Web business successful. Bring your data-collection effort right to the individuals of interest. Pop-up survey invitations or e-mail invitations to customers who've opted in for e-mail communications make it easy to interact.

• **Build an ongoing dialogue with your customers.** The very best way to improve survey response rates is to make communication between your business and your customers a common and mutually rewarding activity. Once customers have seen that you genuinely care about their wants and needs, they'll gladly participate in your research projects. Any combination of these tactics can lead to double- and even triple-digit increases in your online survey response.

• **Focus on site visitors who have a naturally high interest in communicating with you.** This can be accomplished by intercepting visitors after they've made some minimum commitment to do business with your company. These are the customers or prospects who are interested in telling you how to improve their future experiences.

• **Motivate your visitors to communicate with you.** It's been proven in both the offline and the online world that people don't like to give unless they receive. If your research is well thought out, the value of this information should greatly outweigh the cost of collecting it. The cost includes any premiums that you offered.

• **Be sensitive to your visitors' needs.** Anticipate and address obvious issues like time constraints and privacy concerns before you even begin creating the survey.

## To Sum It All Up

- Internet direct mail is only one facet of a total Internet marketing effort. And Internet marketing is only one facet of a company's total marketing effort.
- The more effective you make the website that links to your Internet direct mail, the greater the response and sales will be upon click-through to the site.
- The solo Internet direct mail is not the only e-mail marketing option available. Others include publishing your own e-zine and placing an ad in other e-zines.

# FOLLOWING UP WITH INTERNET PROSPECTS

As ANY EXPERIENCED marketer knows, the more you follow up with prospects and customers, the more sales you close. This chapter deals with following up responses and inquiries generated online, and focuses on two basic e-marketing follow-up systems: autoresponders and data push.

## Automated Response with Autoresponders

An *autoresponder* is a software program or system specifically designed for inquiry fulfillment on the Internet. Think of autoresponders as an "e-mail on demand" technology similar to fax on demand. The prospect sends an inquiry to your e-mail address, and the autoresponder automatically e-mails the information he or she requested.

Why were autoresponders invented? When you are in a hurry to obtain information, you may not have a lot of time to search through numerous links of websites to locate, and then read or print, the information. You may not even have access to the Web at the time, perhaps only being able to reach the Internet via an e-mail account at work or school.

Wouldn't it be wonderful if websites or other online or offline sources provided you with an e-mail address, or addresses, to which you could send a message and then receive an appropriate reply document directly in your e-mailbox within minutes?

That service is becoming more widely available as communicators and webmasters begin using autoresponder technology to enhance their ability to serve website visitors and e-mail users. And, as more and more people become familiar with autoresponders' benefits, links to autoresponder addresses may become expected, essential parts of websites and other online and offline communications efforts, such as letterhead, brochures, ads, product labels, and so on.

What types of information can autoresponders deliver? You name it: company contact details; office hours and policies; restaurant menus; special offers and sales; product descriptions; price lists; order forms; job listings; reports; newsletters; organizational membership information; travel directions; literary works; class lessons; answers to frequently asked questions; news releases; the list of possibilities goes on and on.

Autoresponders are gaining in popularity. For instance, during President Clinton's post-impeachment Senate trial, senators received up to half a million e-mail messages a day—ten times the usual amount. The federal government turned to EchoMail, an advanced autoresponder product, to handle the load. After installing EchoMail, senator response time to individual e-mails was reduced from days or weeks to minutes.

Autoresponders, which are also sometimes referred to as "ARs," mailbots, infobots, or e-mail-on-demand, are computer programs designed to automatically and immediately send an informational document (or documents) via e-mail in response to a request submitted either by e-mail or through an online form. As such, they are, by nature, a nonintrusive, user-invoked Internet communications tool as opposed to intrusive spam. Once set up, ARs respond to inquiries without direct human intervention and enable information seekers to retrieve a document (or documents) via e-mail twenty-four hours a day, seven days a week from anywhere in the world where they have access to an Internet e-mail account.

So, once you know an address for a particular autoresponder document, you can request it even if it's 3 A.M. and you're at a remote location, simply by sending an e-mail message. Depending upon Internet traffic and upon how your own e-mail software is configured to retrieve messages, you should receive the document within minutes.

With many autoresponders the address itself is the actual command to retrieve the document, so you can simply send a blank e-mail message to the address. For other autoresponder programs, you must supply a specific subject or body message, so you'll need to follow any given instructions to retrieve the document you want. Some webmasters provide hypertext "mailto:" links to ARs directly from their website, in which case a menu pops up from which you can e-mail your request; others provide button links that request the document as soon as you click on the graphic. It may also interest you to know that many online forms are linked to AR documents providing you with an automatic standard reply via e-mail after you've submitted the form.

How can you tell the difference between an autoresponder address and a regular e-mail address? Currently, it is difficult to do so unless some specific indication accompanies the address, because the syntax for regular and AR addresses is the same. Also, there is no commonly accepted standard for designating AR addresses.

To help clarify things for e-mail users, Voron Communications, developer of the AutoResponders.com, ReadyInfo, and Sponders websites, suggests the use of the following abbreviations to designate autoresponder addresses:

- AR: (means "autoresponder" address)
- ARS: (means "autoresponder series" address)

Thus, the designation "AR:info@readyinfo.com" means that sending e-mail to that address would retrieve the autoresponder document file named "info" at the ReadyInfo.com domain. Similarly, if we change the designation to "ARS:info@readyinfo.com" it means that sending e-mail to that address would retrieve an autoresponder document file named "info" at the ReadyInfo.com domain, plus a series of one or more follow-up documents.

If you would like to see for yourself how easy it is to retrieve autoresponder documents, send for the demonstration document offered by AutoResponders.com. Just send any e-mail to AR:demo@autoresponders.com. Within a few minutes, a reply document should arrive in your e-mail box. It's that simple!

Say you want to buy something for your kids, such as a fancy hamster wheel. You visit a pet store site on the Web and compare a few high-performance wheels, then log off. The next day, you revisit the site, and you're met with a personalized greeting: "Hello again, Derek! We hope you have found the right wheel for your hamster. Do you also need a water bottle or some cedar wood shavings to line the cage with?"

While you were poking around the Web pages, the site's server stashed a nugget of information on your computer called a *cookie*. In this case, the cookie included a record of your visit and the kinds of information you looked at. When you linked to the pet store's site on the second day, the store's Web server read the cookie on your computer, recognized you as a repeat visitor with an interest in hamster wheels, and responded accordingly.

One company, Merchant Mail Network, automatically prepares and sends rich-media e-mail messages to specific customers, based on their preferences, page visits, and products purchased. These e-mailings typically include color catalog pages along with personalized messages and special offers. For more information on Merchant Mail Network, visit www.digital-impact.com.

## How Do Cookies Work and How Are They Used?

If you have a Web browser on your computer, you also have a cookie file. As you view a web page, HTML code (the language of the Web) directs the browser on your computer to write a cookie in your cookie file, recording whatever data the server specifies. Subsequently, the Web server can read your browser's cookie file. Each website creates a separate file and can read only its own cookies: the pet store can't read a cookie created by another site.

Websites use cookies for several reasons. One is to gather targeted or personalized content, as in the example above. URL cookies can track where you came from, where you go within the site, when you go there (down to the time of day), how long you spend in each area of the site, and whether you buy online.

A cookie could also record the links or advertisements that you click on and add that information to a profile of your interests located in your cookie file. Cookies can remember your member ID and password so that you don't have to retype them every time you visit a membership site. Or a cookie can serve as a shopping cart for an electronic commerce website so that your browser remembers the items you wanted to purchase, even if you leave the site and return later.

The point is to make the website more appealing to you, enticing you to come back again. If the pet store's personalized greeting gets you to buy cedar shavings, then a cookie just generated some additional revenue for the store.

Some privacy groups object to cookies. Their concern is essentially that the technology underlying cookies could be used to read other data off your hard drive. This presents a security risk. Some people also regard cookies as an invasion of privacy: they don't want their browser making a semipermanent record of every page they've visited.

It is now possible to set your browser to reject cookies or to alert you when a Web server attempts to write something to your cookie file. That way, when a website tries to give you a cookie, you can catch it with its hand in the jar.

## The Three Cs of E-Success

Internet specialists talk about the 3 Cs of e-business: *commerce, content,* and *community.*

The first C, commerce, refers to the website's ability to permit the consumer to buy online. Without e-commerce, an e-mail can only generate online leads or offline purchases; you cannot have true one-step mail order on the Internet.

The second C, content, refers to the information and services available on the website. Sites that display only product information are not as interesting to Internet users as those that offer useful information and tools. (An example of a tool is one found on a health website that displays your ideal weight when you enter your height.) The better your content, the more users will favor your site.

The interactivity and graphic nature of the Internet may, on the surface, make it attractive as a marketing tool. But Web surfers are drawn by content, not graphics. "Animation and day-glo colors make the Web lively and inviting," says copywriter Shira Linden, "But it's the content-rich sites that snag browsers and convert them into buyers." She recommends valuable content, refreshed often, so people stay longer and come back more often.

"What was once called 'editorial' is now called 'content,'" observes an article in *Hotline*, the monthly newsletter of the Newsletter Publishers Association in Washington, D.C. The article observes that on the Web, much of the content is created not by professional publishers or writers, but by users, buyers, and consumers—people sharing and talking with each other, rather than a publisher deciding and controlling what they read. "The power of content," the article concludes, "comes from someone with interests or experiences similar to yours writing you about it."

The third C, community, refers to the relationship users have with the website and each other. It's the online equivalent of a neighborhood bookstore, café, or coffee shop. Web surfers begin to feel your site is a good place to go and spend time, especially with other visitors. In an article in *CIO Enterprise* (October 14, 1999, section 2, p. 34), Daintry Duffy identifies three types of online communities:

- Internet communities that serve as a marketing and advertising tool
- extranet communities designed to strengthen relationships with trade partners or customers
- intranet communities that facilitate knowledge sharing within an organization

Chat rooms and forums can help build this sense of community. When you see people in postings talking by name to each other—as they argue a point or share opinions—you know you're on a site with a strong sense of community.

A good example is iVillage.com. The use of the word "village" in the name instantly creates an image of an Internet community.

The website caters to a variety of interests, including news, health, parenting, personal investing, pets, relationships, travel, and even a book club aimed primarily at women. You can send instant messages to other members, participate in chats, post notices on boards, even have your own member's page. Another example is TechRepublic, a community of IT (information technology) professionals, which you can visit at www.trfree.com.

CyberSite Inc. oversees about twenty communities of interest. Their most popular is AncientSites, which is aimed at premedieval history enthusiasts and has ninety thousand registered members. They offer free information as well as related products through affiliate programs. One e-mail promoting ancient coins generated a 74 percent click-through rate, with a 3 percent conversion rate. "It [the community of interest] is a superior environment for selling merchandise," says CyberSites COO Keith Halper.

To the e-mail marketer, community may be the most important C. The greater the sense of community, the stronger the relationship between the users and the website. Therefore, the users who have opted in and are on your e-list (and you can get almost all of them to opt in by requiring them to register to use chat rooms, forums, and other favorite site features) have a great relationship with the site. This maximizes their receptiveness to and willingness to receive e-marketing messages sent both by you and by other companies you allow to rent your e-list. According to an article in *American Demographics* (June 2000, p. 39), members of online communities are 36 percent more likely than regular Internet users to make purchases online.

Other keys to successful e-commerce sites include:

- a large volume of quality traffic
- effective marketing and promotion
- a well-established back end
- plenty of buying opportunities
- outstanding customer service and support

To this we add another item: "Opt-in before communication." Do not send e-mails to website visitors until and unless they opt in on your registration page.

A common e-marketing mistake is to assume a greater affinity with your website than your visitors actually have. Having a person opt in before you send him or her e-mail marketing messages is the minimal requirement, but opt-in doesn't guarantee that the prospect likes and respects your site—or even that he or she remembers the visit!

Too often we don't realize that our business or website is much more interesting to us than it is to the mass of surfers on the Internet. However, the more content and utility you offer, the more visitors will grow to like your site, and the greater the awareness you'll gain.

Measure Web surfer activity. Those who visit and buy more will know you better than those who visit sporadically or never buy.

The bottom line: don't assume a closer relationship between your site and visitors than actually exists. "Your customer dictates the depth of the relationship, which must be based on what he or she needs, so don't try to bond with every visitor to your website," advises self-promotion consultant Ilise Benun. "Just get to know your customers, then keep getting to know them. If you nurture these connections over time, real relationships will develop."

## Viral E-Marketing

Relax. We're not talking about computer viruses. *Viral marketing* refers to the extra reach and response you can potentially gain when recipients of your e-marketing message pass the e-mail on to other people.

Normally this is something that just happens because of the relative ease of passing on an e-mail—just click the "Forward" button and enter the name of the people you want to send it to. (With paper mail, by comparison, you've got to find an envelope, address it, put on a stamp, and take it to a mailbox.)

Sometimes when response to an e-marketing campaign is higher than expected, we suspect viral marketing as the cause. Viral marketing seems to be highest among people on computer and IT e-lists as well as communities of interest.

Most e-marketers just let it happen and enjoy the added reach. It may be worth testing an e-mail that deliberately asks for pass-along and even offers an incentive to do so. For instance, if you are sending an invitation for a free trial subscription to an e-zine for a limited period, you can extend the recipient's subscription for an extra month for everyone they pass the message to who accepts the offer.

An e-mail from gazelle.com, an online hosiery marketer, offers a free gift with purchase. The e-mail encourages pass-along by letting the recipient know anyone she forwards the e-mail to will also be extended the free gift offer. The P.S. reads: "Give this special gift offer to your friends by forwarding them this e-mail now. They'll be glad you did!"

## Make Money Renting Your E-List

Here's another way to profit from e-marketing. After building your house e-list, you can get $100 to $200 per thousand names or more by renting your e-list to other marketers!

A *mailing list manager* is an individual or firm who markets your house mailing list or database of customers and prospects on the open market. The manager promotes your list to mailers, agencies, list brokers, consultants, and others looking to rent mailing lists. A list manager represents one or more specific lists and gets a management fee every time the list is rented. A list broker, by comparison, arranges rental of any list the customer wants, and gets a commission regardless of which recommended lists are rented.

If you have a house list of customers and prospects that you are currently renting to other marketers, a list manager may be able to help you reduce the administrative work of list management while increasing your list rental revenues. If you don't currently rent your house list but are thinking of doing so, the list manager can help you evaluate the list's marketability and profit potential, and then market and promote your list to generate additional income.

Mailing lists rent from $100 to $200 per thousand names and more. As the list owner, you get this income minus commission fees that go to the list manager, broker, or ad agency. A well-managed list can generate $1 to $3 per name per year or more in revenue.

Therefore, if you put your house list of fifty-thousand names on the market, you can make an additional $50,000 to $200,000 or more in income with virtually no extra work or involvement on your part. (In regular direct mail, you can have mailers renting your list return undeliverable addresses to you. This way, you continually update your mailing list, with your list renters paying the cost of the postage.)

There are plenty of list managers you can hire to manage your list. Or, you can do it yourself. How do you decide which path to take?

"For eighteen years, I was the in-house list manager for Lillian Vernon, one of the nation's largest consumer direct marketers. Now I work for a list management firm representing Avon, Egghead, and other lists," says Joy Contreras, an experienced list manager.

"Because I've been on both sides of the desk, direct marketers often ask me, 'Does it make sense for us to manage our list in-house or go to an outside list management firm?' Here's a quick and simple self-assessment to help you decide."

- Do you have access to a creative director, graphic artist, and copywriting team to create ads, data cards, fax promotions, mailing pieces, and other list promotions?
- Do you have a sales force to sell your list? Does this sales force know all the brokers and, more important, which brokers represent which mailers and offers? Remember, 80 percent of list orders are generated through brokers.
- How strong is your sales team's knowledge of your list and how it relates to the mailer's offer? Can they make detailed recommendations to the list broker and mailer with rationales for using your list?
- Does your list sales force have credibility? Will list brokers and mailers take your recommendations seriously?
- Does your organization take the presentation on the road to brokers and mailers to sell them on the benefits of using your file?
- How's your company's visibility? Does your company participate in industry trade shows and functions? Does it have the same visibility and coverage as you could be getting from an outside list manager?
- Does your company have multiple products? If not, you may be losing the opportunity to cross-sell. By comparison, an outside list manager can often sell a broker or mailer on your list after they've received a count request or an order on another similar list.
- Does your in-house list department have the relationships with, and the in-depth knowledge of, the data processing

facilities needed to create subfiles, enhancements, and regression models to make your list more attractive to different types of mailers?

- Can you provide twenty-four-hour turnaround to list users in a crunch?
- Do you have an Internet presence, and can it project your image and list internationally?
- Does your company have the administrative and IT infrastructures to support list management tasks, including tracking of tests and continuations, orders, accounts receivables, and report generation?

We advise you to concentrate your list marketing efforts on brokers, not other marketers. There are perhaps millions of companies that use mailing lists, but—according to SRDS, the list-industry bible—only 754 list brokerage companies. Of those, only a few dozen handle e-lists. Yet 80 percent of list orders are placed by brokers, not mailers.

Therefore, it would make sense to concentrate your list marketing efforts on the brokers. Here are eight offers you can make to get more list brokers to recommend more of your lists for more tests, more often.

*1. Free test.* If you strongly believe your list will do well with a particular mailing, offer to do a five-thousand-name test for free. The potential revenue of the rollout far exceeds the modest cost of giving away a few thousand names for a test. Such an offer catches the broker's attention and shows you are interested in helping users get results rather than making a quick buck with numerous small one-shot tests.

*2. Guarantee.* If you don't want to offer a free test, offer a guarantee of performance. For example, if the list isn't profitable for a proven e-mail campaign, there's no charge, or the mailer can test another five thousand names from one of your other list properties. This strategy works when selling to brokers who shy away from free tests because it costs them a five-thousand-name commission.

*3. Net-net deal.* Help brokers reduce their clients' list rental costs. In a net-net arrangement, your list is merged-purged with other lists the mailer is testing. The mailer pays only for unduplicated names from your list. Depending on the level of duplication, this can make it anywhere from 10 to 50 percent cheaper to use your list.

*4. Discounted run charges.* Run charges for lists are typically $5 to $10 per thousand. A broker who is on the border about your list may be swayed if you offer to cut or even eliminate run charges for a test. The lower the cost, the better the chance of reaching or beating break-even on the test.

*5. Exclusives.* To build closer relationships with key brokers, offer them an exclusive. Special selects are an attractive offer. A broker whose client sells Windows NT applications might be interested in your list of corporate data center managers. By offering a selection of companies that have NT installed (something that is not listed on the data card for this file), you increase the odds the list will pay off for them.

Another exclusive you can offer is a first. When a list is updated, or new opt-in names become available, call your favorite broker, let him or her know, and give the broker first crack at these fresh names.

*6. Variable pricing.* A software company promoting a $250 program can afford a higher cost-per-thousand than a publisher selling a $19 book. Perhaps it's time list owners started offering tiered pricing based on the break-even economics of the particular mailing.

This is a radical idea for mailing lists. But space reps have already adopted this pricing model. Many publications, for example, have one rate for corporate advertisers and lower rates for retail and mail-order advertisers. Why not price your list based at least partially on the mailer's ability to make a test pay off?

In fact, the list industry has taken a small step in this direction for years, offering reduced rates for fund-raising mailings. Adding tiers to pricing can help price list rentals more realistically, so a broader range of mailers have a chance to mail the list at a profit.

*7. Better product.* Keep your list clean by updating daily or weekly. Increase selects with demographic overlays. The better the quality and selectivity of the list, the more likely brokers are to recommend it to their mailers.

Some list owners and managers offer to model their file against the mailer's customers, allowing the mailer to select prospects with similar characteristics. This can multiply response rates many times over on tests and continuations. If you don't know how to do this modeling in-house, there are many database consulting firms ready to assist you.

*8. Superior knowledge.* The more brokers know about the market a given mailing list reaches, the better able they are to make an intelligent decision about whether to recommend the list for a test.

List owners and managers often boast about how many well-known direct marketers have tested their lists, but brokers are much more interested in continuations. What percentage of those who tested the list rolled out? Seventy percent or better is impressive.

Another big selling point is for brokers (two of us, Michelle and Steve, are brokers) to learn that someone with a product similar to the client's product has tested the list and rolled out. That means the odds are good the list will work for the client's mail campaign too.

Incidentally, don't bother trying to sway brokers with fancy brochures and elaborate mailers. Brokers primarily just want to see a data card. It's the information—not the format—that makes or breaks a list promotion.

As a rule, the more data on the data card, the better. Write a clear, descriptive profile of who is on the list and the type of buyers they are. Include such useful things as size of average order, availability of hotline names, whether the prospects are buyers or inquirers, when the list was last updated, and how the names were generated—direct mail, retail, catalog, credit card, sweepstakes, telemarketing, or Internet.

But don't send brokers stacks of data cards that haven't been well targeted to the broker's clientele. If the brokers have to go through the pile to find the relevant lists, they're doing your work—and they'll resent it.

Another thing that rarely works is gifts, giveaways, and other special promotions. There's a conflict in a broker accepting a gift, such as a vacation or laptop computer, for recommending a particular list. It looks especially bad if the list doesn't work.

The biggest mistake a list owner or manager can make is not carefully analyzing the marketing challenges of direct marketers before approaching their list brokers with list suggestions. The quickest way to lose credibility is to recommend your lists when they are clearly inappropriate for the mail campaign. Don't recommend the Omaha Steaks customer file for a fund-raising mailing for Vegetarians Against Animal Slaughter. Do that even one time, and you may never get the broker's ear again. And because direct marketing is a relatively small and close-knit community, that's a mistake you cannot afford to make.

## Sticky Sites

A *sticky* website is one that people want to linger on, spend time with, and revisit frequently. The stickier the site, the more commerce it will generate—if it's an e-commerce site and not just an advertising site consisting of product literature posted on Web pages.

If you have the first C (commerce) taken care of, you'll increase your stickiness and sales by strengthening the other two Cs, content and community. If the content is relevant and interesting, people will use your site more—and buy more. If there is a real sense of community on the site, they'll visit often to see what's happening.

*National Geographic* increased e-commerce by surveying its gift shop to determine the most popular item. It turned out to be greeting cards. Their next e-campaign featured a set of wild animal cards, with four cards displayed per page. An e-mail encouraged prospects to click to the site to view the sample cards. The prospect could then choose to e-mail electronic versions of any card to a friend. People liked what they saw, and the opt-out rate to the e-mail was less than 0.04 percent. The click-through rate was 32 percent, and the campaign added twenty-five thousand new names to the *National Geographic* e-list within three weeks.

## Data Push

*Data push* is a technology that enables an e-marketer to tailor online follow-up to the needs and interests of each customer.

All Internet responses are collected in a database. The database stores unduplicated transaction, demographic, and promotion data.

The database contains rich information on each prospect. For instance, records might tell which sections of your website the prospect visited, the topics of interest, the products bought, the type of computer used, and so on. For example, if you have an entertainment website featuring restaurant menus, the database tells you what types of cuisine the prospect is interested in, and where in town he or she likes to eat—west side, east side, downtown, and so on.

Now let's say a particular downtown restaurant on the website is having a special dinner featuring vegetarian cuisine. With data push, an e-mail advertising the special can be sent just to those people in the database who like vegetarian food and eat downtown.

With cookies, data push, and other database technology, you can focus your e-marketing on the prospects and customers who have the highest likelihood of responding to your offer. What makes database marketing on the Internet so compelling today?

To begin with, database marketing is measurable. In the past, management was likely to place advertising (space, broadcast, outdoor) and automatically assume a cause-and-effect relationship between advertising expenditure and increased sales. Now top management is more bottom-line oriented. They want to know that if they spend X, that they will receive Y return on their investment. The key here is not sales, but profitable sales.

With database marketing, marketers can treat every prospect differently. To stay alive in the new millennium, companies need to "right-size" their sales force. Yet you increasingly need to stay in touch with customers to build awareness and create demand for your offers. With a smaller sales force, it isn't practical to target entire markets as if everyone has the same potential.

Through the use of sophisticated statistical models, database marketing enables you to classify every prospect and customer based on previous historic data and trends. This gives you the ability to predict, accurately and confidently, the potential for each individual's future business. Consequently, marketing programs may be customized to target an individual based on his or her probable return on investment.

This means that an individual with the highest probability for a profitable response can be targeted more often and differently than the individual with a low score, vastly increasing the overall profitability of your mailings while simultaneously reducing your costs.

Database marketing gives you a sustainable advantage to help you stay ahead of your competition. Today's marketers have witnessed an explosion of products all vying for the same target audience. Yet the costs of all forms of advertising have steadily increased. Once again database marketers have the edge. By knowing which individuals have the greatest probability of responding, and armed with in-depth knowledge about the demographics of their prospective buyers, database marketers have an overwhelming competitive advantage. By concentrating your efforts on the most responsive segments, you can deliver personalized messages to your prospective buyers and overpower competitors who use traditional mass-marketing methods.

Database marketing lets you precisely control the number of times and messages reaching your prospective buyer. Through a marketing database you can keep track of how many times an individual has been contacted and which product offerings he or she received. You can also suppress your competitors' names so that they will not know your marketing strategy until it's too late to react.

Another advantage is database marketing's ability to segment your e-market. Some prospects, for example, browse the Internet for information but prefer to buy offline; others are totally into the Internet and want transactions completed online from start to finish. Some prospects do almost all of their shopping on the Internet; some mix online and offline; some buy hardly anything. According to an article in *DM News* (March 1, 1999), three-quarters of all sales on the Internet are made to 25 percent of the people online.

## More About Database Marketing on the Internet

With database marketing, you can gain the information you need to make better marketing decisions. The result is more targeted promotions that reduce your costs (because you're contacting only the best prospects) and boost your results (because you don't waste time contacting people who are unlikely to be interested).

For more than a decade, direct marketing has been making a transition to database marketing. Internet direct mail, only a year or so old, is making an even more rapid transition to "Internet database marketing." Database marketing is a powerful tool in both conventional and online marketing. But the Internet gives it the added benefit of faster delivery of the campaigns you conceive.

With Internet database marketing, you use the information in your company databases as well as any useful external information to either improve or enhance your marketing efforts—as well as evaluate new markets or the potential of new products you plan to launch. Internet database marketing achieves this by extensive use of database systems and database-related tools. You can also gain the ability to send one-to-one personalized e-mail content based on collaborative filtering (discussed in Chapter 4, page 88), buying habits, Internet surfing habits, and buying preferences.

"Companies can leverage Web traffic data for a competitive advantage," explains John Payne of IBM. According to Payne, analysis of Web traffic requires data created by the Web server software. This data contains Web log records known as *hits*. Every item on a Web page generates a hit. Logically, the more pictures a site owner puts on a page, the more hits the Web server records in the log.

*Page views* are simply the number of times Web pages have been seen by a user. *Visits* are the series of pages seen when a user comes to (visits) a website. Typically, there are multiple hits per page view and multiple page views per visit. An analysis by IBM indicates an average rate of five hits per page view and an average of five page views per visit.

There is a maturity cycle all website owners progress through as they experience the power of the Internet. (See Figure 10.1.) As a website becomes an integral and strategic part of a company's business plan, site owners want more information. They realize that reporting on only hits, or even page views, while interesting, does not provide an ability to improve site effectiveness, particularly when this statistic can be easily manipulated by website design.

However, investigating and interpreting visit patterns can be very insightful. Looking at the most prevalent paths site visitors travel, where they came from, and how much time they spend on specific pages or categories of pages are important techniques in

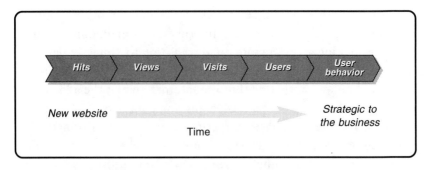

**Figure 10.1. The goal is to turn visitors into customers.**

measuring a site's success. Investigating content affinities and behavior patterns of site visitors can help determine the most effective placement of information.

In addition, understanding the quantity and quality of visitors—for example, understanding new visitor behavior versus repeat visitor behavior—can make a dramatic difference in a website's success. With this analytic capability, companies gain meaningful insight into their users and their users' behavior, allowing them to target their content. They gain improved customer satisfaction and, ultimately, increased sales.

The three elements of website analysis that prove to be most important are path analysis, referral analysis, and advanced data mining. Any such analysis, to be effective, requires a well-designed underlying database and a fail-safe method of populating that database with clean data. This data must be stored in a manner that the sequence of pages each site visitor sees when he comes to a website (visits) can be determined.

Path analysis is a methodology of investigating what pages are seen before and after a specific page. This analysis includes determining time spent on each page as well as entry and exit points from the website. It is an effective technique for measuring content affinities as well as effectiveness of site design. It can also be used to measure the impact of creatives such as animated pictures, added to a specific page with the intent of attracting site visitors to a specific part of the website. The Internet is a wonderful medium for experimentation with marketing and design strategies, for one can change content, immediately measure the results, and take appropriate action based upon those results.

Referral analysis is also very valuable. This process determines where website visitors came from before visiting the site. It can be very effective in measuring the clicks on ads placed on other websites and the subsequent Web pages these clickers investigated. Such analysis can also reveal how long they remained on each page, the duration of the entire visit, and whether a purchase was made. This information can help assess the value of affiliations with other websites or search engine traffic, including search terms used that resulted in those valuable visits to the site. It helps answer the question, "Where do the best customers come from, what are they looking for, and what do they do when they get there?" This analysis allows the website owner to make appropriate modifications and to structure business agreements based upon fact rather than intuition.

Data mining can be an ambiguous term when used indiscriminately by site analysis tool vendors as well as website owners. Many will use the term when they have implemented only a query interface for analyzing data. This application is known to as *verification-driven data mining*, where the user validates a hypothesis such as, "traffic from a specific location is increasing at an x percent rate."

A more sophisticated implementation of data mining known as *discovery-driven data mining* utilizes techniques such as clustering, associations, and neural induction. This application requires advanced software and yields results created by the data relationships and not by hypotheses. This advanced data mining technology can be very valuable in determining content affinities as well as site visitor behaviors, which can lead to increased content effectiveness. One example is the collaborative filtering methodology discussed in Chapter 4, page 88.

Path analysis, referral analysis, and data mining can be effectively implemented without the use of technology that is perceived to invade consumer privacy, such as registration or the use of persistent cookies. However, if either technology is implemented, a significantly more robust analysis can occur, showing, for example, behavior comparisons of new visitors versus returning visitors, or even analyzing demographic patterns by visitor behaviors and content areas, such as, "show me the incomes and age levels of visitors to specific pages or content areas on our website."

"Would it help you to know that 35 percent of your largest customers are golfers?" asks Internet consultant Ed Ziv. "Think what would happen if you then put an article or an ad in *Golf Digest*, or if you sponsored someone on the pro tour."

Or what if you could find out what books your customers read, or what kind of cars they drive, or where they vacation? You would know how to relate to them in terms they find meaningful and could market your product to their lifestyle and needs. The idea is to best position yourself to the people who want to talk with you.

The Internet is a two-way communication tool: you can put customer surveys on your site and provide freebies and drawings for giveaways in return for answering a few questions. But let's kick it up a level. Not all two-way communication requires that the client talk with you. Tracking software called *referrer logs* is a great tool. Products such as Access Watch or Microsoft's Usage Analyst will tell you:

- how many people hit your page
- date and time of each hit to your site
- the times of harvest and lightest traffic
- average number of pages viewed by each visitor
- the pages viewed on your site that were viewed most frequently

This is wonderful information for spotting trends. If, for example, the page dedicated to launching your big new product isn't drawing them in, or if it peaked three weeks ago, you want to know about it. If people are landing on your home page, but not clicking past it, you know you've got to put out a different welcome mat.

Most of the products will also give you specific information, such as the visitor's domain name, browser type, machine, and the page the visitor was on before dropping in on you. If you can know exactly who your users are, you can keep specific user preferences in a database.

Many sites, including Yahoo! and MSN, allow users to customize the look of their personal home page when they access the service. Want to see the local weather? Want to see how your stocks are doing? This information is stored in cookies (small files placed on your hard drive), and the service uses these to configure itself to the user's preferences.

Fortified with this kind of information, you can ensure that your message is getting to the people who want what you've got. But use personalized information carefully—don't overdo it. One national pizza franchise experimented with this a few years ago and found customers were unnerved when the person answering their call could say, without introduction, "Hello Mr. Smith. I guess your wife is out of town. Our profile on you shows a 50 percent chance you'll be pigging out on another pepperoni tonight."

There are two options for storing all this information; either it can be stored on your server, or, to save you storage space and give your customer a little more privacy, you can store the information as cookie files on the customer's machine. These files can collect massive amounts of additional information for you, such as the customer's real name, actual address, demographic information, and even a full history of his or her most recently visited websites.

When using cookies, consider putting a notice somewhere on your site that you use them, Ziv advises. Give users the option of not having you store their information. You may tell people "our lips are sealed," or you may want to have a box that says, "Click here if you don't want us to share your information." Either way, have a privacy policy, post it, and scrupulously honor it.

Why do we urge businesses to support their Internet marketing efforts with database support? For the website owner who truly believes in the power of the Internet to effectively deliver solutions, the time and resources spent in analyzing Web traffic can yield significant competitive advantages. It does require an investment of time and talent to determine those valuable "ahas!" that will deliver a competitive advantage in this new worldwide medium, but it is an investment with a great return.

In an increasing number of markets and product categories, mass-marketing no longer works: customized campaigns and individually tailored messages are necessary. E-mail marketing combined with a database gives you the optimum tool for delivering this degree of customization and personalization.

Return on investment (ROI) calculations are getting more and more important; marketing as an investment increasingly has to justify its returns. Database marketing gives you a tool for putting a meaningful number on answers to questions like, "How much business did your latest e-campaign generate?"

Internet database marketing can help you:

- improve your marketing efforts
- measure results
- enhance customer service
- get to know your customers' preferences and buying habits better
- calculate lifetime customer value
- learn how to distinguish between valuable customers and not-that-valuable ones
- select target markets for your e-marketing activities more carefully
- evaluate diverse propensity-to-purchase indicators
- calculate the potential of new markets, new target groups, and new products within your database

Standard methods often cannot answer these questions. Database marketing, on the other hand, provides a point-and-click graphical user interface (GUI) for ad hoc queries of information. More sophisticated software can perform calculations and generate reports that show the answers to the aforementioned concerns in a clear graphical presentation.

With computer-aided marketing, e-marketers profit in numerous ways. To begin with, being more precise with one's activities saves time and resources, as does targeting your market segmentation more accurately.

More precise targeting, in turn, increases customer satisfaction by providing the right information at the right time to the right customer. Increasing customer satisfaction improves business performance in the long run. Response rates from e-campaigns will dramatically increase, while bounce-backs and especially opt-outs considerably decrease.

With e-marketing, you can dramatically reduce your direct marketing costs, overcoming rising postal rates and production, creative, and printing costs. You can also speed delivery and response times, so you get results in days, not weeks or months. With database marketing, you can fine-tune your e-marketing to deliver relevant messages to the most qualified prospects more often, increasing your response rates significantly. The combination is the most powerful tool available today to marketers selling products and services to defined audiences reachable through the Internet.

## Is Traditional Direct Mail Marketing Dead?

To some of you—most likely the Generation Xers—the e-mail success stories in this book sound like an opportunity made in heaven, a chance to take a leap ahead in e-commerce, open up worldwide markets, and free yourself from the cost, slowness, and clumsiness of paper marketing.

Others—many Baby Boomers and Matures—look at the Internet like a deer caught in the path of an oncoming car looking at the headlights: too stunned to move and scared out of its wits. But aside from its newness and techie nature, is Internet marketing anything to really be frightened about? For example, does it threaten to make traditional (paper) direct mail and catalogs obsolete?

One person who believes so is Ted Wham, director of membership at Excite@Home Inc. in Redwood, California. "Direct mail will remain viable for certain niche markets," said Wham at a Direct Marketing Association meeting, according to a report in *DM News* (September 13, 1999). "It will not remain viable, in my observation, for consumer-based or large-scale business-to-business marketing operations." We, however, disagree.

To be sure, in conventional direct mail, cost per thousand is rising, response rates are dropping, lists are suffering from fatigue, and the universe of available names that you can mail profitably is slipping. At the same time, the Internet beckons to direct marketers with the lure of millions of online prospects reachable in an instant, with no production costs or turnaround time, and at virtually zero cost per thousand.

According to Forrester Research (*CIO WebBusiness*, section 2, October 1, 1999, p. 18), the Internet will siphon off 10 percent of all U.S. ad spending—a total of $27 billion—away from traditional media, with newspapers and direct mail being the hardest hit.

Why then do so many traditional direct marketers, including us, think that even in this electronic age, paper direct mail will continue as a major marketing tool well into the new millennium? Simply because every time pundits predicted the demise of the traditional printed media in the past, it didn't happen. When advocates of CD-ROMs, software, the Internet, and electronic publishing proclaim in loud voices that printed direct mail will soon be dead, we get the feeling of *moo ja vu*—meaning we've heard this bull before.

Futurists have been predicting the death of traditional media for decades. Yet it never comes to pass. Consider Thomas Edison, for example.

When Thomas Edison invented the phonograph in 1876, he did it to bring music into the average American home. In his early model, the "records" were made of cylinders coated with tinfoil, onto which the vibrations from sound waves were impressed with a needle.

Once he got a working model, Edison saw his invention could be used to carry the spoken word as well as music. He publicly proclaimed that the book-on-record (precursor of today's audiobook industry) was a far superior learning tool to the printed page—and that by the end of the millennium, all college students would be learning by listening to recorded texts, and paper textbooks would be obsolete. In 1996, however, textbook sales in the United States grossed more than $4 billion.

In 1964, when Sony introduced the CV-2000, the first home VCR, technologists proclaimed that the new videocassettes heralded the death of the printed word. Futurist and science fiction author Isaac Asimov responded with an essay describing what he called "the ultimate cassette."

Such a cassette, said Asimov, would be lightweight and portable. It would not require a player or need to be plugged into a power supply. It could be searched to look up specific information or access particular sections. And its per-unit cost should be low. At the end of the essay, he revealed that he was, in fact, describing a *book*, to demonstrate that with all these advantages, print media might be supplemented by—but never replaced with—electronic media.

On the other hand, a recent Roper poll shows that 69 percent of Americans prefer to get their news from TV, versus only 37 percent from newspapers—indicating that we are indeed becoming more oriented toward electronic media and less toward print. More evidence: the average American household watches TV fifty hours a week. And from 1980 to 1995, the number of daily newspapers in America dropped from 1,743 to 1,548—a decline of 11 percent.

"In the future, the act of printing words on paper will be as common as writing in stone is today," said Nicholas Negroponte, author of *Being Digital* (Vintage Books, 1996), in a recent interview with *Publisher's Weekly*. "The reason that so many works are printed on paper today in newspapers, magazines, and books is that paper is the most ubiquitous, economical, and easy-to-use display device we have.

"Computer screens are still comparatively rare, far too expensive, and they're anything but easy to use—not to mention uncomfortable in bed. But all these conditions will change. By the year 2050, paper will be rare because it will be far too expensive, and it will be difficult to use. A three-year-old child of that year will have to be told why paper doesn't make sounds, show movies, or read a story to him by itself when he's ready to doze off."

According to Dan Poynter, author of *The Self-Publishing Manual*, 80 percent of U.S. families did not buy or read a book last year. Seventy percent of U.S. adults have not been in a bookstore in the past five years, and 58 percent of the adult population never reads another book after high school.

On the other hand, notes Poynter, U.S. adults spent $25.6 billion on books in 1996—almost five times the $5.4 billion they spent going to the movies. "The pessimist says our market is smaller than we thought," Poynter tells die-hard print fans. "The optimist says our potential market [for print] is larger than we thought."

Newspaper columnist Charles Krauthammer predicts that print will all but vanish in the next century. "The Gutenberg age will end with the 20th century," writes Krauthammer. "First to go will be the newspaper. Then the magazine. Then the book. Their paper versions, that is. They will all find a new life on screen, on disk, on line. What is dying is printing, not writing. It is our way of transmitting words—not words themselves—that is obsolete."

Are consumers proving Krauthammer right? "The appearance of new means of information does not destroy earlier ones; it frees them from one kind of constraint or another," argues writer Umberto Eco, noting that painting and drawing did not die with the invention of photography and cinema.

There is growing anecdotal evidence to support the conclusion that electronic information will not eliminate paper anytime soon. Sarah Stambler, editor of *Marketing with Technology News*, reports that a major study found businesses are ordering 10 percent more paper due to people printing out the e-mail they receive. Consultant Marlene Jensen reports that in a promotion offering a newsletter aimed at webmasters, 96 percent chose the printed version over the e-mail version—even though the print version cost $100 more.

The "paperless office" and the Internet's threat to make paper obsolete may never come to pass, especially in marketing. In an article in *Metalworking Marketing* (December 1999, p. 4), Michael Menaker points out that print has many advantages over computer-based communications, including resolution, portability, and ease of use. "In this interactive age, is there still a place for the traditional corporate capabilities brochure? Absolutely!" he concludes.

The Direct Marketing Association economic forecasts paint a bright picture for traditional direct mail—at least in the short-term future. In 1999, expenditures for traditional direct mail advertising in the United States were approximately $41.8 billion versus only $1.1 billion for interactive advertising (e-mail, the Web). According to the Direct Marketing Association's List Usage Survey, two-thirds of respondents reported increasing the quantity of their mailings in 1998, while only 11 percent decreased (as reported in *Sales & Marketing Management*, November 1999, p. 118).

By 2003, annual expenditures in the United States will increase to $52.7 billion for direct mail and $5.27 billion for interactive advertising. That means traditional direct mail marketers will outspend Internet marketers by ten to one.

At the same time, $5.27 billion spent on interactive advertising in 2003 is almost *five times* the $1.1 billion spent four years earlier. This fivefold increase in Internet direct mail volume may actually relieve some of the fatigue from overuse that traditional lists are currently suffering.

A recent article in *Memo to Mailers*, a newsletter published by the U.S. Post Office, cites a study by the Papercom Alliance indicating that the Internet helps traditional direct marketing rather than hurts it. According to the study, "steady growth in mail order was boosted by sales over the Internet." Total mail-order sales grew by 10 percent in 1998 to $358.8 billion. Growth from traditional mail-order sources *excluding* the Internet was 7.91 percent.

What's more, there are some chinks even in the shining armor of the marketing knight called the Internet. To begin with, the model for e-mail marketing is permission-based, whereas traditional direct marketing does not currently require permission to mail. This means the Internet does not give you the kind of universe availability that traditional mailing lists do.

And with millions of websites and countless e-mail messages being sent daily, recipients are already on overload. As the number of people using the Internet increases, the situation will only get worse; more than four trillion e-mail messages were sent last year. This may decrease response rates while causing more users to begin opting out of receiving further e-mail.

Marketers know that form follows function, and that the medium should fit the message—and the Internet, while perfect for some offers, is less than ideal for others. The Internet is a great medium for software marketers, who can advertise, take orders, and actually deliver their products completely online.

The Internet is also ideal for marketers who need to provide customers with access to product and service information and ordering capability on a round-the-clock basis. This factor is part of the reason for the growing popularity of online stock trading (the other reason being the reduced trading fees brokerages can offer by eliminating the live broker).

Graphics-intensive marketing, on the other hand, requires bandwidth and speed the current Internet infrastructure lacks. That's probably why Victoria's Secret mails us a catalog every other week or so, even though they have an active website complete with e-commerce. For example, when Victoria's Secret broadcast its first live online fashion show in February 1999, the extraordinary volume of traffic it generated created technical problems that prevented users from seeing the show.

Does this mean we don't consider the Internet as a force to be reckoned with? On the contrary, IBM predicts Internet commerce to reach $400 billion annually by 2002. But we see the Internet and traditional snail mail as more complementary than competitive.

Yes, there will be mailings that don't happen because the direct marketer opts for Internet direct mail instead. But just as some catalog customers prefer an order form and others prefer a toll-free number, some consumers prefer the Internet and others prefer a piece of paper.

Add the Internet to your marketing arsenal? Certainly. That's what this book is all about. Tighten the focus of paper direct mail, catalogs, and print ads to improve your return on investment? Yes. But cut them off instantly and go 100 percent electronic? Do so only at your peril—and at the risk of having many of your customers go somewhere else.

## To Sum It All Up

The e-maillennium is here. Welcome to the age of the Internet. The race to win in e-business is on. By mastering e-mail marketing, you gain an edge that will soon leave your competitors in the dust. Too bad for them—but good for you.

# Sources and Resources

## Software

AWeber Systems
4547 Old Oak Road
Suite B
Doylestown, PA 18901
Phone: 800-531-5065
Web: www.aweber.com
*Autoresponder*

Crown Industries
1630 N. Main Street  #310
Walnut Creek, CA 94596
Phone: 925-938-0770
E-mail: info@moneyfun.com
Web: www.moneyfun.com

Email King
1040 S. Mt. Vernon Avenue #G146
Colton, CA 92324
Phone: 909-797-5424
Web: www.netbillions.com
*Bulk e-mail program*

ENN
6711 Glenray Drive
Houston, TX 77084-1067
E-mail: enn@phoenix.net
Web: www.phoenix.net/~enn/$autoenn.html
*Autoresponder*

Exactis
707 17th Street
Suite 2850
Denver, CO 80202
Phone: 800-699-7006
E-mail: expresssales@exactis.com
Web: www.exactis.com
*Bulk e-mail program*

Frontier Productions
69A Liberty Ship Way
Sausalito, CA 94965
Phone: 415-331-4900
Fax: 415-331-4904
E-mail: justin@frontierproductions.com
Web: www.frontierproductions.com
*E-mail broadcasting and management software*

General Interactive
66 Church Street
Cambridge, MA 02138
Phone: 617-354-8585
E-mail: info@interactive.com
Web: www.echomail.com
*Autoresponders*

LivePerson
665 Broadway
Suite 1200
New York, NY 10012

Phone: 212-277-8950
Web: www.liveperson.com
*Software that enables your visitors to chat online with your cus-
tomer service reps*

L-Soft International, Inc.
8100 Corporate Drive
Suite 350
Landover, MD 20785-2231
Phone: 800-399-5449
E-mail: sales@lsoft.com
Web: www.lsoft.com
*LISTSERVER and other e-mail software*

Macromedia, Incorporated
600 Townsend Street
San Francisco, CA 94103
Phone: 800-326-2128 or 415-252-2000
Web: www.macromedia.com
*Collaborative filtering and other e-business applications*

Microsoft bCentral
Phone: 800-426-9400
Web: www.bcentral.com
*ListBot automatically lets you collect Internet addresses of visitors
to your website and send them e-mail.*

Net Perceptions
7901 Flying Cloud Drive
Eden Prairie, MN 55344-7905
Phone: 800-466-0711
E-mail: info@netperceptions.com
Web: www.netperceptions.com
*Collaborative filtering software*

RevNet
3305 West Mill Drive

Huntsville, AL
Phone: 888-999-1420
*E-mail list merge, database, and transmission software*

Servicesoft
Phone: 800-737-8738
Web: www.servicesoft.com
*High-end autoresponder*

Vertex Inc.
1041 Old Cassatt Road
Berwyn, PA 19312
Phone: 800-355-3500
Web: www.vertexinc.com
*EQuantum software for calculating sales and use tax on e-commerce transactions*

Voron Communications
8001 Castor Avenue
Suite 199
Philadelphia, PA 19152
Phone: 215-742-2440
E-mail: admin@voron.com
Web: www.voron.com
*Autoresponder*

WorldProfit
16912 - 111 Avenue
Edmonton, AB, Canada T5N 4G9
Phone: 780-444-7477
Web: www.worldprofit.com
*Listserver and autoresponder*

# E-Mail List Brokers and Service Bureaus

Act One
165 Pleasant Street
Suite 19

Village Plaza 1
Marblehead, MA 01945-2308
Phone: 800-228-5478
E-mail: actlist@ma.ultranet.com
Web: www.actonelists.com

Acxiom/Direct Media
200 Pemberwick Road
Greenwich, CT 06830
Phone: 203-532-1000
Web: www.directmedia.com
*E-lists, transmission, merge-purge*

Admail.net
DM Group
251 West Garfield Road
Aurora, OH 44202
Phone: 330-995-0864
Web: www.admail.net
*E-list brokerage, management, hygiene, merge-purge, database management, bulk e-mailing*

ALCi Interactive
88 Orchard Road CN-5219
Princeton, NJ 08543
Phone: 800-ALC-LIST
E-mail: sgirt@amlist.com
Web: www.amlist.com
*Database marketing, e-list rentals, e-list management, transmission*

Applied Information Group
100 Market Street
Kenilworth, NJ 07033
Phone: 908-241-7007
E-mail: daveb@appliedinfogroup.com
Web: www.appliedinfogroup.com
*HTML and visual e-mail, online campaign tracking, e-mail transmission, database management*

Bigfoot Interactive
1841 Broadway
Suite 609
New York, NY 10023
Phone: 212-262-1118
Web: www.bigfootinteractive.com
*E-lists, transmission, Internet database management, consulting*

CertifiedMail.com
140 Mountain Avenue
Springfield, NJ 07081
Phone: 973-467-1024
Web: www.certifiedmail.com
*Online certified e-mail services*

Digital Impact
177 Bovet Road, #200
San Mateo, CA 94402
Phone: 650-356-3400
E-mail: info@doubleclick.net
Web: www.digitalimpact.com
*Personalized e-campaigns*

DoubleClick
450 West 33rd Street, 16th floor
New York, NY 10276
Phone: 212-381-5705
E-mail: info@doubleclick.net
Web: www.doubleclick.com
*Closed-loop banner ad and e-marketing*

EClass Direct
625 Miramontes Street
Half Moon Bay, CA  94019
Phone: 650-712-6700
E-mail: info@eclassdirect.com
Web: www.eclassdirect.com
*E-mail marketing and transmission bureau*

eGain Communications
455 W. Maude Avenue
Sunnyvale, CA 94086
Phone: 888-603-4246
E-mail: sales@egain.com
Web: www.egain.com
*Software and services for e-commerce sites*

e-PostDirect
1 Blue Hill Plaza
Pearl River, NY 10965
Phone: 800-409-4443
Fax: 914-620-9035
E-mail: michelle.feit@edithroman.com
Web: www.epostdirect.com
*Opt-in e-mail list management; e-mail list brokerage; I-marketing consultation; personalized Internet campaign creation, execution, and tracking; HTML and Visual Mail, transmission, e-mail address appending, merge-purge, website design, banner ad placement, e-commerce*

iQ.com
12950 Saratoga Avenue
Suite B
Saratoga, CA 95070
Phone: 408-777-4000
E-mail: info@iq.com
Web: www.iq.com
*Online e-mail and Web-based promotions for e-marketers*

Walter Karl
1 Blue Hill Plaza
Pearl River, NY 10965
E-mail: kathye@walterkarl.com
Phone: 914-620-0700

Merchant Mail Network
Phone: 650-286-7300

Web: www.digital-impact.com
*Specializes in transmitting targeted rich-media e-mail to existing customers*

MessageMedia, Inc. Headquarters Boulder, Colorado
6060 Spine Road
Boulder, CO 80301
Voice: 303-440-7550
Toll-Free 888-440-7550
Sales: 800-565-0198
Fax: 303-440-0303

Millard Group
10 Vose Farm Road
P.O. Box 890
Peterborough, NH 03458-0890
Phone: 603-924-9262, ext. 313, Frank Quaranta
Fax: 603-924-7810

Net Masters
Phone: 800-242-0363, ext. 2082
E-mail: netmasters@grabmail.com
*Bulk mailing, URL submission, search engine ranking, e-lists, website design*

OakNet Publishing
2630B NW 41st Street
Gainesville, FL 32606
Phone: 352-376-5822
E-mail: editor@oaknetpub.com
Web: www.oaknetpub.com
*Transmission of e-zines*

Pinpoint Media
1400 East Hill Boulevard
Deerfield Beach, FL 33441
Phone: 954-725-6455
E-mail: info@pinpointmedia.com

Web: www.pinpointmedia.com
*Opt-in e-lists*

PostMasterDirect.com
A NetCreations Company
379 W. Broadway
Suite 202
New York, NY 10012
Phone: 212-625-1370
E-mail: sales@postmasterdirect.com
Web: www.postmasterdirect.com
*Opt-in e-lists, merge-purge, transmission*

ROI Direct.com
100 Bush Street
San Francisco, CA 94104
Phone: 800-420-4224
E-mail: info@roidirect.com
Web: www.roidirect.com
*E-commerce site development and hosting, e-mail marketing programs, e-list and database services, inbound e-mail customer service*

24/7 Media
1250 Broadway, 28th Floor
New York, NY 10001
Phone: 212-231-7100
E-mail: mtuohy@247media.com
Web: www.247media.com
*Opt-in e-lists*

SparkList
1800 W. Mason Street
Green Bay, WI 54303
Phone: 920-490-5901
E-mail: info@sparklist.com
Web: www.sparklist.com
*E-list hosting and management services, online discussion hosting*

# Website Design Firms

Rabi Das, President
Etensity
2070 Chainbridge Road
Suite 180 West
Vienna, VA 22182
Phone: 703-827-5840
E-mail: bdas@etensity.com

Barry Fox
FoxTek
49 West Street
Northport, NY 11768
Phone: 516-754-4304

Kent Martin
Network Creative
104 Mountain Avenue
Gilette, NJ 07930
Phone: 908-903-9090

Susan Mintzer
Quadrix
255 Old New Brunswick Road
Suite South 220
Piscataway, NJ 08854
Phone: 732-235-2600
*E-commerce websites*

Jason Petefish
Silver Star Productions
87 Aspen Ledges Road
Ridgefield, CT 06877
Phone: 203-894-1849

# E-Business Solutions Providers

A2.com
Phone: 742-741-8913

Web: www.a2.com
*E-mail with "live" response forms built into message. Data is completed in forms captured in the mailer's database.*

BizRate Inc.
4053 Redwood Avenue
Los Angeles, CA 90066
Phone: 310-305-3506
Web: www.bizrate.com
*Rating service for e-commerce sites that lets managers get customer feedback at low cost*

CyberCash
2100 Reston Parkway, 3rd Floor
Reston, VA 20191
Phone: 703-620-4200
Web: www.cybercash.com
*Provider of secure Internet credit card processing services*

Digital Storage
SubmitOrder.com
7003 Post Road, 3rd Floor
Dublin, OH 43016
Phone: 877-719-6010 or 740-548-0253
*Outsourced e-commerce services including website design, deployment, operation, order processing, payment verification, product picking, packaging, shipping, phone support, and data mining*

e-centives
6903 Rockledge Drive
Suite 1200
Bethesda, MD 20817
Phone: 877-323-6848
Web: www.e-centives.com
*Personalized digital coupons, printed coupons, and other special offers delivered to Web surfers based on their unique shopping profiles and interests*

EContacts
20 Pickering Street, 2nd Floor
Needham, MA 02492
Phone: 781-449-1440
Toll-Free: 888-718-1845
Fax: 781-455-6526
E-mail: info@econtacts.com
Web: www.econtacts.com
*E-mail-based relationship management program*

ETracks.com
A division of Learn2.com
White Plains, NY
Web: www.etracks.com
*AdaptiveProxy Tracking tracks e-mail recipients who respond to a particular URL in reply to an e-mail broadcast. Measures click-throughs to the site as well as online purchases.*

Flash Creative Management
433 Hackensack Avenue
Hackensack, NJ  07601
Phone: 201-489-2500
*Management consultants*

Henry Haugland
Quest Systems Group
24 Arbor Circle
Natick, MA  01760
Phone: 508-647-4710
Fax: 508-650-3517
E-mail: info@questgroup.com
*Personalized URLs for response to e-marketing messages*

IBM
New Orchard Road
Armonk, NY 10504
Phone: 800-426-2255

Web: www.ibm.com
*Full suite of applications for e-commerce includes Net.Commerce, which enables companies to market and sell in a secure and scalable way on the Internet*

Mercury Interactive
1325 Borregas Avenue
Sunnyvale, CA 94089
Phone: 800-TEST-911
E-mail: info@merc-int.com
Web: www.merc-int.com
*Tools for testing e-commerce websites' ability to handle varying traffic loads*

MyEvents.com
245 Vallejo Street
San Francisco, CA 94111
Phone: 415-344-4800
Web: www.licensing.myevents.com
*Customized calendars, contact managers, photo albums, bulletin boards, messaging, and other groupware capabilities you can add to your website to give it greater value to visitors*

MyPoints.com
565 Commercial Street, 4th Floor
San Francisco, CA 94111-3031
Phone: 415-676-3700
E-mail: steve.markowitz@mypoints.com
Web: www.mypoints.com
*Internet bonus-point rewards programs*

Net2Phone
171 Main Street
Hackensack, NJ 07601
Phone: 877-732-8693
E-mail: bizdev@net2phone.com
Web: www.net2phoneprofits.com/bus

*Allows customers to visit your site and speak with a service representative using only one phone line. Customer service agent can push Web pages to the customer.*

Network Solutions
505 Huntman Park Drive
Herndon, VA 20170
Phone: 703-742-0400
Web: www.networksolutions.com
*Search for and register domain names online.*

2Share Corporate Edge
221 Main Street
Suite 800
San Francisco, CA 94105
Phone: 800-815-7612
Web: www.2bridge.com
*Third-party managed corporate intranets and extranets*

Vicom Computer Services, Inc.
60 Carolyn Boulevard
Farmingdale, NY 11735
Phone: 631-694-3900
Fax: 631-694-2640
E-mail: vverola@vicomnet.com
Web: www.vicomnet.com
Contact: Victor V. Verola
*Authoring creative animated Internet direct mail for marketing*

Web Cards
Web: www.printing.com
*Specializes in printing promotional postcards to promote websites*

## Internet Direct Mail Copywriters

Bob Bly
22 E. Quackenbush Avenue

Dumont, NJ 07628
Phone: 201-385-1220
E-mail: rwbly@bly.com
Web: www.bly.com

Al Bredenberg Creative Services
71 Franklin Street
Danbury, CT 06810
Phone: 203-791-8204
E-mail: ab@copywriter.com
Web: www.copywriter.com

Trevor Levine
Marketing Experts
3284 Adeline Street, Suite B
Berkeley, CA 94703
Phone: 510-665-6520
E-mail: levine@marketingexperts.com
Web: www.marketingexperts.com

Ivan Levison
14 Los Cerros Drive
Greenbrae, CA 94904
Phone: 415-461-0672
E-mail: ivan@levison.com
Web: www.levison.com

Yanik Silver
14312 Fairdale Road
Silver Spring, MD 20905
Phone: 301-656-2424
E-mail: yanik@surefiremarketing.com
Web: www.instantsalesletters.com

Scott T. Smith
Business Copywriting.Net
116 Silverwood Drive
Bozeman, MT 59715

Phone: 800-798-4471
Web: www.copywriting.net

## Get Your Website on Search Engines

Fee-Based Services
SubmitIt! www.submitit.com
!Register-It! www.registerit.com
*Will submit your site to as many as 400 search engines and directories*

Search Directories
Yahoo! www.yahoo.com
LookSmart www.looksmart.com
Excite www.excite.com
Lycos www.lycos.com
*Can take weeks or months to get your website categorized*

www.searchengine.com
*Information on how to maximize the use of search engines to promote your website*

Search Service
AltaVista  www.altavista.com
Infoseek www.infoseek.com
*These two are the quickest way to index site selections (usually within days)*

## Books

*Advertising on the Internet* by Robbin Zeff and Brad Aronson (John Wiley & Sons)

*Business-to-Business Internet Marketing* by Barry Silverstein (Maximum Press)

*Connections: A Guide to On-Line Writing* by Daniel Anderson, Bret Benjamin, and Bill Paredes-Holt (Allyn and Bacon)

*Cybertalk That Sells* by Herschell Gordon Lewis and Jamie Murphy (Contemporary Books)

*Cyberwriting* by Joe Vitale (Amacom)

*How to Make a Fortune on the Information Superhighway* by Laurence A. Canter and Martha S. Siegel (HarperCollins)

*The Internet Marketing Plan* by Kim Bayne (John Wiley & Sons)

*Making Money on the Internet* by Alfred and Emily Glossbrenner (McGraw-Hill)

*Marketing on the Internet* by Judy Strauss and Raymond Frost (Prentice Hall)

*Marketing Online* by Marcia Yudkin (Morris Publishing)

*The One-to-One Fieldbook* by Don Peppers, Martha Rogers, and Bob Dorf (Bantam Books)

*Online Marketing Handbook* by Daniel S. Janal (John Wiley & Sons)

*Permission Marketing* by Seth Godin (Simon & Schuster)

*Poor Richard's E-mail Publishing* by Chris Pirillo (Top Floor Publishing)

*Poor Richard's Internet Marketing and Promotions* by Peter Kent and Tara Calishain (Top Floor Publishing)

*Roger C. Parker's Guide to Web Content and Design* by Roger C. Parker (MIS Press)

*Relationship Marketing on the Internet* by Roger C. Parker (Adams Media)

*Simple Steps to E-Mail Success* by Joy Van Skiver (WREXpress)

*A Small Business Guide to Doing Business on the Internet* by Brian Hurley and Peter Birkwood (Self Counsel)

*The 3 Rs of E-Mail* by Diane B. Hartman and Karen Nantz (Crisp Publications)

*Untangling the Web* by Michael L. Kasavana (Educational Institute)

*Web Site Wizardry* by Marianne Krcma (Coriolis Group Books)

*Web Wealth* by Dr. Jeffrey Lant (JLA Publications)

*Writing Effective E-Mail* by Nancy and Tom Flynn (Crisp Publications)

*Writing for New Media* by Andrew Bonime and Ken C. Pohlman (John Wiley & Sons)

*Writing.com* by Moira Anderson Allen (Allworth Press)

## Credit Cards, Merchant Accounts

1ClickCharge
Web: www.1clickcharge.com
*Specializes in low-dollar online credit card purchases*

American Express
Phone: 800-The-Card
Web: www.americanexpress.com

Bancard, Inc.
1233 Sherman Drive
Longmont, CO 80501
Phone: 800-666-7575

Cardservice West
4505 Las Virgenes Road, #206
Calabasas, CA 91302
Phone: 800-735-4171
E-mail: cards@cswcom.com
Web: www.cswcom.com

Carte Blanche
Data Capture Systems
231 Quincy St.
Rapid City, SD 57701
Phone: 605-341-6461

Diner's Club
Phone: 800-2-Diners
Web: www.citibank.com/dinersus

Discover
Phone: 800-347-2683
Web: www.discovercard.com

Electronic Bankcard Systems
2554 Lincoln Boulevard
Suite 1088
Marina Del Rey, CA 90291
Phone: 213-827-5772

Electronic Credit Services
Phone: 800-755-4327
Web: www.esccards.com

Electronic Transfer Inc.
3107 E. Mission
Spokane, WA 99202
Phone: 800-757-3107

Elite Merchant Services
Phone: 888-840-1079
E-mail: info@elitecardservice.com
Web: www.elitecardservice.com

Frontline Processing Corporation
Phone: 888-999-1523
Web: www.frontlineprocessing.com

Gold Coast Bankcard Center
Ft. Lauderdale, FL
Phone: 305-492-0303

Harbridge Merchant Services
681 Andersen Drive, 4th Floor, Building 6
Pittsburgh, PA 15220
Phone: 412-937-1272

MasterCard International
2000 Purchase Street
Purchase, NY 10577
Phone: 914-249-2000
Web: www.mastercard.com

Peachtree Software/World Wide Wallet
Web: www.peachtree.com/os/

Teleflora Creditline
11444 W. Olympic Boulevard
Los Angeles, CA 90064
Phone: 800-321-2654, ext. 2690
Web: www.creditline.com

Total Merchant Services
100 Elk Run Drive
Suite 225
Basair, CO 81621
Phone: 888-84-TOTAL
E-mail: info@totalmerchantservices.com
Web: www.totalmerchantservices.com

U.S. Merchant Services
611 S. Federal Highway
Stuart, FL 34994
Phone: 561-220-7515
Web: www.pos-systems-solutions.com

Visa International
P.O. Box 8999
San Francisco, CA 94128-8999
Web: www.visa.com

## Periodicals

*Adweek*
*IQ Interactive Report*
1515 Broadway
New York, NY 10036
Phone: 212-536-5336

*CIO WebBusiness*
492 Old Connecticut Path
P.O. Box 9208
Framingham, MA 01701-9208
Phone: 800-788-4605
Web: www.cio.com

*eMarketer Newsletter*
Web: www.emarketer.com

*E-ZineZ: The E-Zine About E-Zines!*
1112 First Street
Suite 167
Coronado, CA 92118
Phone: 800-305-8266
E-mail: kate@e-zinez.com
Web: www.e-zinez.com

*Industry Standard*
315 Pacific Avenue
San Francisco, CA 94111
Phone: 415-733-5401

*Interactive Week*
Quentin Roosevelt Boulevard

Suite 400
Garden City, NY 11530
Phone: 516-229-3700

*Internet Marketing Report*
Progressive Business Publications
376 Technology Drive
Malvern, PA 19355-1315
Phone: 800-220-5000
Web: www.pbp.com

*Internet Week*
600 Community Drive
Manhasset, NY 11030
Phone: 516-562-5000

*Internet World News*
50 E. 42nd Street, 9th floor
New York, NY 10017
Phone: 212-547-1811

*I-Marketing News*
100 Avenue of the Americas
New York, NY 10013
Phone: 212-925-7300

*Marketing with Technology News*
370 Central Park West, #210
New York, NY 10025
Phone: 212-222-1713
E-mail: sarah@mwt.com
Web: www.mwt.com

*Search Engine Report*
Web: www.searchenginewatch.com

*Silicon Alley Reporter*
Rising Tide Studios
101 E. 15th Street, 3rd floor

New York, NY 10003
Phone: 212-475-8000

*Wall Street & Technology*
Miller Freeman
P.O. Box 1054
Skokie, IL 60076-8054
Phone: 800-682-8297
Web: www.wstonline.com

*Web Techniques*
600 Harrison Street
San Francisco, CA 94107
Phone: 415-908-6643

*What's Working Online*
Georgetown Publishing
1101 30th Street NW
Washington, DC 20007
Phone: 800-915-0022

## Websites

www.clickz.com
*Articles, news, and services for Internet direct mail, website design, banner advertising, and other Internet marketing*

www.edithroman.com
*Search more than 30,000 postal and e-mail lists online for free*

www.faqs.org/faqs/www/webannounce-faq/
*Good source of information on newsgroups*

www.hitbox.com
*Ranks websites by traffic*

internet.com Corporation
20 Ketchum Street
Westport, CT 06880

Phone: 203-662-2800
Fax: 203-222-1679
Research Web: www.allnetresearch.com
Corporate Web: www.internet.com
*"The Superstore for Internet Research."*

www.marketingcentral.com
*Web-based applications for marketers*

www.mrfire.com
*Articles on offline and online marketing*

www.robfrankel.com
*Website from a leading Web marketing consultant and author.
Subscribe to his e-zine, FrankelBiz.*

www.statmarket.com
*Internet statistics and user trends*

www.theadstop.com
*Online media buying service for banner advertising. Includes list-
ings of sites that accept banner advertising with descriptions, traffic, and pricing.*

Direct Marketing Association
www.the-dma.com
*Opt-out form for preventing spam to your e-mail address*

http://thomas.loc.gov/home/thomas.html
*E-marketing legislation*

www.vertex.com
*Updates on taxation affecting e-commerce*

Web Digest
www.webdigest.com
*Sign up on this website to receive e-mail messages with the
URLs of websites that match your areas of interest. Choose*

*from business, finance, health, sports, travel, technology, and more.*

Webstat
www.webstat.net
*Measures visitor activity on your website*

Web Site Garage
http://websitegarage.netscape.com
*Online website tune-up and optimization*

www.worldprofit.com
*Products, services, and information for Internet marketers*

## Seminars and Conferences

ComNet
P.O. Box 9127
1400 Providence Highway
Norwood, MA 02062
Phone: 800-545-EXPO
E-mail: information@comnetexpo.com
Web: www.comnetexpo.com
*Covers the Internet and other communications technology, including local area networks (LANs) and wide area networks (WANs)*

Electronic Commerce World
2021 Coolidge Street
Hollywood, FL 33020-2400
Phone: 877-ECWORLD
Web: www.ecomworld.com
*Conference on how to Web-enable your business*

Giga Information Group
One Longwater Circle
Norwell, MA 02061
Phone: 781-792-2669

Web: www.gigaweb.com
*E-business conferences*

Institute for International Research
708 Third Avenue
New York, NY 10017-4103
Phone: 212-661-3500
Toll-Free: 888-670-8200
Web: www.iir-ny.com
*Seminars on e-mail marketing*

International Quality and Productivity Center
150 Clove Road
P.O. Box 401
Little Falls, NJ 07424-0401
Phone: 800-882-8684
Web: www.iqpc.com
*Seminars on Internet marketing*

Web: www.thestandard.com/netreturns
*Net Returns—annual conference on business use of the Internet*

Jupiter Communications
627 Broadway
New York, NY 10012
Phone: 800-405-4413
E-mail: customerservice@jup.com
Web: www.jup.com
*Conferences on online advertising*

Opt-in E-Mail Marketing Strategies Annual Conference
World Research Group
1120 Avenue of the Americas
New York, NY 10036
Phone: 800-647-7600
E-mail: info@worldrg.com
Web: www.worldrg.com

Penton
20 Ketchum Street
Westport, CT 06880
Phone: 800-500-1959
E-mail: fiwprogram@fiwprogram.com
*Annual Internet World Conference*

Siebel e-Business Conferences
Siebel Systems
1855 South Grant Street
San Mateo, CA 94402-2667
Phone: 800-394-5287
Web: www.siebel.com/ebusinessworld

Thunder Lizard Productions
1619 Eighth Avenue North
Seattle, WA 98109
Phone: 800-221-3806
E-mail: webmarketing@thunderlizard.com
Web: www.thunderlizard.com
*Conferences on Web marketing*

Web 2000
Millar Freeman
600 Harrison Street
San Francisco, CA 94107-9602
Phone: 888-234-9476
Web: www.mfweb.com
*Conference for Web professionals*

# SAMPLE E-MAILS

SOME PRACTITIONERS, A minority at present, advocate long copy Internet direct mail, saying that short copy is insufficient to do a complete selling job for many direct marketing offers.

Trevor Levine is perhaps the premier advocate of long form e-mail copy. Recently Trevor was hired by newsletter publisher Scott Britton to generate new subscribers.

The offer in previous mailings had been a free issue. This mailing offers a special bonus premium.

At a 1998 real estate convention, Britton had tape recorded one of his lectures. But he'd done little to market the recording. So Levine came up with a grabber name for it: "Real Estate Secrets the 'Experts' Don't Want You to Know About." Levine also turned Britton's collection of money-making classified ads (which were in one of his back issues) into a second bonus premium.

"We began mailing 100 letters at a time to our house list. This list is comprised of inquiries and other product sales we have generated over the past three years. Some of these names are admittedly old, but the response was tremendous," reports Britton. "Of the first 100 sales letters mailed, we generated sixteen paid orders, with eleven letters coming back as undeliverable. The response to each successive mailing has been at least this good, if not better." This result was obtained with a house list comprised of people who knew Britton, most of them personally.

Skip the Years of Hard Knocks, Avoid the Pitfalls, Stay off the Road to Bankruptcy, and Achieve the Lifestyle You've Always Dreamed Of . . .

Yours Free: "Real Estate Secrets the Experts Don't Want You to Know About," Plus 11 Magnetic Classified Ads That'll Make Your Phone Ring off the Hook With Red-Hot Real Estate Deals!

"Use just one of my real estate profit strategies, and I guarantee that you'll make $10,000 or more over the next 12 months. Otherwise, these secrets (and over $774 worth of gifts) are yours to keep. Absolutely free. How can I be so confident?"

"Unlike the 'TV experts,' I earn almost all of my money actually doing what I teach. I've spent 21 years developing a no-nonsense, street-smart approach to real estate investing. That's why my subscribers love me. Don't lose this time-sensitive opportunity to start profiting too. Don't let someone else beat you to it. Read this letter now." *Scott Britton*

When you get your hands on these secrets (now captured on tape!), you'll discover:

- Why you can't live on rental income alone
- Why today, the old "buy and hold" strategy could leave you dead broke
- The five new investment strategies, and how to stack them for maximum advantage
- The "rags-to-riches" secret that gets you cash upfront—even if you have no cash or credit
- WARNING: don't invest any money until you activate this profit center first!
- Nothing down . . . nothing a month . . . how to profit without financing
- How to find and buy properties at 40 to 50% below market value (then instantly resell them for a profit!)

From: Scott Britton
Monday, 4:02 p.m.

Dear Friend,

If you do what the "experts" tell you to—if you overborrow and overextend yourself—you could wind up spinning your wheels, throwing your hard-earned money away, and living "cash poor" for decades—Or, worse yet, filing for bankruptcy.

The Truth About Their Dangerous "Buy and Hold" Strategy
If you've listened to the "experts," you might think that once you own enough properties, you'll enjoy an easy full time income—just collecting rents. Come on. That's a load of crap!

Sure, those "projected" incomes look great on TV. Your income, you learn, equals your rents minus your mortgage, property tax, and insurance payments. But—oops!—they "forget" to tell you about hidden costs, like vacancies, heating and air conditioning systems, new roofs, and other capital improvements. Come on, guys.

$50,000 checks? Sure, you can borrow a lot of money. But borrowed money isn't profit. It's a liability. Plain and simple. And when you overborrow, you can get crushed under enormous debt. It's no joke.

Even Some of the "Experts" Have Gone Bankrupt, Doing Exactly What They Tell You and Me to Do!

And even if you succeed at building a big net worth on paper, that doesn't mean you'll have an income.

Like plenty of other real estate "millionaires," you can wind up without enough cash to even buy groceries. You can find yourself tied down to your properties, unable to ever go on vacation. Unable to have the life you really want for yourself. Unable to ever be free. So what's the solution?

If You Want to Make a Full Time Income in Real Estate . . .

You've got to learn the secrets to buying AND selling. This is the low-risk, street-smart approach. It's how you earn the cash you need to do everything else.

Friend, this technique—turning quick profits through buying AND selling—is just one example of the real-world strategies you'll learn to master, if you're fortunate enough to get your hands on my unpublicized tape set, "Real Estate Secrets the 'Experts' Don't Want You to Know About." (Only 100 people will get a copy.) Here are some of the other strategies you'll discover:

- How to make wholesale offers that get accepted!
- How to guarantee your profit when you buy!
- How to keep sellers from going behind your back!
- How to invest for the freedom and lifestyle you really want!
- How to develop your "x-ray vision" so you can recognize the $1,000 bills lying around your market, waiting to be picked up!
- Why now is the best time in history to sell your home!
- How to make $100,000 per year (tax-free!) by selling just one house every two years!
- Single family homes, duplexes, or apartment buildings—find out which is the best investment and why!

Now about these tapes: this information was recorded live at J.P. Vaughan's 1998 Creative Real Estate Online Convention in Las Vegas. J.P. and I go way back. And when she decided to do the convention, well, I owed her a few favors.

So, after quite a bit of arm twisting, I agreed to expose these strategies, but only to the small handful of investors who attended her convention. (And who paid $329 plus travel expenses.)

Even so, my colleagues were up in arms. (If they were my relatives, most of them would've disowned me.) Until now, nobody but my colleagues, and the investors at J.P.'s convention, has even gotten a peek at these strategies. However . . .

As part of our deal, J.P. let me record and make 100 copies of my presentation. (It's a two-tape set.) And because of a formatting problem at the duplication house, I just got them back this month. That's why you've got this time-sensitive opportunity.

Just Take a Look at What a Couple of Other Investors Say About the Material on These Tapes:

NOTE: These guys were already buying properties when they discovered my strategies, so they know what they're talking about.

"I completely agree with Scott. A year ago I wanted to buy investment properties for monthly income. What I bought was an additional job. I have three income properties and that is all I can handle or want to handle.

"I am now looking to buy smart and make long-term and short-term cash. Listen to Scott and appreciate his experience now instead of learning the hard way as I did."

—Jennifer Munson New Hampshire

"Scott . . . I've been to many seminars . . . Your honest down-to-earth presentation is much better than the usual pie-in-the-sky crap. I've been doing rehabbing for a long time and was looking for ways to improve and expand what I've been doing.

"My wife and I have finally gotten our children interested in working with us (three boys and two girls) . . . your ideas will help us start."

—Rob Snyder Cumming, GA

If you're fortunate enough to get a set of these tapes (before they've all been claimed), here are some more of the real-world, street-smart strategies you'll discover . . .

- How to convert your competitors into your business allies
- Why you don't need cash to make "all cash" offers
- How you can take advantage of the "power of cash," even if you're dead broke
- Seven guerrilla marketing tactics that'll accelerate your profits
- The secret power of becoming a "new school" thinker
- How to use "The Most Powerful Negotiating Technique in the World"
- Three people you must sell . . . or you're dead in the water
- The ultimate strategy for selling your properties fast
- Why the "Pavlov dog" approach makes prospects think of you
- The proper use of leverage (a frank discussion the gurus hope you'll never hear)

NOTE: If you don't get these tapes, you could wind up making the same fatal mistakes that have killed the careers of countless others.

Hurry and You'll Also Get 11 Magnetic Classified Ads That'll Make Your Phone Ring off the Hook with Hot Real Estate Deals!

If you're one of the next 100 people to say "Yes," I'll also send you my 11 MOST profitable classified ads. These ads are the cumulative result of 21 years—and $31,873—worth of testing, monitoring, and tweaking. A big investment, but absolutely worth the effort . . .

Today, these babies make me anywhere from 4 to 87 times what they cost to run. One of these ads produced a deal where I was able to make $8,350 just flipping one property. With no money out of my pocket. Total time invested: two hours!

Another of these ads made me over $49,000 last year. And it won't stop bringing money in.

How I Started with Nothing and Built a Fortune

Listen: I wasn't born into money. I didn't inherit a fortune. In fact, I flunked out of law school. Then I got burned in the restaurant business.

But all the while, I pictured having the kind of lifestyle that you probably imagine having now . . . a life where you don't have to go to work every day . . . you can go on vacation when you want to . . . you can live where you want to . . . and you can send your kids to the best schools.

And the more I learned about real estate, the more I realized that buying property, and immediately selling it, is perhaps the best way to create that freedom.

You don't have to be a landlord. You don't have to hassle with tenants. You don't have to plunge toilets at 11 P.M.

Sure, I tried the methods the "experts" teach. (I still spend over $10,000 per year on real estate education.) And like most amateurs, I started out buying distressed properties (probates, divorces, HUD foreclosures, and so on). But eventually,

I Discovered That There Are Much Better Opportunities in Real Estate. So Why Don't the "Experts" Tell You About Them?

Well, most of them compile their "techniques" by going to other experts' seminars.

Then, instead of going out and actually applying the principles, they repackage and sell their own versions of the same information! (You can't really blame them; those books and tapes do make them lots of money!)

But that means you only get part of the story. After all, most of their tired techniques put you heavily into debt. And like I've said, borrowing doesn't increase your net worth.

It's not profit. And it hurts your cash flow. The more you owe, the bigger your payments. And the less you have to live on.

What's more, the real estate market, and the strategies that'll be most profitable for you, are constantly changing. Information starts going stale the day it's produced.

Information You Find in Books and Tapes Published Today Could Be Obsolete in 6 to 12 Months. Even My Information.

That's why I'm offering you, risk-free, the next twelve issues of my newsletter, "Scott Britton's University Of Real Estate Letter."

Like two semesters of the best real estate training you could ever hope for, these newsletters are packed with proven, up to date strategies for maximizing your real estate profits.

Every month, you'll discover a new approach to investing that'll give you more cash flow, more freedom, and more of the lifestyle you want. Just take a look at what others have said about it . . .

"Your recent 'Negotiations' newsletter . . . definitely put money in my pocket . . . (it) brought to my attention . . . that I should make my best offer and stand firm. A recent seller said they had a person willing to pay $12,000 for a 4 bedroom house.

"My offer was $8,000. After 30 days and the seller's buyer flaking out, the seller called me back to take my deal. I since found a person willing to pay $12,000 for the house. The $4,000 profit is directly attributable to your sound advice . . ."

—Walter Wofford, President Good Neighbor Management, Jackson, MS

"I was enthralled by your superb description of real *Creative Real Estate* . . . your real world advice about overleveraging . . . is rock solid, sound advice for everyone from novice to veteran . . . If you write an occasional 800 word article for *Creative Real Estate* magazine . . . we would be pleased to publish it."

—A.D. Kessler, Publisher *Creative Real Estate* magazine, Rancho Santa Fe, CA

"Your excellent publication . . . It's GREAT!! I would be glad to recommend it to any of my *Lease Purchase Times* or *Success Stories* readers . . . You have some very original ideas that obviously come from years of hands on experience."

—Claude Diamond Diamond Consulting Group, Chula Vista, CA

So what will you learn? Here are highlights from the 1998 newsletters:

Low-Cost and No-Cost Ways to Become a Powerful Magnet, Attracting Hot Deals to Your Doorstep Every Day of the Week

- The $10 marketing device that brings you more calls than all of your other marketing efforts combined
- How a one-time investment of $75 can bring you deals for the rest of your working life.
- Dialing for dollars: the four groups of people who'll lead you to the deals, and exactly what to say to them
- The single most powerful thing you can do to grow your business (and it's free!)
- How to generate an easy second income stream from realtors
- What to offer on your business card (that virtually no one else offers!) to make prospects line up at your doorstep
- How to get other people to help you locate properties and buyers!
- Five yard signs that'll flood your telephone line with prospects (and they only cost about $10 each to produce)!

I know this all sounds terrific. But when you implement these strategies, I want to warn you about one problem:

You're Going to Be Flooded with More Phone Calls Than a Human Being Can Handle!

And believe me, it's a real problem. Because there just isn't enough time in the day to handle them all—especially when you're out meeting people and looking at properties all the time.

That's why I also cover:

- How to put your marketing on "autopilot" with simple, inexpensive technology
- How to never again spend hours making the same sales pitch over and over again!
- How to prequalify prospects before ever speaking with them!
- How, using this technique, you can screen out nonmotivated sellers
- Which telephone features allow you to advertise a single number, but be reached by all of your new prospects, anytime, anywhere!

Believe it or not, though I've bought and sold hundreds of properties during my 20-year career, I'm still learning new ways to make money in real estate.

And as a subscriber, you'll be privy to all of my developments, breakthroughs, and discoveries. The information you get each month will be absolutely current. But best of all . . .

You'll Get Over $744 in Free Bonuses, If You're One of the Next 100 People to Say "Yes"!

SUPER BONUS #1: All twelve newsletter back issues from 1998. (A $195 value!) If you like the strategies you just read about, here's your chance to make them start working for you (along with MANY more)—at no extra cost. Instead of waiting eagerly by your mailbox all year, you can have twelve months' worth of profit strategies right now.

SUPER BONUS #2: "Real Estate Secrets the 'Experts' Don't Want You to Know About." (Worth a lot more than $329!) Like I mentioned, you'll get sound strategies for boosting your profits, your net worth, and your cash flow—NOT your debts. The cost to investors who learned these strategies in Las Vegas was $329 plus travel expenses.

SUPER BONUS #3: The eleven classified ads I described above. Like I said, these magnetic ads are the result of 21 years—and $31,873—worth of testing, monitoring, and tweaking. This one bonus is worth more than 100 times the pocket change you'll spend on my newsletter.

SUPER BONUS #4: The most profitable 30 minutes you'll ever spend, especially if you're a beginner. (A $250 value!) You'll get to spend 30 minutes on the phone with me, where you can get sound advice about the specific deals you're involved in.

Unlike nonsubscribers, you won't have to pay my normal fee of $500/hour.

Just Try Getting Ron LeGrand, Carleton Sheets, Or "Millionaire" Russ Whitney on the Phone to Advise You Personally!
(Even if you have bought their books, tapes, or high-priced seminars.)

Take a look at what these beginning investors say about the value of these consultations:

"Your willingness to help and the care and interest you show are wonderful. Ever since I tuned in to you, I've been amazed by this. You've apparently consciously chosen to cater to the beginning investor.

"I'd be willing to bet that if you directly marketed your willingness to help (which you probably shouldn't), your materials would be worth 10+ times their cost. My two cents . . ."

— David Hecht, Marlborough, MA

"We can't begin to express how much your help and others means to us. We find it remarkable that successful folks such as yourself take the time to answer questions and offer advice to rank amateurs. We are convinced that we have finally found the way to take back control of our lives."

— Charles & Susan DeFiore, Las Vegas, NV

You Get This Complete, No-Risk, 12-Month $10,000 Satisfaction Guarantee

Listen: I'm so confident that you'll profit from the strategies you learn from me (my cancellations are zero) that I'm standing behind my offer with this unprecedented guarantee:

If you don't make at least $10,000 using one of my strategies, or if for any reason you're not completely satisfied with my newsletter, you can cancel your subscription at any time within the next twelve months. You'll then get a complete 100% refund of your subscription price—no matter how many issues you've already received.  No questions asked. Best of all, the free bonuses are yours to keep, no matter what you decide.

Friend, that's a guaranteed gain just for reviewing my material!

Now there's one little thing I've got to tell you about. When you get the two tapes, "Real Estate Secrets the 'Experts' Don't Want You to Know About," they're not going to come in a fancy, 4-color case. They're going to come in simple plastic boxes with plain black and white labels.

And because my presentation was recorded live, the recording quality is not quite "hi fi." Though you won't have any problem hearing me speak, just be aware that this recording is not as "professionally produced," with music and all, as the more polished tapes you've probably bought.

The price for all this?

For two semesters (twelve months) of the best, most profitable real estate training you'll ever get—a program that's guaranteed to make you at least $10,000 over the next twelve months, or your full subscription price back? Just $195!

"Now hold on just a minute," you might be thinking. "Why in the world is Scott offering to give me all of his expertise, secrets that others paid $329 to learn about, twelve months of his real estate profit strategies, all of last year's strategies, a personal consultation, AND his eleven most profitable ads for only $195?"

Here's why:

Once you've spent twelve months profiting from my strategies, I'm confident that you'll be a subscriber for years to come. That's because subscribers who make money with my strategies don't even think of canceling their subscriptions. In fact, I'm so confident that if you . . .

Subscribe Within the Next 7 Days, I'll Put $98 in Your Pocket Right Now.

Here's my thinking. I don't know your financial situation. And if you're in a cash crunch today, but you're serious about using my strategies to profit in real estate, I know that $195 will seem like pocket change next year—when it's time to renew.

So, if you subscribe within the next 7 days, I'll let you take this entire package, with all of the bonuses (assuming you're one of the next 100 people to subscribe) for a paltry $97!

Now ask yourself this: Why lose sleep, worrying that you might've made a poor buying or selling decision? Or feel burdened by a difficult real estate decision that grinds away at you?

Why spend 21 years and over $30,000 in advertising (like I did!) to find out which ads are profitable, and more important, which ads bring you the really BIG profits?

Why struggle through years of trial and error when you can find out, right now, exactly what you need to know to start profiting from every dollar, and every hour, you invest in your business?

Why face all these struggles when—right now—you can discover the guaranteed strategies that my subscribers are raving about?

You can have a clear track to run on. Get 30 minutes of expert advice about any deal you're involved in. Start earning immediate cash profits—without falling dangerously into debt.

And Never Again Waste Your Hard-Earned Money on Losing Ads.

You've read the testimonials. You've read my guarantee. Let's face it: you can't lose! You will make at least $10,000 over the next 12 months—guaranteed;

otherwise, all of my secrets, newsletters, and bonuses are yours to keep. Period.

And even if you cancel (very unlikely!) you'll get 100% of your money back, no matter how many issues you've already received.

Friend, don't throw away another dollar. Don't waste another hour. Don't spend another year in the trenches. Phone, fax, or mail your order today.

Sincerely,

Scott Britton

P.S. Don't forget: to get the $98 discount, you must act within the next 7 days . . . sorry, no exceptions.

P.P.S. I only have 100 copies of the tape set, "Real Estate Secrets the 'Experts' Don't Want You to Know About." To get your copy (and all of the other bonuses) free of charge, you must be one of the next 100 people to subscribe. Phone, fax, or mail your order today.

\_\_\_ YES! I want to turn real estate into wealth with minimal risk or stress. I want to profit from your no-B.S., always up-to-date, safe, stress-free strategies for turning real estate into real wealth. Please enter my one-year subscription for your University of Real Estate Letter, and send me my first issue now. If, within the next 12 months, I don't make at least $10,000 using one of your strategies, or if for any reason I'm not satisfied with your newsletter, I understand that I can cancel my subscription and get a complete 100% refund of my subscription price—no matter how many issues I've already received.

\_\_\_ On this basis, Scott, I'm subscribing at the normal price of $195.

\_\_\_ Scott, I'm responding within 7 days, so give me the incredible rate of just $97.

\_\_\_ DOUBLE YES! If I'm one of the next 100 people to subscribe, please also rush me (by 2nd day air) "Real Estate Secrets the 'Experts' Don't Want You to Know About," all 12 newsletter back issues from 1998, and the 11 classified ads described above. And, please reserve a 30-minute consultation slot for me.

I understand that these free bonuses are mine to keep, even if I cancel my subscription and receive a 100% refund.

# E-Mail Series

Here are the first four sales messages Levine wrote for AWeber Systems. AWeber's computer will send your prospects, via e-mail, an automatic response and a sequence of six additional follow-up messages.

Prospects who visit AWeber's website are invited to receive the following sequence of messages. Levine took some of AWeber's "standard features" and repositioned them as "free bonuses." He also helped AWeber come up with additional bonuses. "By tying these bonuses to deadlines, we created fear of loss—a very strong motivator," says Trevor.

## MESSAGE #1 *(instant reply)*

Dear Trevor,

Just moments ago, you turned the key for a "test drive" of AWeber's profit-boosting follow-up system. And your timing was great! Because you checked out our website at just the right time, you're qualified for SIX FREE GIFTS . . . NOTE: Three of these gifts are unusually valuable, so you must subscribe by March 7th, 1999, to get them. (See details below.)

Now Trevor, imagine how impressed YOUR prospects will be when—like you— they ask for information, and it's delivered to their e-mail boxes INSTANTLY . . .

Imagine how many MORE sales you'll make, when your prospects are motivated AGAIN and AGAIN by a SERIES of follow-up messages . . . a stream of messages that give you SO much credibility, and build SO much rapport with your prospects, that buying from you becomes the ONLY sensible choice!

And imagine (the best part) . . .

- All of this follow-up is done for you . . .
- By a state-of-the-art computer . . .

- 24 hours every day . . .
- With no mistakes, ever . . .

Trevor, if your goal is to:

- Convert the MAXIMUM number of leads to customers . . .
- Make the MAXIMUM number of sales, and . . .
- Get the MAXIMUM profit out of every dollar you spend on advertising . . .

Then read every word of this message!

Heck, once you write your sales messages (and we can even help you with that), the AWeber system will e-mail each of your prospects a sequence of SEVEN messages—AUTOMATICALLY!

AND IT'S GUARANTEED TO MAKE YOU MONEY

If it doesn't make you money, you can cancel, get a 100% refund, and KEEP the free bonuses! (See details below.)

WHY WILL SEVEN MESSAGES "MAXIMIZE" YOUR RESPONSE?

In test after test, marketers have found that most prospects won't buy from you after just one contact. After all, you're still a stranger to them! (Not to mention that when they first hurry through your sales message, or your website, your message doesn't fully sink in.)

That's why repeated contact is so powerful. When your prospects hear from you again and again . . .

- You become more credible . . .
- You become more trustworthy, and . . .
- You get to motivate them again and again . . .

According to marketers, your prospects must hear from you SEVEN times. That's what it takes for many of them to respond.

THE AUTOMATED SYSTEM THAT MAKES FOLLOW-UP A BREEZE!

Trevor, once you activate your account, here's what you can look forward to:

- When your prospects request information via your AWeber e-mail address or your website, it's delivered automatically—within seconds.
- Your messages are sent and your prospects' addresses are automatically added to your database, saving you hours of endless data entry.
- You spend more time with your family, since the AWeber system is doing all the work.
- A total of SEVEN messages are sent, automatically, to each of your prospects, at regular predetermined intervals. This builds trust and rapport with your prospects.
- Your effective, efficient AWeber follow-up system MAXIMIZES the conversion of prospects into customers, all without any intervention from you.
- You save time, save money, reduce stress, build customer loyalty, increase conversion ratios, and make more money!

ALL THIS IS POSSIBLE THANKS TO AUTORESPONDERS

An "autoresponder" is like an ONLINE version of "fax-on-demand." Once you paste your sales message into an autoresponder, prospects can get your information any time of the day, just by sending a message to your autoresponder e-mail address. (Any message!) It's an instant reply device that:

- Delivers your message to your prospects within seconds, via e-mail . . .
- Works for you 24 hours per day . . .
- Delivers information even when you're not at your computer . . .
- Saves you hours of manually fulfilling information requests . . .

HOW IS THE AWEBER SYSTEM DIFFERENT FROM OTHERS?

Glad you asked! There's one downside to regular, single-reply autoresponders: they only send ONE message to your prospects! Like these regular autoresponders, the AWeber system delivers an instant reply to your prospects. HOWEVER . . .

The AWeber system will also:

- Follow up with your prospects SEVEN times . . .
- Completely automatically . . .
- And you get to tell it how many days should pass between each of your messages . . .

Trevor, we're talking about a completely automated marketing system that makes you money around the clock!

And because you checked out our website at just the right time, you're entitled to some cool bonuses not usually offered by autoresponder companies:

1. FREE setup of your account! (Other companies charge $15 to $50!)

2. FREE PERSONALIZATION. Trevor, do you notice how this message is personalized with YOUR name? Thanks to our personalization feature, our system can merge a prospect's first name into every message (s)he gets from you. Not only does this keep your message from looking like a "mass mailing," but personalizing your messages has been PROVEN to build rapport and get you a higher response!

3. FREE instant forwarding of your prospects' e-mail addresses. Most other autoresponder companies can't send you the e-mail addresses of your prospects! And those that do make you wait for days, weeks, or even months to get the e-mail addresses of your prospects. Subscribe within seven days, and we'll program our system to send you every name and e-mail address instantly.

PLUS, IF YOU SUBSCRIBE BY MARCH 7TH, 1999, YOU'LL ALSO GET THESE THREE EXTRA GIFTS:

4. A FREE copy of "Insider Internet Marketing." (Normally costs $23.95.) This "down and dirty" publication, straight from the mouth of Internet marketing "insider" Jim Daniels, exposes EVERY marketing strategy, method, secret, resource, tool, and trick that Daniels (as well as other prominent Internet marketers) has employed to explode online profits. You'll learn to compete with the big players, "correctly" harness the power of direct e-mail, the ten keys to building a marketing-friendly website, and MUCH more.

5. Jim Daniels's PERSONAL directory of fifty e-zines that'll give you the BIGGEST bang for your advertising dollar.

6. A FREE copy of "Why Your Prospects Forget About You—And How to Turn Them Into Customers." In this special report, you'll find out why "typical" follow-up gets meager results, why a carefully planned SEQUENCE of messages will DRAMATICALLY increase your sales, how to TIME your messages for MAXIMUM response, what to SAY in each of your messages, and the special offer you MUST include in your LAST TWO messages.

DON'T DECIDE NOW—YOU'VE GOT 60 DAYS TO USE AWEBER
—RISK-FREE!

Trevor, if you subscribe today, I GUARANTEE that you'll enjoy bigger profits within the next 60 days. If you don't, or if for ANY reason you're not completely satisfied with our service, just cancel your subscription within 60 days, and we'll cheerfully refund 100% of what you've paid. No questions. No hard feelings. And (the best part!) no matter what you decide, the FREE BONUSES are YOURS TO KEEP!

That's a guaranteed gain, just for trying out our system!

ALL THIS FOR JUST $15 TO $20 PER MONTH?
THIS IS GREAT! HOW DO I SUBSCRIBE?

To get your own AWeber Follow Up Autoresponder, go to our website right now at http://www.aweber.com/

Once you're there, simply click on the "Order Today" link at the top of any page. Fill out our online form, choose a payment method, and your account will be set up in less than five minutes.

Trevor, can you picture yourself, ten minutes from now, activating YOUR new account (with just a few clicks of the mouse)? Grab your SIX FREE BONUSES and boost your profits now. Go to http://www.aweber.com/

Best Regards,

Tom Kulzer

CEO & President AWeber Systems http://www.aweber.com/

P.S. Tomorrow, the AWeber system will send you the second message in my message sequence—automatically—just like it will when it's working for YOU.

P.P.S. Want to share the Aweber program with your friends and associates? In tomorrow's message, you'll find out how you can enjoy an easy month-after-month income as an AWeber affiliate. (Affiliate signup is free, and you don't even have to be a subscriber!) For more details right now, go to http://www.aweber.com/affiliate.php

P.P.P.S. If you haven't subscribed yet, what are you waiting for? You do want to save time, make more sales, and boost your profits, don't you? Then go to our website and grab your SIX FREE BONUSES right now! Go to http://www.aweber.com/

## MESSAGE #2 *(one day later)*

Trevor, why in your right mind would you let someone else take money that could've been yours?

Just since yesterday, when you started your "test drive" of the AWeber system, AWeber affiliates around the world have been raking in easy money—just by mentioning our service to others . . .

With each day that goes by, more and more of your online friends and associates are hearing about our service. And every time they subscribe, SOMEONE gets richer—thanks to our generous month-after-month commission of 20%. Why shouldn't that someone be YOU?

(It's NOT a misprint, Trevor—you'll get 20% EVERY month, for as long as your referrals remain customers!)

The more you realize how much this system will do for you, the more you'll also realize how helpful it'll be to your friends and associates. And the best part is:

AWEBER AFFILIATE SIGNUP IS FREE!

Just tell your online friends and associates about AWeber and give them your special affiliate link for them to order from. Any order placed from your special affiliate link will earn you a 20% affiliate commission!

On a single monthly account, you'll earn $47.88 every year! And when a customer buys a year's worth of service up-front, you'll get an immediate $35.88. Plus, you'll get another $35.88 every year, for as long as that person renews service!

PLUS, GET PAID FOR FINDING OTHER AFFILIATES!

To encourage you to find other affiliates, we'll even pay you 10% on the sales made by your subaffiliates.

"This sounds too good to be true," you think. "How can a FREE affiliate program be so generous?"

Frankly, of all the advertising methods we've used, we've found that word of mouth recommendations have been the most effective, the FASTEST way to get the word out. So, when you tell your friends and associates about us, we're happy to share our profits with you.

To become a FREE AWeber affiliate visit our website and fill out the form. http://www.aweber.com/signup.php

Best Regards,

Tom Kulzer
CEO & President AWeber Systems http://www.aweber.com/

P.S. In two days from today, the AWeber system will send you the third message in my message sequence—automatically—just like it will when it's working for YOU.

P.P.S. Want to attract hundreds of FREE leads every month? In my next message, you'll learn about FIVE ways to make people EAGER for your sequence of messages. Can't wait? Go to http://www.aweber.com/demo/started.php

P.P.P.S. If you haven't become an affiliate yet, what are you waiting for? Like you, your friends and associates want to save time, make more sales, and boost their profits. Why not be their hero? Go to http://www.aweber.com/signup.php

## MESSAGE #3 (three days after message #1)

### Subject: Five Ways to Get FREE Leads

By now, Trevor, you're excited by the power of motivating your prospects AGAIN and AGAIN—with a SEQUENCE of compelling messages (just like the sequence you've been getting from me).

By now, you can picture the HUGE increase in your revenue, as you convert more and more of your prospects into customers. And by now, you realize how dirt cheap our service is (especially when you think of all the money it's going to make you)!

Heck, you've probably already subscribed. But just in case you haven't . . .

I'm going to sweeten the deal with ONE MORE FREE BONUS. However, to get it, you must subscribe by March 7th, 1999. (See details below. Current customers: you qualify as well. Just contact us.)

NOW FOR THE "MEAT" OF TODAY'S MESSAGE:

Trevor, right here in this message, I'm going to show you how to EASILY generate hundreds of FREE leads every month, using . . .

- Signature files . . .
- Newsgroups . . .
- Message boards . . .
- Articles, and . . .
- Your website . . .

But be careful; when you use these methods, you're going to generate more inquiries than one human being can handle. So you WON'T want to respond to them MANUALLY. That could take you all day.

An autoresponder can help by sending an automatic reply to every one of your inquiries. However . . .

As I mentioned before, if all you have is a regular, SINGLE-REPLY autoresponder, you're going to LOSE 50% or more of the sales you SHOULD be making—sales you WILL make with AWeber's personalized, automated COMPLETE follow-up system.

With that in mind, here are five methods to generating free leads:

1. YOUR SIGNATURE FILE:

When you attach a signature file to the bottom of your e-mail, and you use it to offer FREE information, or a BENEFIT to your prospects, then every time you send a message, it's like sending a FREE AD! Here's an example of a signature I use in my e-mail program:

Are you wasting time on the phone? FREE report details how to save valuable hours of phone time. mailto: esa@aweber.com

For specific directions, just consult the "Help" file in your e-mail program.

2. NEWSGROUPS:

Newsgroups are a GREAT place to use your "signature file" as a FREE AD. But here's the thing: never place a blatant ad in a newsgroup. Instead, find a group that has discussions about something you know well, and contribute your knowledge to the group.

When others see the FREE information, or the BENEFIT you're offering in your signature file, they'll naturally send an e-mail to your autoresponder.

3. MESSAGE BOARDS:

These are like newsgroups, except that they're on the Web. Although you usually can't use signature files, you can often participate in the discussion, and leave your website link at the bottom of the message. Just make sure you post "on topic" and do not blatantly advertise.

## 4. WRITING ARTICLES:

This is absolutely my FAVORITE way of gaining publicity online. There are literally thousands of very targeted publications on the Internet. Simply pick a topic that you know well, and write an article about it. It doesn't have to be a literary work of art, just something that's informative.

It's customary that an author gets several lines at the end of his or her article to promote what he or she is selling. For examples of articles I've written, visit my other website at www.electsuccess.com

## 5. YOUR WEBSITE:

If you have a website, you can capture e-mail addresses directly, using a special "opt-in form" you'll get from us—FREE—when you subscribe. It allows your prospects to type in their names and e-mail addresses, and receive your sales messages automatically. A simple form looks like this:

For More Information
Your Name:

Your E-mail Address:

SPECIAL 7th FREE BONUS IF YOU SUBSCRIBE BY $DATE+4

Trevor, if you subscribe by $DATE+4, I'll throw in ONE MORE free bonus: a copy of Trevor Levine's "How to Explode the Response to Any Ad, Sales Letter, or Website" . . .

In this special report, you'll discover:

- The #1 mistake made in writing ads and sales messages...
- A PROVEN way to boost your response by 500% . . .
- How to create urgency . . .
- How to reverse the risk . . .
- How to motivate your prospects to respond to or buy from you IMMEDIATELY . . .

Like I said, when you use these techniques, you're going to generate more free leads than one person can possibly handle. You don't want to spend all day responding to them manually, do you? And you sure don't want your prospects to think of you as unprofessional because you didn't get back to them right away. Do you?

If not, you NEED AWeber's personalized, automated COMPLETE follow-up system. Not to mention that . . .

. . . You only have FOUR DAYS LEFT to qualify for the three time-sensitive bonuses I mentioned in my first message, plus the EXTRA special report I just described. Trevor, take one more look at what you'll lose if you don't act quickly:

7. A FREE copy of "Insider Internet Marketing." (Normally costs $23.95.) This "down and dirty" publication, straight from the mouth of Internet marketing "insider" Jim Daniels, exposes EVERY marketing strategy, method, secret, resource, tool, and trick that Daniels (as well as other prominent Internet marketers) has employed to explode online profits. You'll learn to compete with the big players, "correctly" harness the power of direct e-mail, the ten keys to building a marketing-friendly website, and MUCH more.

8. Jim Daniels's PERSONAL directory of fifty e-zines that'll give you the BIGGEST bang for your advertising dollar.

9. A FREE copy of "Why Your Prospects Forget About You—and How to Turn Them into Customers." In this special report, you'll find out why "typical" follow-up gets meager results, why a carefully planned SEQUENCE of messages will DRAMATICALLY increase your sales, how to TIME your messages for MAXIMUM response, what to SAY in each of your messages, and the special offer you must include in your LAST TWO messages.

DON'T DECIDE NOW—YOU'VE GOT 60 DAYS TO USE AWEBER —RISK-FREE!

Trevor, if you subscribe today, I GUARANTEE that you'll enjoy bigger profits within the next 60 days. If you don't, or if for ANY reason you're not completely satisfied with our service, just cancel your subscription within 60 days, and we'll cheerfully refund 100% of what you've paid. No questions. No hard feelings. And (the best part!) no matter what you decide, the FREE BONUSES are YOURS TO KEEP!

That's a guaranteed gain, just for trying out our system!

ALL THIS FOR JUST $15 TO $20 PER MONTH?
THIS IS GREAT! HOW DO I SUBSCRIBE?

To get your own AWeber follow-up autoresponder, go to our website right now at http://www.aweber.com/

Once you're there, simply click on the "Order Today" link at the top of any page. Fill out our online form, choose a payment method, and your account will be set up in less than five minutes.

With a few clicks of the mouse, you can be using your new account in the next ten minutes!!

Best Regards,

Tom Kulzer
CEO & President AWeber Systems http://www.aweber.com/

P.S. In three days from today, the AWeber system will send you the fourth message in my message sequence—automatically—just like it will when it's working for YOU.

P.P.S. How would you like to work FEWER hours, while earning twice—or even three times—your current income? In my next message, you'll learn how AWeber's automated follow-up system can save you fifteen hours every month!

P.P.P.S. Don't wait until my next message to subscribe! Don't lose your chance to get the FOUR FREE BONUSES. After all, it's obvious that you'll profit from our service, isn't it? Since the free bonus offer expires on March 7th, 1999, doesn't it make sense to grab your FREE BONUSES right now, while you still have the chance? To get them, go to our website right now at http://www.aweber.com/

P.P.P.P.S. Want to share the AWeber program with your friends and associates? Affiliate signup is FREE, and you don't even have to be a subscriber! You get 20% each time someone pays for their service. And when you recommend the affiliate program to others, you make 10% on their sales! You have nothing to lose by simply filling out a short online form and becoming an AWeber affiliate. For more details right now, go to http://www.aweber.com/affiliate.php

## MESSAGE #4 *(seven days after message #1)*

Dear Trevor,

In a moment, you'll find out how the AWeber system can save you fifteen hours every month. But first, a reminder:

TODAY is your FINAL CHANCE to get the FOUR FREE BONUSES!

That's why you've already subscribed to AWeber, right?

By now, I'm sure you have. By now, you realize that AUTOMATING the follow-up process is going to:

- Save you lots of time . . .
- Generate more sales . . .
- Boost your profits (in the SAME way that it's boosted my sales and profits). . .

By now, too, your brain is sizzling with all of the HOT marketing and advertising strategies you've been gleaning from your FOUR FREE BONUSES:

- Jim Daniels's hit book, "Insider Internet Marketing." (Normally costs $23.95.)
- Jim Daniels's PERSONAL directory of fifty e-zines that'll give you the BIGGEST bang for your advertising dollar.
- "Why Your Prospects Forget About You—and How to Turn Them into Customers."
- "How to Explode the Response to Any Ad, Sales Letter, or Website."

What? You haven't subscribed yet? . . . Then ask yourself this:

In the seven days since you started your "test drive," how much of your valuable time did you squander on boring, repetitive follow-up work? (And how many more IMPORTANT things did you neglect because you didn't have "enough time"?!)

Did every prospect hear from you at least FOUR times?

If the AWeber system had been working for you, they would have!

Trevor, stop losing sales you COULD be closing. Stop frittering your time away on boring follow-up work. Today is your LAST chance to claim your bonuses, so grab them right now by going to http://www.aweber.com/signup.php

NOW FOR THE "MEAT" OF TODAY'S MESSAGE:

Trevor, if you want to convert the MAXIMUM number of leads to sales, there's no question about it: your prospects must hear from you at least seven times. That's what it takes for many prospects to respond.

Now suppose you have a regular, single-reply autoresponder. And it brings you just ten responses per day.

If you're a "good marketer," you're following up with each of these prospects SIX TIMES after his or her initial request. Now, multiply 10 responses per day by 6 follow-up messages per response, and you'll find that you're sending out 1,800 follow-up messages every month!

Trevor, if you're doing this MANUALLY, and it takes you 30 seconds to cut and paste each follow-up message into an e-mail message, those 1,800 messages are adding FIFTEEN HOURS to your already-too-busy schedule every month! That's almost TWO entire work days!

And that means you're working for LESS than $1.33/hour!!

Figure it out: if you're doing 15 hours of follow-up work, and all you're saving is $15 to $20 (the cost of having AWeber's system do it for you, AUTOMATICALLY), your actual profit is a laughable $1.00 to $1.33 per hour!!

(FYI: Not exactly a *Success* magazine cover story.)

Trevor, when you think about it like that, doesn't it just make sense to put the whole thing on autopilot? After all, when the AWeber system is working for you, you'll be able to:

- Work fewer hours
- Enjoy more free time and less stress
- Build credibility and trust with your prospects (hands-free!)
- Convert the MAXIMUM number of leads to customers
- Get the MOST from every dollar you spend on advertising
- NEVER AGAIN lose sales you could've closed with better follow-up
- Multiply your sales and profits
- All this with no extra work on your part

If you're in business, Trevor, NOT having an automated follow-up system is like NOT having a bank account. Or NOT having a phone. Sure, you could save a few dollars each month by getting rid of your bank account. Or your phone. But that would be nuts! Wouldn't it?

Well, when you spend time and money to generate leads, only to let them slip through your fingers (because you aren't contacting them SEVEN times), isn't that just as self-defeating? Don't be penny-wise and dollar-foolish. Increase next week's profits, right now, by clicking here: http://www.aweber.com/signup.php

DON'T DECIDE NOW—YOU'VE GOT 60 DAYS TO USE AWEBER —RISK-FREE!

Trevor, if you subscribe today, I GUARANTEE that you'll enjoy bigger profits within the next 60 days. If you don't, or if for ANY reason you're not completely satisfied with our service, just cancel your subscription within 60 days, and we'll cheerfully refund 100% of what you've paid. No questions. No hard feelings. And (the best part!) no matter what you decide, the FREE BONUSES are YOURS TO KEEP!

That's a guaranteed gain, just for trying out our system!

ALL THIS FOR JUST $15 TO $20 PER MONTH?

THIS IS GREAT! HOW DO I SUBSCRIBE?

To get your own AWeber follow-up autoresponder, go to our website right now at http://www.aweber.com/

Once you're there, simply click on the "Order Today" link at the top of any page. Fill out our online form, choose a payment method, and your account will be set up in less than five minutes.

Don't lose out on the three FREE bonuses I mentioned above. To get them, you must subscribe TODAY. Let's go! Click on this link right now: http://www.aweber.com/signup.php

Sincerely,

Tom Kulzer
CEO & President AWeber Systems http://www.aweber.com/

P.S. Here's a recent testimonial from one of our subscribers:

"Using the AWeber system, I was able to have close to 300 people go through my online pipeline in a little over a month. By having all of the follow up, e-mailing, and record-keeping automated, I saved myself several hours of work each day for more productive activities.

If I tried to do what AWeber does, it would take at least an hour a day, probably closer to two. But nothing would be instant. It would have to wait until I had time or was logged in to reply with the first message. Then the other six messages would have to be sent once a day. I guess I would set up an address book for each day. It would get messy, become increasingly time consuming, and after a while I would probably pay twice what you are offering to do it for me (or just give it up.)"

Kevin Wilke, VisionPro Newsletter Editor

P.P.S. Five days from today, the Aweber system will send you the fifth message in my message sequence—automatically—just like it will when it's working for YOU. It's a letter from the president of ForeclosureWorld.com, an AWeber subscriber who reports a $10,000+ increase in weekly sales since activating his AWeber account!

P.P.P.S. But don't wait until then to subscribe! Today is your LAST CHANCE to get the FOUR time-sensitive bonuses. Grab them right now by going to http://www.aweber.com/signup.php

P.P.P.P.S. Want to share the AWeber program with your friends and associates? Affiliate signup is FREE, and you don't even have to be a subscriber! You get 20% each time someone pays for their service. And when you recommend the affiliate program to others, you make 10% on their sales! You have nothing to lose by simply filling out a short online form and becoming an AWeber affiliate. For more details right now, go to http://www.aweber.com/affiliate.php

For example, Kelly Schwedland, President of American Business Dynamics (ABD), hired Trevor Levine of Marketing Experts, an Internet copywriting firm, to write several online sales letters. Schwedland and members of his staff are Certified E-Myth Consultants. They use the principles in Michael Gerber's book *The E-Myth* to help businesses become more efficient and profitable.

The first letter was e-mailed to business owners who'd visited www.abdynamics.com, but taken no action. The goal was to dangle ABD's "bait"—a free business needs analysis—in front of their prospects over and over again. So ABD created a twelve-part "course" and hired Trevor to write the "thank you" letter that let prospects know they'd been selected to receive the course.

This gave ABD twelve opportunities to offer its free business needs analysis to its prospects. Actually, thirteen, since ABD also offered the analysis right in the postscript of the thank you letter.

Notice that copy didn't just state that the course was worth $149. The e-mail explained *why* ABD was temporarily waiving the price. This is what made the $149 price believable.

After e-mailing just this Thank You, ABD reported back: "Our request for analysis has gone from average twenty-two in the previous three months to forty-seven last month alone. That's an average increase of 114% after utilizing these marketing pieces."

# MESSAGE #1

For Trevor Levine

The Marketing Experts

Trevor:

Use this exciting "thank you" to take your business to the next level—so you can start enjoying more freedom, more money, more control over your business, and more time off . . .

That's right. Because you checked out our E-myth website at just the right time, you're one of a select group of people to get free help with problems like these:

- Your business depends too much on your being there
- Not enough profit
- Not enough time
- Not enough sales/customers
- You can't find good people
- You can't develop capable managers
- Inadequate cash flow
- You need more working capital

Soon, business owners who face these problems—your colleagues—will be able to access these solutions right from their desktop computers. Solutions that'll come in the form of our no-holds-barred twelve-part program "The E-Myth Advocate." This one-year program will be $149.00.

YOU, HOWEVER, ARE GOING TO GET ALL TWELVE SOLUTION-PACKED SEGMENTS FOR FREE.

Why?

Partly, as our way of saying "thanks" for your interest in the E-Myth. And partly so that we can learn more about the problems that you—our website visitor—encounter each day.

See, before we start selling paid programs, we want to get feedback from business owners like you, business owners who are already familiar with the E-Myth concepts. We want to know for certain that our content is exactly what you need.

To do this, we're including a brief questionnaire with each segment. After you read a segment, please take just a minute to complete the questionnaire. That'll help us give you even more useful information in the future.

To receive your first segment right now, "Why Your Small Business Isn't Reaching Its Potential, Reason #1: You Need Management Systems," click here: http://abdynamics.com/E-Myth_Advocate/A153.htm

To more life,

Kelly Schwedland
President
American Business Dynamics
http://www.abdynamics.com

P.S. CAN'T WAIT?
GET THE SOLUTIONS TO YOUR PROBLEMS RIGHT NOW—WITH A FREE BUSINESS NEEDS ANALYSIS http://abdynamics.com/analysis.htm

When you checked out our site, you must have skipped over the offer for a FREE business needs analysis. (It's a $500 value—but it's yours for free.)

In this exciting analysis, you and one of our certified e-myth consultants will look together at the gap between where your business is today and where you'd like it to be. Then you'll determine how to:

• Bridge that gap
• Make your business run like a franchise
• Develop systems that eliminate mistakes, problems, and frustrations
• Make your employees eager to give you what you want
• Have complete control over your business, without having to always be there

Perhaps for the first time ever, you'll be able to really see your business from the e-myth point of view. And once you do, you'll naturally be able to:

- Increase your personal income
- Increase your business's profits
- Increase your productivity

As well as:

- Increase your people's productivity
- Enjoy a business that runs itself

Arrange for yours right now. Just click here:
http://www.abdynamics.com/analysis.htm

In a follow-up campaign, ABD arranged for Seth Lederman—a self-made E-Myth success story—to host a teleconference for some of its prospects. After hearing how Lederman profited from the E-Myth principles, participants were invited to enroll in the E-Myth Mastery Program (that is, to become consulting clients of ABD).

Trevor was again hired to write the invitation. ABD reported back with these results:

- 575 prospects were sent the invitation
- 65 clicked on the web site to see more
- 22 registered (online and phone)
- 7 more wanted to come but couldn't make it
- 16 showed up for the teleconference
- 6 enrolled in the first month of the mastery program

In short, 3.83 percent of those invited registered, and 27.27 percent of those who registered became clients. Notice how the copy uses fear of loss to create urgency.

## MESSAGE #2

For: Trevor Levine
The Marketing Experts

Hoping to reach you before it's too late . . .

As of this moment, Trevor (Wednesday, 5:17 P.M.), we still have room for you on the upcoming free teleconference with self-made millionaire Seth Lederman. Incredibly, the call is free, so it's filling up fast . . .

If you're fortunate enough to be included, you'll find out how Lederman used magnetic "E-Myth" strategies to explode his income and cut his workweek down to just 10 hours. But here's the best part:

Lederman was like you. He owned a small business. He struggled with the frustrations you face every day. For example . . .

- Not enough free time
- Not enough customers, sales, or profits
- Your business depends too much on your being there
- You work longer hours than your employees
- You can't find good people
- Too much stress

But using "E-Myth" strategies, he solved ALL of these problems. And on the call, he'll tell you how he . . .

- Designed his business to run itself, so it no longer depended on his being there . . .
- Cut his workweek from 60 hours down to just 10 hours . . . and . . .
- Simultaneously grew his firm from $500,000 to $4,000,000 in just THREE years . . .

You'll get to hear firsthand from Lederman how you can use "E-Myth" strategies to produce these SAME benefits in your business:

- Work fewer hours
- Make more sales
- Make more money
- Enjoy a business that runs itself
- Have complete control over your business without having to always be there

Because callers will get to participate, the conference is limited to just 25 people.

The bottom line: if you're interested, don't wait. Don't lose your chance be included on this call. Visit http://www.abdynamics.com/seminar.htm RIGHT NOW. Or call 1-888-888-8888. Either way, you'll be able to reserve your place on the call, or get more information.

Sincerely,

Kelly Schwedland
President, American Business Dynamics

P.S. If you miss this opportunity to speak directly with Lederman (for free), when WILL you get to hear a self-made millionaire reveal how he transformed his business, multiplied his income, and cut his workweek down to just 10 hours?

Visit http://www.abdynamics.com/seminar.htm right now. Or call 1-888-888-8888.

# Glossary

*Ad click rate* Sometimes referred to as *click-through*, this is the percentage of ad views that resulted in an ad click.

*Ad clicks* Number of times users click on an ad banner.

*Address* A unique identifier for a computer or site online, usually a URL for a website or marked with an @ for an e-mail address. This is how your computer finds a location on the information super-highway.

*Ad views (impressions)* Number of times an ad banner is down-loaded and presumably seen by visitors. If the same ad appears on multiple pages simultaneously, this statistic may understate the number of ad impressions, due to browser caching. Corresponds to net impressions in traditional media. There is currently no way of know-ing whether an ad was actually loaded. Most servers record an ad as served even if it was not.

*Affiliate marketing* A system of advertising in which site A agrees to feature buttons from site B, and site A gets a percentage of any sales generated for site B. It can also be applied to situations in which an advertiser may be looking for marketing information, rather than a cash sale. Popular among startups with very small marketing budgets.

*Affiliate program* An arrangement in which a company pays you a percentage of the sale for every online customer they get through a link from your website to theirs.

*Affinity Marketing* Marketing efforts—including e-mail promotions, banners, or offline media—aimed at consumers on the basis of established buying patterns. (For example, "Dear Cowpoke, as a valued cattle-restraint equipment customer, you're invited to a special Webcast sneak peek of our newest product: the Heifer Holder. Act now!")

*Anchor* A word, phrase, or graphic image, in hypertext, it is the object that is highlighted, underlined, or "clickable" that links to another site.

*Applet* An application program written in Java that allows viewing of simple animation on Web pages.

*ARPA (Advanced Research Project Agency)* The U.S. Department of Defense agency that, in conjunction with leading universities, created ARPAnet, the precursor of the Internet.

*ASP (application service provider)* Third-party vendors that develop and host Internet and intranet applications for customers, tailoring the applications to the customer's business requirements and processes.

*ATM (asynchronous transfer mode)* A high-speed switching technique that uses fixed-size cells to transmit voice, data, and video.

*Auditor* Third-party company that tracks, counts, and verifies ad-banner requests or verifies a website's ad reporting system.

*Avatar* A digital representation of a user in a virtual reality site.

*Backbone* A high-speed line or series of connections that forms a large pathway within a network. The term is relative to the size of network it is serving. A backbone in a small network would probably be much smaller than many non-backbone lines in a large network.

**Bandwidth** How much information (text, images, video, sound) can be sent through a connection. Usually measured in bits per second. A full page of text is about 16,000 bits. A fast modem can move approximately 15,000 bits in one second. Full-motion full-screen video requires about 10,000,000 bits per second, depending on compression.

**Banner ad** A banner is the small boxed message that appears atop commercial websites (usually the home page)—or on the first page of an e-zine—and are usually hotlinked to the advertiser's site.

**Beta** This term has migrated from computer and software development, and it is usually used as "beta site." It means test site or test version. Beta is not the final version of a product or website, but it's close enough to show in public and work the bugs out.

**Bookmark** A bookmark is an easy way to find your way back to a website—just like a bookmark helps you keep your place in a book you are reading.

**Bounce** This is what happens when e-mail returns as undeliverable.

**Branding** A school of advertising that says, "If the consumer has heard of us, we've done our job." Fortunately for agencies, brand value is extremely difficult to measure, so branding campaigns can be easily defended with grandiose predictions of future glory.

**Broadband** A data-transmission scheme in which multiple signals share the bandwidth. This allows the transmission of voice, data, and video signals over a simple medium.

**Browser** An application used to view information from the Internet. Browsers provide a user-friendly interface for navigating through and accessing the vast amount of information on the Internet.

**Browser caching** To speed surfing, browsers store recently used pages on a user's disk. If a site is revisited, browsers display pages from the disk instead of requesting them from the server. As a result, servers undercount the number of times a page is viewed.

*Browsing* A term that refers to exploring an online area, usually on the World Wide Web.

*BBS (bulletin board system)* Software that enables users to log into e-mail, Usenet, and chat groups via modem.

*Buttons* Objects that, when clicked once, cause something to happen.

*Cache* A storage area for frequently accessed information. Retrieval of the information is faster from the cache than from the originating source. There are many types of cache, including RAM cache, secondary cache, disk cache, and cache memory, to name a few.

*CD-ROM* Compact Disk-Read Only Memory, a storage medium popular in modern computers. One CD-ROM can hold 600 MB of data.

*Centrex* A central office-based business communications system that provides direct dialing capability and advanced calling features normally found only on an onsite PBX.

*CGI (common gateway interface)* An interface-creation scripting program that allows Web pages to be made on the fly based on information from buttons, checkboxes, text input, and so on.

*Chat room* An area online where you can chat with other members in real time.

*Click* The opportunity for a visitor to be transferred to a location by clicking on an ad, as recorded by the server.

*Click-through rate* The percentage of people receiving an e-mail who will click on a URL embedded in the message to reach a specific Web page.

*Cookie* A file on your computer that records information such as where you have been on the World Wide Web. The browser stores this information, which allows a site to remember the browser in future transactions or requests. Since the Web's protocol has no way to remember requests, cookies read and record a user's browser type and IP address, and store this information on the user's own computer. The cookie can be read only by a server in the domain that stored it. Visitors can accept or deny cookies by changing a setting in their browser preferences.

*CPC* Cost per click.

*CPL* Cost per lead.

*CPM* CPM is the cost per thousand for a particular site. A website that charges $15,000 per banner and guarantees 600,000 impressions has a CPM of $25 ($15,000 divided by 600).

*CPT* Cost per transaction.

*CPTM* Cost per targeted thousand impressions.

*CPU (central processing unit)* The central processing unit is the main "brain" of the computer, where the information is processed and calculations are done.

*Coverage* The percentage of a population group covered by the Internet.

*Creative* The technology used to create or develop an ad unit. The most common creative technology for banners is GIF or JPEG images. Other creative technologies include Java, HTML, or streaming audio or video. These are commonly referred to as *rich-media banners*.

*Cyberspace* Coined by author William Gibson in his 1984 novel *Neuromancer, cyberspace* is now used to describe all of the information available through computer networks.

*Demographic overlay* Adding demographic data to a prospect or customer list by running it through the computer and matching it against other lists that already contain the data.

*Direct response*   The school of advertising that says, "The Internet is an interactive medium. If the consumer interacts with our marketing efforts, we've done our job." Unfortunately for agencies, there's nowhere to hide with interactive campaigns, as they produce precise success or failure measurements.

*Domain*   Part of the DNS (domain naming system) name that specifies details about the host. A domain is the main subdivision of Internet addresses, the last three letters after the final dot, and it tells you what kind of organization you are dealing with. There are six top-level domains widely used in the U.S.: .com (commercial), .edu (educational), .net (network operations), .gov (U.S. government), .mil (U.S. military), and .org (organization). Other, two-letter domains represent countries, thus, .uk for the United Kingdom, and so on.

*Domain consolidation level*   Data reflect the consolidation of multiple domain names and/or URLs associated with the main site.

*Drill down*   A term used to express what a surfer does as he or she goes further into a website—deeper into the back pages, deeper into data. Make certain that when someone takes the time to "drill down" into your site that they come back with information worth digging for.

*Dynamic rotation*   Advertisements rotate on a timed basis.

*E-commerce*   Using electronic information technologies on the Internet to allow direct selling and automatic processing of purchases between parties.

*E-list*   A direct mail list containing Internet addresses and used to distribute promotional messages over the Internet.

*E-mail*   An abbreviation for *electronic mail*, which is a network service that allows users to send and receive messages via computer. Once confined to a closed group within a particular network, the

Internet and common message protocols make it possible to send and receive messages worldwide.

***Emoticons*** The online means of facial expressions and gestures. Examples: :) Tip your head to the left and you will see the two eyes and smiling mouth. Use them where applicable in chats and e-mail. Other emoticons include: :( *sad* :0 *surprised* o:) *innocent.*

***E-maillennium*** The era, at the beginning of the twenty-first century, when direct marketing evolved from paper mail to electronic delivery over the Internet.

***E-zine*** A part-promotional, part-informational newsletter or magazine distributed on the Internet.

***FAQ (frequently asked questions)*** FAQ is a commonly used abbreviation for "frequently asked questions." Most Internet sites will have a FAQ to explain what is in the area and how to use its features.

***Firewall*** A security barrier placed between an organization's internal computer network—either its IS system or intranet—and the Internet. It keeps your information in, and unwanted people out. It consists of one or more routers, which accept, reject, or edit transmitted information and requests.

***Flame*** 1. An intentionally crude or abusive e-mail message or Usenet post. Rule: Don't do it. Ever. Not only is it bad netiquette, you leave a trail. 2. A complaint message from a spam recipient sent over the Internet to the advertiser.

***Forms*** The pages in most browsers that accept information in text-entry fields. They can be customized to receive company sales data and orders, expense reports, or other information. They can also be used to communicate.

***Frames*** The use of multiple, independent sections to create a single Web page. Each frame is built as a separate HTML file, but with one "master" file to identify each section. When a user requests a page with frames, several pages will be displayed as panes. Sites using frames may report one page request with several panes as multiple page requests. Most audit firms count only the master HTML page request and therefore can accurately report the page requests.

*Frame relay*  A form of packet switching that allows high-speed, statistically multiplexed connectivity over a shared network. The technology depends on high-quality transmission facilities and makes the intelligent end-points responsible for the integrity of the data.

*Freeware*  Shareware, or software, that can be downloaded off the Internet for free.

*Frequency*  The number of times an ad is delivered to the same browser in a single session or time period. A site needs to use cookies in order to manage ad frequency.

*FTP*  File transfer protocol, a protocol that allows the transfer of files from one computer to another. *FTP* can also be used as a verb.

*Gateway*  A link from one computer system to a different computer system.

*GIF (graphic interchange format)*  GIF (rhymes with "gift") is a graphics format that can be displayed on almost all Web browsers. It is a common compression format used for transferring graphics files between different computers. Most of the "pictures" you see online are GIF files. They display in 256 colors and have built-in compression. GIF images are the most common form of banner creative.

*GIF89a (animated GIF)*  A GIF animation tool that creates sequences of images to simulate animation and allows for transparent background colors. Animated GIFs can generate higher response rates than static banners.

*Gross exposures*  Each time a Web server sends a file to a browser, it is recorded in the server log file as a "hit." Hits are generated for every element of a requested page (including graphics, text, and interactive items). If a page containing two graphics is viewed by a user, three hits will be recorded—one for the page itself and one for each graphic. Webmasters use hits to measure their server's workload. Because page designs vary greatly, hits are a poor guide for traffic measurement.

*Hacker* Originally used to describe a computer enthusiast who pushed a system to its highest performance through clever programming.

*Helper application* This term refers to software programs that run along with browser programs, enabling them to perform additional functions. Good examples are Shockwave for downloading and viewing moving images, and RealAudio for hearing sounds and music online.

*History list* Most browsers have a pull-down menu that displays the sites you've recently visited so you can return to a site instantly or view your latest surfing session. The same mechanism makes it possible for servers to track where you were before visiting a particular site—better viewing habit information than television networks ever dreamed of providing.

*Hit* The sending of a single file, whether text, graphic, audio, or other type of file. When a page request is made, all elements or files that comprise the page are recorded as hits on a server's log file. While there is no accurate formula for determining the number of visitors to a page or site based on the number of hits—one visitor could go back and forth twenty times, or twenty people could visit a single time each—a hit at least indicates somebody was there. Thus, hits can be far more valuable than the tracking devices in any other media.

*Home page* The page designated as the main point of entry of a website (or main page) or the starting point when a browser first connects to the Internet. Typically, it welcomes you and introduces the purpose of the site, or the organization sponsoring it, and then provides links to the lower-level pages of the site. In business terms, it's the grabber. If your home page downloads too slowly, or it's unclear or uninteresting, you will probably lose customers.

*Host*  An Internet host used to be a single machine connected to the Internet (which meant it had a unique IP address). As a host, it made certain services available to other machines on the network. However, virtual hosting now means that one physical host can actually be many virtual hosts.

*Hotlists*  These can be pull-down or pop-up menus on browsers that contain new or popular sites. Major browser and search engine home pages also contain updated hotlists, and there are entire sites, such as Cool Site O' the Day.

*HTML (hypertext markup language)*  Hypertext markup language is a coding language used to make hypertext documents for use on the Web. HTML resembles old-fashioned typesetting code, where a block of text is surrounded by codes that indicate how it should appear. HTML allows text to be "linked" to another file on the Internet.

*HTTP (hypertext transfer protocol)*  A standard method of publishing information as hypertext in HTML format on the Internet, HTTP is the format of the World Wide Web. When a browser sees "HTTP" at the beginning of an address, it knows that it is viewing a WWW page.

*HTTPS*  HTTP with SSL (secure socket layer) encryption for security.

*Hyperlink*  This is the clickable link in text or graphics on a Web page that takes you to another place on the same page, another page, or a whole other site. It is the single most powerful and important function of online communications. Hyperlinks are revolutionizing the way the world gets its information.

*Hypertext*  Electronic documents that present information that can be read by following many different directions through links, rather than just read linearly like printed text.

*Impression (ad impression or page impression)*  The ad impression is the metric a site uses for measuring inventory. Different definitions exist for this term: 1. The viewing of a page or ad by the user. The assumption is that the page or ad images were successfully downloaded and the user viewed the page or ads. 2. The request for a page or ad. Agencies usually collect a fee for every thousand impressions (hence the term CPM, cost per thousand).

*Infopreneur* Someone who starts up a business in information technology or online communications.

*Interactivity* If your website isn't interactive, it's dead.

*Internet* 1. A collection of approximately 60,000 independent, interconnected networks that use the TCP/IP protocols and that evolved from ARPANet of the late '60s and early '70s. "The Net" is a worldwide system of computer networks providing reliable and redundant connectivity between disparate computers and systems by using common transport and data protocols. 2. Generally, any network made up of two or more interconnected local or wide area networks.

*Internet domain name* The unique name that identifies an Internet entity.

*Interstitial* Means "something in between" and is a page that is inserted in the normal flow of content between a user and a site. An interstitial ad is an "intrusive" ad unit that is spontaneously delivered without specifically being requested by a user. Blocking the site behind it, interstitial ads are designed to grab consumers' attention for the few nanoseconds it takes them to close the window. Interstitials can be full pages or small daughter windows. Also referred to as "pop-ups." 2. A banner appearing in a location other than a home page or near the masthead of an e-zine.

*Intranet* Intranets are private networks, usually maintained by corporations for internal communications, which use Internet—usually Web—protocols, software, and servers. They are relatively cheap, fast, and reliable networking and information warehouse systems that link offices around the world. They make it is easy for corporate users to communicate with one another, and to access the information resources of the Internet.

*Inventory*   The number of ads available for sale on a website. Ad inventory is determined by the number of ads on a page, the number of pages containing ad space, and the number of page requests.

*IP address*   Internet protocol address. Every system connected to the Internet has a unique IP address, which consists of a number in the format A.B.C.D where each of the four sections is a decimal number from 0 to 255. Most people use domain names instead, and the resolution between domain names and IP addresses is handled by the network and the domain name servers. With virtual hosting, a single machine can act like multiple machines (with multiple domain names and IP addresses).

*IRC (internet relay chat)*   A facility that allows people—from many different places in the world at one time—to chat in real time. The chats, or forums, are typed remarks, and they can be either public or private. This, understandably, is a wildly popular consumer area of the Internet. A sort of "ham radio" for today, it offers intimacy combined with autonomy. Many celebrities are also talking to the public at preannounced times, so IRC has commercial publicity uses, too. Business meetings can be conducted in the same way.

*ISDN (integrated services digital network)*   ISDN lines are high-speed dial-up connections to the Internet. That's good. What's bad is that their cost and availability are determined by local telephone companies, which means in some places they are available, in other places not; and sometimes they're cheap, and at other times wildly expensive. It is a lot of commotion for a connection roughly four times faster than a 28.8 modem. (The joke among communications experts is that ISDN stands for "it still does nothing.") Wait for fiber optic lines, which will be thousands of times faster—that's the future.

*ISP (Internet service provider)*   1. A business that provides access to the Internet. Its services are available to either individuals or companies, and include a dial-in interface with the Internet, software supply, and often website and intranet design. There are currently more than 3,000 ISPs in the U.S. alone. It's a growth business, and, as a result, pricing is highly competitive, so shop around. 2. A company that, for a fee, provides businesses and consumers with access to the Internet.

*IVR (interactive voice response)* A communication device that provides interactive menus for callers to use to input data using a touch-tone telephone keypad.

*Java* Java is an object-oriented programming language created by Sun Microsystems that supports enhanced features such as animation, or real-time updating of information. If you are using a browser that supports Java, an applet (Java program) embedded in the Web page will automatically run.

*JPEG (joint photographic experts group)* JPEG (pronounced "jay peg") is a graphics format newer than GIF that displays photographs and graphic images with millions of colors. It also compresses well and is easy to download. Unfortunately, not many browsers currently support it, so don't use it for your logo.

*Keyword* A word or phrase used to focus an online search.

*Killer app* A term that migrated from software development to online. It is nothing more than tech-talk for the eternal search for next big idea.

*Lag* The amount of time between making an online request or command and receiving a response. Until lag time becomes no time at all, the Internet will not be consumer-friendly, and its profit potential will remain limited.

*LAN (local area network)* A computer network—which for some reason is pronounced "land"—limited to a certain area, usually a single floor or building. The Web is a network, but not a LAN.

*Link* An electronic connection between two websites (also called *hotlink*). When an item on one Web page is clicked on, the user is transferred to another page or another area on the same page.

*Listserver* A program that automatically sends e-mail to a list of subscribers. It is the mechanism that is used to keep newsgroups informed.

*Load* Usually used with *upload* or *download*, it means to transfer files or software—to "load"—from one computer or server to another computer or server. In other words, it's the movement of information online.

*Log or log files* File that keeps track of network connections.

*Login* The identification or name used to access—log into—a computer, network, or site.

*Mailing list* An online mailing list is an automatically distributed e-mail message on a particular topic going to certain individuals. You can subscribe or unsubscribe to a mailing list by sending a message via e-mail. There are many good professional mailing lists, and you should find the ones that concern your business.

*Metatags* Used to identify the creator of a Web page, what HTML specs the page follows, and the keywords and description of the page.

*MIME (multipurpose Internet mail extensions)* A method of encoding a file for delivery over the Internet.

*Modem* A contraction for "modulation/demodulation," it is the device that converts a digital bit stream into an analog signal (and back again) so computers can communicate across phone lines.

*Modem speeds* The speed at which you connect to the Internet through your computer's modem. They include 14.4, 28,8, 33.6, and ISDN. T1 and T3 are high-speed connections that don't require a modem.

*Mosaic* Developed by the NCSA, the National Center for Super-computing Applications at the University of Illinois in Urbana, this is the breakthrough browser that revolutionized the Internet. It brought clickability and graphics to a hard-to-navigate, text-heavy information system and made the Web—and its vast commercial possibilities—a reality.

*MPEG*  The file format that is used to compress and transmit movies or video clips online.

*Multimailing*  Direct mail campaign using both e-mail and postal direct mail.

*Netiquette (Internet etiquette)*  The rules of how to behave on the Internet. The most important one relevant to e-mail marketing is not to send promotional or commercial messages to anyone you don't know or who has not agreed to receive them.

*Netizen*  An active Internet user.

*Net monthly circulation*  The number of unique Web users in the panel that visited the site over the course of the reporting period, expressed as a percentage of the in-tab.

*Network (ad network)*  An aggregator or broker of advertising inventory from many sites—for example, 24/7 Media.

*Newbie*  A term to describe anyone new to an area, whether it be a particular forum online or the Internet.

*Newsgroup*  A discussion group on Usenet devoted to talking about a specific topic. Currently, there are over 15,000 newsgroups. Also called usenets, newsgroups consist of messages posted on electronic bulletin boards. Many of them cover professional subjects and societies and are rich sources of business information; others are junk and contain little but mindless drivel.

*Online*  It's where you are right now—and where the rest of the world is heading to get its information and entertainment, to communicate, and to buy products and services.

*Online service*   A business that provides its subscribers with a wide variety of data transmitted over telecommunications lines. Online services provide an infrastructure in which subscribers can communicate with one another, either by exchanging e-mail messages or by participating in online conferences (forums). In addition, the service can connect users with an almost unlimited number of third-party information providers. Subscribers can get up-to-date stock quotes, news stories hot off the wire, articles from many magazines and journals—in fact, almost any information that has been put in electronic form. Of course, accessing all this data carries a price.

*Opt in*   To agree to receive promotional e-mails when registering on a particular website from the site owner and other companies to whom he or she may rent your e-mail address.

*Opt out*   To request that an e-list owner take your name off the list or at least make sure you are not sent any promotional e-mails.

*Page*   All websites are a collection of electronic "pages." Each Web page is a document formatted in HTML that contains text, images, or media objects such as RealAudio player files, QuickTime videos, or Java applets. The *home page* is typically a visitor's first point of entry and features a site index. Pages can be static or dynamically generated. All frames and frame parent documents are counted as pages.

*Page request*   The opportunity for an HTML document to appear in a browser window as a direct result of a visitor's interaction with a website (IAB). The page request is for a browser to "get" a page from a site and is recorded by the server log.

*Page views*   Number of times a user requests a page that may contain a particular ad. Indicative of the number of times an ad was potentially seen, or "gross impressions." Page views may overstate ad impressions if users choose to turn off graphics (often done to speed browsing).

*Pay-per-click*   An advertising pricing model in which advertisers pay agencies based on how many consumers clicked on a promotion.

Condemned by advertisers and agencies alike for its many marketing vagaries and technical loopholes. '

*Pay-per-impression*  An advertising pricing model in which advertisers pay agencies based on how many consumers see their promotions.

*Pay-per-sale*  An advertising pricing model in which advertisers pay agencies based on how many consumers actually buy something as a direct result of the promotion. Despised by agencies for the wretched accountability it brings to their lives.

*PCMCIA*  An acronym for Personal Computer Memory Card Industry Association. Many laptop computers use these devices as modems.

*PDF (portable document format)*  Word processing software, business applications, or desktop publishing files on the Web that look exactly like the originals. Must have Adobe Acrobat Reader to view.

*PDF files*  Adobe's portable document format (pdf) is a translation format used primarily for distributing files across a network or on a website. Files with a .pdf extension have been created in another application and then translated into .pdf files so they can be viewed by anyone, regardless of platform.

*PID (personal information destination)*  There are millions of pages of information on the Web, but if you are looking for a specific item, there is only one page—or very few—that contains exactly the information you need. That's your PID. Think of it as a needle in a haystack.

*Plug-in*  A program application that can easily be installed and used as part of a Web browser. Once installed, plug-in applications are recognized by the browser, and its function is integrated into the main HTML file being presented.

*POP (point of presence)*  POP is a service provider's location for connecting to users. Generally, POPs refer to the location where people can dial into the provider's host computer. Most providers have several POPs to allow low-cost access via telephone lines.

*Pop-up*  Any screen, box, or message that suddenly appears on the computer screen during a session.

*Portal*  A website or service that offers a broad array of resources and services, such as e-mail, forums, search engines, and online shopping malls. The first Web portals were online services, such as AOL, that provided access to the Web, but by now most of the traditional search engines have transformed themselves into Web portals to attract and keep a larger audience.

*POTS (plain old telephone service)*  Unless you are reading this at a high-tech company or large corporation with ISDN or T1 lines, chances are you accessed over POTS, copper wires that transmit at about 28.8K—which means surfing for you is a fairly slow business.

*PPP (point to point protocol)*  The language that enables a computer to use telephone lines and a modem to connect to the Internet. Gradually replacing SLIP as the preferred means of connection.

*Protocol*  A set of rules that governs how information is to be exchanged between computer systems. Also used in certain structured chat rooms to refer to the order in which people may speak.

*Push*  Is the delivery ("pushing") of information that is initiated by the server rather than being requested ("pulled") by a user. Pointcast is the best-known push service that pushes information based on the user's profile.

*Query*  A request for information, usually to a search engine.

*Rank*  An ad's standing in comparison to other ads, based on the graphical click-through rate. Rank provides advertisers with information on an ad's performance across sites.

**Reach** Unique Web users who visited the site over the course of the reporting period, expressed as a percentage of the universe for the demographic category. Also called *unduplicated audience.*

**Real time** Events that happen in real time are happening virtually at that particular moment. When you chat in a chat room or send an instant message, you are interacting in real time since it is immediate.

**RealAudio** A commercial software program that plays audio on demand without waiting for long file transfers. For instance, you can listen to National Public Radio's entire broadcast of "All Things Considered" on the Internet.

**Registration** A process for site visitors to enter information about themselves. Sites use registration data to enable or enhance targeting of ads. Some sites require certain registration in order to access their content. Some sites use voluntary registration. Fee-based sites conduct registration in the form of a transaction (taking a credit card to pay for the content). A registered user is a user who visits a website and elects, or is required, to provide certain information. Nonregistered users may be denied access to a site requiring registration.

**RFP** Request for proposal.

**RFC** *(request for comment)* The documents that contain the protocols, standards, and information that define the Internet. Gathered and published by the Internet Engineering Task Force, a consensus-building body made up of institutions and corporations involved with online communications, they are preceded by RFC and followed by a number. RFC archives can be found at InterNIC.

**Rich media** Interactive multimedia presentations in Internet direct mail, banner ads, and Web pages.

**ROI** Return on investment.

*Router* The hardware or software that handles connections between networks online. In other words, it tells your computer where to go.

*Screen name* The name you use to represent yourself online.

*Search engine* A program that searches documents for specified keywords and returns a list of the documents where the keywords were found. Although *search engine* is really a general class of programs, the term is often used to specifically describe systems like AltaVista and Excite that enable users to search for documents on the World Wide Web and Usenet newsgroups.

*Server* Servers are the backbone of the Internet, the computers that are linked by communication lines and "serve up" information in the form of text, graphics, and multimedia to online computers that request data—that's you. (When a server "goes down," it loses its online link and the information it holds cannot be accessed.)

*Session* A series of transactions or hits made by a single user. If there has been no activity for a period of time, followed by the resumption of activity by the same user, a new session is considered started. Thirty minutes is the most common time period used to measure a session length.

*Shareware* Software programs that are openly available and usually can be downloaded online. They are often free, though not always.

*Shovelware* Shovelware is software that is inflated in value by "shoveling" in all kinds of information, usually free to anyone and generally worthless. The term is being expanded by usage to the Web, where a lot of irrelevant information is shoveled onto many sites.

*Shockwave* A plug-in that allows for multimedia movies to play through a browser.

*SIC (standard industrial classification) codes* Classifies establishments by the type of activity in which they are engaged.

*Signature file* A personal footer that can be automatically attached to e-mail.

*SLIP (serial line Internet protocol)* SLIP refers to a method of Internet connection that enables computers to use phone lines and a modem to connect to the Internet without having to connect to a host.

*SMDS (switched multimegabit data services)* A high-speed data transmission service that provides wide area connectivity through the public telephone network.

*Snail mail* A term for traditional land and air mail services, which take days to deliver a message versus seconds for delivery of e-mail.

*Spam* The use of mailing lists to blanket Usenet groups or private e-mail boxes with indiscriminate, unsolicited messages of a promotional nature. Very bad netiquette. Even worse, it's bad business. The future of marketing online is about customizing products and information for individual users. Anyone who tries to use old mass-market techniques in the new media environment is bound to fail.

*Spider* A term used to describe search engines such as Yahoo! and AltaVista, because of the way they cruise all over the World Wide Web to find information. It is a software program that combs the Web for new sites and updated information on old ones, like a spider looking for a fly.

*Splash page* A bridge page between a banner advertisement and an advertiser's website that provides product information and hotlinks. Splash pages are replacing many home pages—particularly on sites more involved with news and publishing—as gateways into Web content. They start with a bigger "splash," more graphics, and timely information, and change often, like the cover of a magazine.

*Static rotation* Advertisements rotate based on the entry of users into a screen. Regardless of the amount of time a user spends with a screen, advertisements will remain on the screen for the entire time and will not change.

*Stickiness*  A measure used to gauge the effectiveness of a site in retaining individual users. The term is typically used in promotional material when traffic numbers are too low to be effective in lauding a site's performance. Never mind the quantity, feel the stick. *Sticky* refers to a website people want to stay on and frequently revisit.

*Surfing*  Exploring the World Wide Web. Commonly seen as "surfing the Net."

*SYSOP*  The person responsible for the day-to-day operations of a computer system or network. In large corporations, this person can be the head of the IS (information systems) department.

*T-1*  A high-speed (1.54 megabits/second) network connection.

*T-3*  An even higher-speed (45 megabits/second) Internet connection.

*Targeted marketing*  Banners or other promotions aimed, on the basis of demographic analysis, at one specific subsection of the market.

*TCP (transmission control protocol)*  TCP works with IP to ensure that packets travel safely on the Internet. This is the method by which most Internet activity takes place.

*Throughput*  The amount of data transmitted through Internet connectors in response to a given request. The more "throughput" you deliver to your customers, the better (if you're charging enough).

*Undernet*  An alternative IRC that is accessed through a normal, or public, chat area. Its access is limited, and it is usually used for private conversations. But be warned: unless you are behind a sophisticated firewall, little on the Net is truly private.

*Unique users*  The total number of different users, or different computer terminals, that have visited a website. This is measured using advanced tracking technology or user registration.

*Upload* To send a file from one computer to another via modem or other telecommunication method.

*URL (uniform resource locator)* An HTTP address used by the World Wide Web to specify a certain site. This is the unique identifier, or address, of a Web page on the internet. URL can be pronounced "you-are-ell" or "earl." It is how Web pages, FTPs, gophers, newsgroups, and even some e-mail boxes are located.

*Usenet* Internet message boards, also known as newsgroups. Each board has a theme, and there are tens of thousands of usenets concerning every imaginable topic. Many of them cover professional subjects and societies and are rich sources of business information; others are junk and contain little but mindless drivel.

*Valid hits* A further refinement of *hits*, valid hits are hits that deliver all information to a user. Excludes hits such as redirects, error messages, and computer-generated hits.

*Viewer* Another name for a help application.

*Viral marketing* Any advertising that propagates itself. When Hotmail users send e-mail, they unwittingly infect the recipient with the tagline at the bottom of the message.

*Virus* A virus is a program that can be downloaded onto your computer or network from the Internet. Some are harmless, while others are programmed to destroy your system, trash your files, and disable your software. No kidding. So be careful. Use antivirus programs. They take a few extra minutes every day to use, but the protection is worth it.

*Visual mail* E-mail containing animation.

*Visits* A sequence of requests made by one user at one site. If a visitor does not request any new information for a period of time, known as the *time-out period*, then the next request by the visitor is considered a new visit. To enable comparisons among sites, I/PRO uses a thirty-minute time-out.

*Visual mail*   Interactive e-mail containing graphics, animation, and sound, pioneered by E-PostDirect.

*VRML (virtual reality modeling language)*   This is an online programming language for creating three-dimensional programs. Looks pretty, but at current bandwidths it's pre-e-e-etty slow . . .

*WAIS (wide area information server)*   WAIS, pronounced "ways," search for data through online gopher databases. Unless you are looking for scientific or technical information, look somewhere else.

*Web page*   An HTML document on the Web, usually one of many together that make up a website.

*Website*   A collection of files that are arranged on the World Wide Web under a common address and allows retrieval via a browser.

*Webmaster*   The individual assigned to administering a corporation or organization's website. This person lays out the information trees, designs the look, codes HTML pages, handles editing and additions, and checks that links are intact. In addition, he or she monitors, routes, and sometimes responds to e-mail generated by the site.

*Website*   The virtual location for an organization's presence on the World Wide Web, usually making up several Web pages and a single home page designated by a unique URL.

*World Wide Web (WWW or Web)*   The Web allows computer users to access information across systems around the world using URLs to identify files and systems, and hypertext links to move between files on the same or different systems. The Web is a client/server information system that supports the retrieval of data in the form of text, graphics, and multimedia in a uniform HTML format. Allowing hypertext links and interactivity on an unprecedented level, its introduction transformed a sleepy, academic communications system into a powerful marketing tool linking businesses and customers around the world.

*'zine* Magazines that are published digitally, rather than on paper. Some are mainstream, while others are oddball and cover almost every topic imaginable.

---

**Emoticons and E-Mail Acronyms**

*Emoticons*, also known as *smileys*, are symbols used in electronic communication to help replace facial gestures you normally see when talking directly to someone. They help communicate someone's mood or indicate when someone's joking. The most typical smiley is :), which, if you tilt your head to the left, is two eyes and a smiling face. Following are other common smileys and their meanings:

| | |
|---|---|
| :) | Smile |
| ;-) | Wink |
| :( | Frown |
| :-D | Laugh |
| :-X | No comment |

Frequently used acronyms are:

| | |
|---|---|
| MSG | Message |
| JIC | Just in case |
| CUL | See you later |
| FAQ | Frequently asked questions |
| IMHO | In my humble opinion |
| BTW | By the way |
| <g> | Grin |
| TTFN | Ta-ta for now |
| LOL | Laughing out loud |
| ROFL | Rolling on the flour laughing |
| INAL | I'm not a lawyer |
| TIA | Thanks in advance |
| PMFJI | Pardon me for jumping in |

# Bibliogrpahy

## Introduction

Ciabattari, Jane, "Intelligence Report," *Parade*, October 10, 1999, p. 7.

Kahn, Mickey Alam, "English-Language Sites Rule W. Europe Web," *DM News International*, December 13, 1999, p. 9.

Lundberg, Abbie, "In Box," *CIO-100*, August 15, 1999, p. 14.

Meyers, Bill, "Small Businesses Flock to the Net," *USA Today* (date unknown).

## Chapter 1

"Americans Spend 65 Million Hours Per Day on the Internet," *Research Alert*, August 20, 1999, p. 3.

Baldwin, Howard, "Bitten by the ASP," *CIO*, November 1, 1999, p. 88.

Barshack, Lenny, "E-Mail: The Net's Killer App," *Target Marketing*, February 1999, p. 102.

Conlon, Ginger, "No Turning Back," *Sales & Marketing Management*, December 1999, pp. 51, 58.

Daly, James, "Giving Away the Store," *Business 2.0* (date unkown).

"Did You Know?" *Sales and Marketing* (date unknown).

"Direct Mail Usage Goes Up," *Sales & Marketing Management*, November 1999, p. 118.

Jahnke, Art, "Truth in Advertising Numbers," *CIO WebBusiness*, section 2, June 1, 1999, p. 20.

Kemp, Ted, "New School Marketer Teaches Old-School DMers New Tricks," *DM News*, September 13, 1999, p. 1.

Kemp, Ted, "Peet's Coffee Sees 20% E-Mail Response Rate," *DM News*, May 10, 1999, p. 6.

"Leave Me a Message at the Tone," *New Man*, February 2000, p. 13.

Leuthold, Steve, "Heads Will Roll on E-Guillotine," *Investment News*, November 22, 1999, p. 8.

McCreary, Lew, "Fast, Cheap, and Out of Control," *CIO Enterprise*, section 2, May 15, 1999, p. 28.

Mendoza, Martha, "Nothing but the E-Mail," *Daily News*, June 16, 1999, p. 37.

"Online Consumers Lining Up," *Record*, November 23, 1998.

Peppers, Don, and Martha Rogers, "The Profits Are in the Mail," *Sales & Marketing Management*, July 1999, p. 24.

"Percent of Small Business on Web," *Sales & Marketing Executive Report*, December 6, 1999, p. 1.

Shrake, Scott, "Survey Says Mail Quantities Up," *Target Marketing*, October 1999, p. 56.

Slayton, Gregory, "Benefiting from Request-Based E-Mail," *DM News*, September 27, 1999, p. 28.

Stansberry, Porter, "The Risks and Rewards of the Pinnacle Effect," *Oxford Club Communiqué*, May 1, 1999.

Woo, Kevin, "Making E-Mail Marketing Work," *Target Marketing*, February 1999, p. 107.

# Chapter 2

Halpin, John, "Shopping the E-Stores," *Daily News*, special section, September 9, 1999, p. 3.

"Internet Commerce Increases as Security Concerns Abate," *Research Alert*, August 20, 1999, p. 1.

"Internet Shopping: An Ernst & Young Special Report," *Stores*, section 2, January 1998, p. 1.

"Internet Taxes," *Record*, December 26, 1999, p. RO-6.

Margherio, Lynn, "The Emerging Digital Economy," U.S. Department of Commerce.

Monarko, Sherry, "Don't Make Me Hate You," *Maximum PC*, January 2000, p. 39.

Morgan, Cynthia, "Who Buys What Online, and Why," *Computer-World*," May 10, 1999, p. 74.

"Need Credit," *American Demographics*, January 2000, p. 9.

Ratnesar, Romesh, "A Hex on Your Taxes," *Time*, December 27, 1999, p. 129.

Waitley, Denis, "You're Online or in the Bread Line," *Priorities*, volume 4, issue 1, p. 24.

Weissman, Rachel X., "Who Are Those Netizens?" *American Demographics*, February 1999, p. 34.


# Chapter 3

Bonim, Andrew, and Ken C. Pohlman, "The Grammar of Interactivity," *Writer's Digest*, 1999 Yearbook, p. 26.

Levison, Ivan, "How to Use E-Mail to Fire Up Sales," www.levison.com.

Meyer, Julie, "Effective E-Mail," *Opportunity World*, October, 1999, p. 46.

Moores, Chris, "Are Customers Ready for Rich Media?" *DM News*, December 13, 1999, p. 26.

Singer, Jonathan, "New Customers Reap Unlimited Rewards," *DM News*, December 13, 1999, p. 22.

## Chapter 4

Andrews, Kelly J., "Opt-in E-Mail," *Target*, February 1999, p. 105.

Andrews, Kelly J., "Raising the Permission Bar," *Target*, January 2000, p. 22.

Andrews, Kelly J., "Tips on Choosing E-Mail Lists," *Target Marketing*, December, 1999, p. 24.

"Getting Wary Reps to Help Build a Database," *Sales & Marketing Management*, January 2000, p. 76.

"Industry Viewpoint," *TM Tipline*, December 27, 1999, p. 1.

Love, Todd, "List Principles Will Work with E-Mail," *DM News*, May 3, 1999, p. 32.

Nunley, Kevin, "Biz-Tips," *Opportunity World*, September 1999, p. 78.

Overby, Bruce, "Letter to the Editor," *Intercom*, May 1999, p. 5.

## Chapter 5

Aaron, Michael, "E-Mail Marketing Has Many Faces," *DM News*, April 26, 1999, p. 20.

Chae, Lee, "The Latest Word on E-Mail," *Network Magazine*, December 1998, p. 66.

DiBlasi, Al, "E-Mail Lists: One-to-One Marketing Tools," *DM News*, December 13, 1999, p. 32.

Hansard, Sara, "Debate Rages Over E-Signatures," *Investment News*, December 6, 1999.

Lavelle, Louis, "Firms Keeping Electronic Eye on More Staff," *Record*, April 16, 1999.

"Targeted E-Mails," www.m2kinteractive.com/presenta tion/prese-mail.html

## Chapter 6

"Be Wary of Using Web Page to Promote," *Newsletter on Newsletters*, December 15, 1999, p. 4.

Fleishman, Glenn, "Better Address Your Customers," *Business 2.0*, January 2000, p. 128.

## Chapter 7

"Cahners Advertising Research Reports," #810.12A, 824.0B1, 861.0A.

Darviche, Michael, "E-Mail Test Strategies," *DM News*, April 23, 1999, p. 22.

Kirsner, Scott, "The Dirty Dozen," *CIO WebBusiness*, section 2, September 1, 1999, p. 22.

Lewis, Maura, "Making Sense of Internet Metrics," *DM News*, April 23, 1999, p. 25.

LoCascio, Robert, "Ten Tips for Live Customer Service," *DM News*, September 20, 1999. P. 22.

McCrea, Bridget, "E-Mail Campaigns Done Right," *Web Merchant*, Summer 1999, p. 26.

## Chapter 8

Bredenberg, Al, "Advertising by E-Mail—Without Raising Hackles," *Al Bredenberg Business Reports*.

Clarke, Tad, "Be Careful What You E-Mail," *DM News*, December 6, 1999, p. 104.

"Cyber Slander," *Business News*, May 31, 1999, p. 3.

Davidson, Jeff, "Commonsense in E-Mailing," *Opportunity World*, September 1999, p. 42.

Deckmyn, Dominique, "When Customers Want E-Mail, Not Spam," *ComputerWorld*, June 21, 1999, p. 81.

"E-Mail User Protection Act: 106th Congress, 1st session, HR 1910.

"Is E-Mail Marketing Hot?" *Hotline*, June 1, 1999, p. 2.

Magill, Ken, "DMA Finally Reaches Accord with Anti-Spam Advocates," *DM News*, December 14, 1998, p. 21.

Moore, Pamela, "7 Fired for Inappropriate E-Mail," *North Jersey Jobs*, October 10, 1999, p. 2.

Smith, Susanne A., and Emily Woodson Davis, "Is Spam Edible?" *CIO WebBusiness*, section 2, December 1, 1998, p. 32.

Strout, Erin, "E-Mail Marketers Beware," *Sales & Marketing Management*, January 2000, p. 11.

Thibodeau, Patrick, "States Put Spam Under Attack," *ComputerWorld*, April 5, 1999.

# Chapter 9

"Banner Daze," *B2B Direct*, July 1999.

Blumenthal, Robin, "Webster Likely Would Be Speechless at These Sales," *Barron's*, December 20, 1999, p. 13.

Bonji, Peter, "Integrating Offline and Online Channels," *DM News*, September 20, 1999, p. 35.

Bredenberg, Al, "Direct Response Techniques Enhance Internet Efforts," *The Advantage from Microsoft Corporation*, August 1999, p. 5.

Conderino, Paul, "Drive Traffic to Your Web Site," *NPA Hotline*, September 13, 1999, p. 3.

Cohen, Andy, "Banner Ads vs. E-Mail Marketing," *Sales & Marketing Management*, August 1999, p. 15.

D'Arcangelo, Jim, "Path to E-Commerce Is Measurement," *DM News*, September 20, 1999, p. 28.

Devlin, Catherine, "Why Your Banner Ads Don't Work," *The Business to Business Marketer*, July 1999, p. 3.

Dodson, Jody, "Increase Your Online Survey Response," *DM News*, September 13, 1999, p. 25.

Doyle, Jim, "Five Reasons Why You Must Get a FAQ Page," *Opportunity World*, October 1999, p. 24.

Forringer, Paul, "Web Marketing Equals Constant Change," *DM News*, April 23, 1999, p. 24.

Frankel, Rob, "9 Easy Steps: How to Screw Up a Banner Campaign," www.searchz.com, July 30, 1999.

Goldblatt, Dan, "Collect and Use Visitor Web Data," *Business News* (date unknown).

Goldblatt, Dan, "You Have Eight Seconds," *Business News*, August 23, 1999, p. 8.

Hennerberg, Gary, "Measuring Your Web Site Profitability," *DM News*, October 4, 1999, p. 24.

Kadanoff, Marcia, "The Changing Face of Rich Media," *DM News*, September 20, 1999, p. 26.

Kahn, Mickey, "Ads Focus on E-Commerce," *DM News*, September 27, 1999, p. 24.

Payne, John, "Leveraging Data to Gain Competitive Advantage," *DM News*, September 20, 1999, p. 24.

Resnick, Rosalind, "Niche Mailers Choose E-Mail Marketing," *DM News*, May 10, 1999, p. 23.

"Search Engines Are Failing," *Internet Marketing Report*, July 28, 1999, p. 1.

Sexton, Sean, "Excite@home Seminar Tout's Rich Media's Arrival," *DRTV News*, September 13, 1999, p. 4.

Voron, Neil, "The Latest in E-Mail Information Technology," *Web Bound* (date unknown).

## Chapter 10

Benun, Ilise, "Connecting with Clients," *The Art of Self Promotion*, September 1999, p. 1.

Duffy, Daintry, "It Takes an E-Village," *CIO Enterprise*, section 2, October 15, 1999, p. 34.

Kemp, Ted, "Virtual Communities Bring in Real Dollars," *DM News*, October 25, 1999, p. 32.

McKim, Robert, "Database Marketing on the Internet," *DM News*, March 1, 1999, p. 28.

Menaker, Michael, "Internet vs. Print," *Metalworking Marketer*, December, 1999, p. 4.

"Name, Rank, Serial Number," *PC Magazine*, March 23, 1999, p. 28.

"New York Conference Features Two Must-Hear Internet Speakers," *NPA Hotline*, November 9, 1999, p. 1.

Slater, Derek, "Virtual Desserts," *CIO Enterprise*, section 2, April 15, 1999, page 86.

Stuart, Anne, "Electronic Electorate," *CIO WebBusiness*, section 2, August 1, 1999, p. 14.

Voron, Neal, "The Latest in E-Mail Information Technology," *Web Bound*, p. 24.

# INDEX

# ABOUT THE AUTHORS

**Steve Roberts** is president of Edith Roman Associates, Inc., one of the largest and fastest growing information companies in the business. Steve has twenty-four years of experience in conventional and Internet direct marketing. He specializes in high technology, publishing, mail order, entertainment, education, and finance, assisting companies in achieving maximum profitable growth through the application of sophisticated direct marketing methods. Steve possesses in-depth knowledge of postal and e-list resources, e-commerce and banner capabilities, e-mail address enhancements, database marketing, data processing, multivariate regression modeling, and market penetration profiling.

Steve's clients include Hewlett-Packard, Elron Software, IBM, Digi-Key, Fred Pryor, CareerTrack, AT&T, Hearst, Ancestry.com, Barnesandnoble.com, Columbia House, International Data Corporation, McGraw Hill, Miller Freeman, Avon, GM, Microsoft, Oracle, Egghead.com, and Real Networks. He contributed to *The Direct Marketing Handbook* and is a frequent contributor to *DM News, I-marketing News, Datapro, Target Marketing, Direct, Catalog Age,* and *Telemarketing Magazine.*

**Michelle Feit** is president of e-POSTDIRECT, a full-service Internet marketing agency. E-POSTDIRECT offers opt-in e-list management and brokerage; I-marketing counsel; personalized Internet campaign creation, execution, and tracking; HTML and Visual Mail; e-mail transmission; e-mail address appending; merge-purge; website design, banner ad placement; and e-commerce. Clients include

Columbia House, Real Networks, Egghead.com, Hearst, Pension, New Pig, Cahners, CareerTrack, Ancestry.com, foofoo.com, send.com, cameraworld.com, net2phone, and dash.com.

Michelle's articles on Internet direct mail have appeared in *Target Marketing*, *I-Marketing*, *Direct*, and *DM News*.

**Bob Bly** is an independent copywriter specializing in traditional and Internet direct marketing.

He has written lead-generating sales letters, direct mail packages, ads, scripts, websites, Internet direct mail, and PR materials for more than 100 clients including IBM, AT&T, The BOC Group, EBI Medical Systems, Associated Air Freight, CoreStates Financial Corp., PSE&G, Alloy Technology, M&T Chemicals, ITT, Takeda Chemicals, UniSys, Phillips Publishing, Fala Direct Marketing, Citrix Systems, and Grumman Corp.

Bob is the author of more than forty books including *The Copywriter's Handbook* (Henry Holt), *Selling Your Services* (Henry Holt & Co.), *Business-to-Business Direct Marketing* (NTC), *The Advertising Manager's Handbook* (Prentice Hall), and *The Elements of Technical Writing* (Macmillan).

Bob's articles have appeared in *Direct*, *Business Marketing*, *Computer Decisions*, *Chemical Engineering*, *Direct Marketing*, *Writer's Digest*, *Amtrak Express*, *DM News*, *Cosmopolitan*, *New Jersey Monthly*, *City Paper*, and many other publications. A winner of the Direct Marketing Association's Gold Echo Award, Mr. Bly has presented seminars on direct marketing and related business topics to numerous organizations including IBM, Foxboro Company, Arco Chemical, Thoroughbred Software Leaders Conference, Appliance Parts Distributors Association, and Dow Chemical.

Steve Roberts
Edith Roman Associates
1 Blue Hill Plaza
Pearl River, NY 10965
Phone: 800-223-2194
Fax: 914-620-9035
E-mail: steve_roberts@edithroman.com
Web: www.edithroman.com

Michelle Feit
e-Post Direct
1 Blue Hill Plaza
Pearl River, NY 10965
Phone: 800-409-4443
Fax: 914-620-9035
E-mail: michelle.feit@epostdirect.com
Web: www.epostdirect.com

Bob Bly
Copywriter
22 E. Quackenbush Avenue
Dumont, NJ 07628
Phone: 201-385-1220
Fax: 201-385-1138
E-mail: rwbly@bly.com
Web: www.bly.com